Computer Communications and Networks

Springer

London
Berlin
Heidelberg
New York
Barcelona
Hong Kong
Milan
Paris
Singapore
Tokyo

The **Computer Communications and Networks** series is a range of textbooks, monographs and handbooks. It sets out to provide students, researchers and non-specialists alike with a sure grounding in current knowledge, together with comprehensible access to the latest developments in computer communications and networking.

Emphasis is placed on clear and explanatory styles that support a tutorial approach, so that even the most complex of topics is presented in a lucid and intelligible manner.

Also in this series:

An Information Security Handbook
John M.D. Hunter
1-85233-180-1

The Quintessential PIC Microcontroller
Sid Katzen
1-85233-309-X

Andy Sloane and Dave Lawrence (Eds)

Multimedia Internet Broadcasting

Quality, Technology and Interface

Springer

Andy Sloane, BSc, PhD, CertED, MIEEE
CoNTACT Research Group, School of Computing and IT,
University of Wolverhampton, Lichfield Street, Wolverhampton, WV1 1LY, UK

Dave Lawrence, BSc, PhD
MinT Research Group, School of Computing Science, Middlesex University,
Trent Park, London N14 4YZ, UK

Series editor
Professor A.J. Sammes, BSc, MPhil, PhD, FBCS, CEng
CISM Group, Cranfield University, RMCS, Shrivenham, Swindon SN6 8LA, UK

ISBN 1-85233-283-2 Springer-Verlag London Berlin Heidelberg

British Library Cataloguing in Publication Data
Multimedia Internet broadcasting : quality, technology and
   interface. – (Computer communications and networks)
   1. Webcasting
   I. Sloane, Andy II. Lawrence, Dave, 1958-
   005.7'776
ISBN 1852332832

Library of Congress Cataloging-in-Publication Data
Multimedia Internet broadcasting : quality, technology and interface / Andy Sloane and
Dave Lawrence (eds.)
      p. cm – (Computer communications and networks)
   Includes bibliographical references and index.
   ISBN 1-85233-283-2 (alk. paper)
   1. Multimedia systems. 2. Internet. 3. Broadcasting. I. Sloane, Andy, 1954- II.
Lawrence, Dave, 1958- III. Series.
   QA76.575 .M83329 2001
   005.7'776—dc21
                                                          00-052661

Typesetting: Electronic text files prepared by editors
Printed and bound at the Athenæum Press Ltd., Gateshead, Tyne and Wear
34/3830-543210 Printed on acid-free paper SPIN 10759669

Preface

Multimedia Internet Broadcasting (MIB) is a relatively recent phenomenon—and yet already many Internet users have experienced it in some way, be it as a user, producer or researcher of broadcast material. In just a few short years activity in this area has exploded—the increasing plethora of websites that carry and provide multimedia broadcasts is clear evidence. A very recent development is the hosting of online events (which are very often associated with terrestrial events) that are dedicated to the streaming of multimedia content. Clearly, the multinational corporate sector has recognised the immense power of the Internet, and in particular the role that the delivery of on demand and "live" multimedia content plays in making the connection with a whole range of online communities. Meanwhile, this same area of activity attracts the interest and attention of individuals—people not necessarily with any other access to broadcasting their original content, nor opportunity to produce such content. Multimedia Internet broadcasting therefore, as with the Internet itself, provides a dynamic blend of commercial opportunity and creative empowerment. It is also an activity and subject area that has attracted substantial academic interest and indeed the many issues raised demand continued and increased research attention.

To serve high quality and interactive multimedia to a wide Internet is not yet generally achievable. The main active barriers appear to be out-dated infrastructures, low capacity user connections, high user interest, inappropriate design approaches, and increasing demands/expectancy. There are many problems to overcome in order to effectively broadcast to an Internet audience—and many of these difficulties require in-depth study and analysis before they can begin to be resolved in a meaningful way. The difficulties and associated issues revolve around the notions of "Quality of Service", usability, and technical performance/efficiency. The discussion of investigations into these aspects occupies the majority of space in this book.

An exacerbating feature is that as improvements in delivery are made in these areas, broadcasting activity and audiences tend to increase—placing new levels of demand on the system.

This book is the first of its kind—bringing together a wide variety of research relating specifically to key areas of multimedia Internet broadcasting, and utilising a comprehensive and detailed treatment. This is a rapidly evolving specialised area of research, and the intention is for the content of the individual chapters to lead to extended discussions on the supporting website (http://mib.mdx.ac.uk). New developments and emerging research directions will be presented online for discussion.

The book looks at many different aspects of the multimedia Internet experience and there are chapters here that will be of interest to users, practitioners, researchers, planners and systems designers. The work reported represents a number of different directions in current research in the area of multimedia Internet broadcasting and there are several themes and threads that can be found in the book. The first three chapters deal with various aspects of the user experience and their behaviour.

The development of MIB tends to be dominated by technological concerns such as protocols and compression algorithms. However, in a market-driven environment, user satisfaction is also important. From the user's perspective, the unique feature of MIB is the potential to make quality of service (QoS) choices. In addition to content choices, users can potentially choose different compression algorithms and different compression rates for video and audio, as well as different frame rates and screen sizes. User satisfaction will depend, to a large extent, on the user's ability to make choices that satisfy their viewing needs. This raises two issues: what sort of options should the broadcaster offer and how should they be communicated to the user, and how easy is it for the user to evaluate the options in relation to their particular needs? In Chapter 1, an examination of these issues is presented. A review and research results focuses on both the user-centred design of MIB interfaces and the psycho-physics of MIB viewing and evaluation. A comprehensive overview of the issues and options is also presented, highlighting the areas most likely to negatively impact user satisfaction. Specific suggestions are made in terms of issues to focus on in usability testing and ways to psycho-physically evaluate the subjective aspects of MIB viewing.

In Chapter 2, some of the latest methods and tools of Advanced Digital User Behaviour Analysis (ADUBA) are discussed. In the first part an overview is given as to the history and current status of the methods and tools of Internet usage analysis. In the second part, the evolution of the Internet from a text-based to a multimedia network and the implications for user behaviour analysis is described. In the third section a summary of some new ways to predict and analyse Internet usage is given, including some showcases of ADUBA tools and experiments. In the final section, conclusions are drawn and an outlook for the future of the ADUBA is undertaken.

While many businesses are keen to develop multimedia Internet broadcasting for in-house services, their deployment raises important practical issues, both for user departments and for corporate network managers. These range from fitness for purpose and usability on the one hand, to the implications for network infrastructure on the other. The study outlined in Chapter 3 was motivated by the need to address these issues. An experimental evaluation of a multimedia Internet broadcasting service designed to support staff training within a large UK bank is described. The focus of the investigation is the influence of different kinds of media content and of network quality of service upon subjects' memory for, and comprehension of, information. In particular, the findings are that degraded quality of service has a greater influence on subjects' uptake of emotive/affective content than on their uptake of factual content. In general, it was found that subjects rated the usability of the system to be quite low, even under ideal network conditions. The results have implications for the more general application of multimedia Internet broadcasting.

Chapters 4 to 6 are concerned with modelling and providing an infrastructure for broadcast events and there are a number of common points in Chapters 4 and 5, particularly the use of the ISABEL application. This provides a platform for the development of customised collaboration services. One extreme case is the organisation of global distributed conferences, with presentations and attendants located in rooms at different sites. It builds its own inter-communication network for providing a uniform Quality of Services through the variety of interconnected sub-networks. Technical problems concerning network and application are not the main problems on this kind of event. In planning, management and realisation of a distributed conference covering several continents, a great variety of networks (including several satellite links) is directly related to the problems of technology management and co-operation between persons and computer systems. Chapter 4 explains how ISABEL provides support for the definition, creation and realisation of this kind of service. Also covered are the technical and organisation problems involved in the realisation of a distributed conference.

The first phase of the videoconference technology evolution was complete by 1996–7. It resulted in videoconferencing becoming a standard and accessible service. Chapter 5 deals with a review of the specifics and main trends inherent to the second phase of the evolution of this service. During this second phase, videoconferencing technologies were progressing under the prevailing conditions when a broadband telecommunication infrastructure became available to a wide scope of corporate and individual users. Videoconferences were considered as a part of the computer-supported co-operative work of distributed groups rather than as an isolated service. The outputs of the NICE/ACTS project (within the 4th Framework program of the European Commission) are given detailed consideration in this chapter since they resulted in the formulation of a new model of a distributed network event. The model has been successfully used for running a number of global network events, which proved that it could be recommended as a standard technical solution.

The final chapter in the modelling section, Chapter 6, looks at QoS architectures. Interactive multimedia (IMM) applications impose many requirements on the transmission of data. These requirements range from high data rates to stringent temporal constraints. Many of today's networks are not able to provide the guarantees required by IMM applications. Not only do the network components need to provide quality of service guarantees, but there is also a need for an overall end-to-end framework that is configurable and able to control and manage delivery of real-time multimedia flows. This chapter reviews functions and parameters for quality of service management to be used in networks and by applications. A novel architectural model that is based on the concept of reflection serves as a reference architecture for the design of new advanced QoS architectures and for the evaluation of existing architectures.

The third section of the book is directed to the trends associated with the use and regulation of the Internet around the world. Chapter 7 is concerned with the challenges of this medium. It postulates that personalisation of Internet services will probably be the main factor for future success of Internet media, where the user obtains the content they want, and is not overwhelmed with unnecessary material. The Internet is the first electronic medium with which this interactive personalisation has been possible. This trend will also be developed by online radio and television, as they move away from general and special interest programming, towards narrowcasting and supply on demand. At the same time, the user is turning into Toffler's pro-sumer, creating the product they themselves desire. Involving users in production of content and the creation of communities increases attractiveness and thus profitability. Personalisation is also aided by two technical means: agents and collaborative filters. These approaches to personalisation are currently being used by several webcasters, to develop their webcasting services.

Accordingly, the other major trend on the Internet is away from globalisation towards niche marketing: content is focussed more and more by interest or locality, dividing the former masses using a single medium into many different users with their "own" medium. These very small target groups (fewer than 10,000 people) can be provided with their own webcasted programme. Former mass media thus become first meso-media on the Internet and finally the fully personalised "Me-channel".

The study in Chapter 8 examines regulatory trends of webcasting in the US, the EU and Japan by taking an approach that is concerned with the convergence between telecommunications and broadcasting. It focuses on universal service because universal service concerning the Internet lays the essential groundwork for webcasting growth and vitality. The study finds that all three nations have attempted to achieve their universal service goals by creating competitive marketplaces. All the approaches are adequate in terms of technological convergence. In particular, the US webcasting sector is likely to evolve without any restrictions owing to the adherence to an unregulated Internet. However, the chapter shows that both the EU's grander aim to cohere different national approaches and the Japanese endeavour to succeed in a secondary info-communications reform have been hampered by different levels of development in the Internet environment in EU member states and by distinctive cultural atmospheres, respectively.

Finally, the book has a section on some of the technical developments of the underlying protocols, algorithms and systems involved in the broadcasting of multimedia data around the Internet.

Layered transmission of data is often recommended as a solution to the problem of varying bandwidth constraints in multicast applications. In the case of video multicast, this technique encodes multiple interdependent layers of video at arbitrary target rates in order to address heterogeneous bandwidth constraints between the source and multiple receivers. However, multi-layered encoding alone is not sufficient to provide high video quality and high bandwidth utilisation, because bandwidth constraints change over time. Adaptive techniques capable of adjusting the rates of video layers are required to maximise video quality and network utilisation.

In Chapter 9 a class of algorithms known as Source-Adaptive Multi-layered Multicast (SAMM) algorithms is defined. In SAMM algorithms, the source uses congestion feedback to adjust the number of generated layers and the bit rate of each layer. Furthermore, an end-to-end SAMM algorithm is introduced, in which only end systems monitor available bandwidth and report the amount of available bandwidth to the source. Using simulations that incorporate actual multi-layered video codecs, it is demonstrated that the proposed SAMM algorithm exhibits better scalability and responsiveness to congestion than algorithms that are not source-adaptive.

Multimedia teleservices require many resources both in the network and in user terminals. Due to the limited availability of such resources, teleservices are competing with each other on the network and can fail, if they cannot have all the resources that would satisfy the resource demand of the teleservice configuration. The work of Chapter 10 describes a better reservation scheme for such teleservices where an adaptive resource broker can adjust the teleservice configurations and their resource requirements to the actual resource utilisation on the network. The broker can realise a teleservice configuration that is as close to the user's desired configuration as it can be while its resource demands are fully satisfied. The broker acts not only at service set-up time but also during the whole teleservice session, adjusting the configuration to the changing network conditions. This has a great advantage in rapidly changing environments such as mobile networks.

Many new applications like groupware systems, news and file distribution or audio and video systems are based on multicast as a prerequisite for scalability. Many of these applications need a reliable multicast support, which is realised in a scalable way by tree-based multicast transport protocols, where the receivers are organised in a so-called ACK tree. Tree-based approaches raise the problem of setting up and maintaining the ACK tree, which is usually done by variations of the expanding ring search (ERS) approach. In the final chapter an alternative approach for building up ACK trees that is based on the concept of a distributed token repository service is presented. Our analysis and simulations show that our approach leads to a significantly lower message overhead compared with ERS and results in better shaped ACK trees, which has a positive effect on reliability and delay.

As will be clear from the above summary, this book covers the crucial aspects of multimedia Internet broadcasting that are relevant in today's network environment. Whilst there are many more areas that could have been included in the book, the overall necessity to provide a useful and timely research-based volume has been achieved.

Andy Sloane and Dave Lawrence
November 2000

Acknowledgements

The editors would like to thank all the referees who helped with the compilation of the papers that make up the chapters of this book, the team at Springer who have been so supportive of the project and the many colleagues who have helped in various ways.

The research for Chapter 1 was supported by grants from Communications and Information Technology Ontario to Professor Richard F. Dillon and from the National Sciences and Engineering Research Council of Canada to Professor Robert L. West. The authors wish to acknowledge the invaluable contributions made to this research by Jo Wood, Stephen Moore, Michael Caspi, Sanjay Chandrasekharan, Diana DeStefano, and Martin Kessner at Carleton University.

The authors of Chapter 3 would like to thank Mark Hartswood for his help with running the experiments, and George Howat of Edinburgh University Computing Services for creating the network and load simulations. They would like also to thank Scottish Bank for their help in providing the necessary resources. Scott Gallacher is supported by an Economic and Social Research Council and Scottish Bank studentship.

In Chapter 6 the authors are indebted to Jürgen Dittrich from GMD-FOKUS for his critical review of, and his contributions to, the CORBA related parts of this paper.

The research for Chapter 8 is supported by the National Science Foundation through grant NCR-9628109. It has also been supported by grants from the University of California MICRO program, Hitachi America, Standard Microsystem Corp., Canon USA, Novell, Tokyo Electric Power Co., Nippon Telegraph and Telephone Corp. (NTT), Nippon Steel Information and Communication Systems Inc. (ENICOM), Fujitsu and Matsushita Electric Industrial Co., and Fundação CAPES/Brazil.

The work for Chapter 9 was supported by the High Speed Network laboratory of Technical University of Budapest, Hungary and the Department of Network Services of Telia Research AB, Sweden.

Contents

Contributors.. xv

1. Human Computer Interaction, Quality of Service, and Multimedia Internet
   Broadcasting
   Robert L. West, Ronald L. Boring, Richard F. Dillon and Jeff Bos................... 1

2. Advanced Digital User Behaviour Analysis (ADUBA)
   Balz Wyss, Christian Scheier and Steffen Egner................................ 17

3. The Influence of Network Quality of Service Factors on the Usability and
   Effectiveness of Multimedia Internet Broadcasting
   Andy McKinlay, Rob Procter and Scott Gallacher.. 35

4. Distributed Global Conferences over Heterogeneous Networks
   *Tomás Robles, Juan Quemada, Tomás de Miguel, Santiago Pavón, Joaquín
   Salvachúa, Manuel Petit, Gabriel Huecas, Hector L. Velayos and Eva
   Castro*... 53

5. Global360/NICE Video Conference Model
   *Andrei S. Mendkovich, Alexei P. Galitsky, Evgeny V. Mironov and Dmitri I.
   Sidelnikov*.. 73

6. Towards an Advanced Quality of Service Architecture
   Jan deMeer and Armin Eberlein.. 93

7. Changes and Challenges: Mass Customised Media and the Internet
   Klaus Goldhammer...121

8. Regulatory Trends in Webcasting in the United States, the European Union, and Japan: Focusing on Universal Service
Jae-Young Kim.. 137

9. A Source-adaptive Multi-layered Multicast Algorithm for Internet Video Distribution
Célio Albuquerque, Brett J. Vickers and Tatsuya Suda.................................... 161

10. An Adaptive Resource Broker for Multimedia Teleservices
Gábor Fehér and István Cselényi 185

11. The Token Repository Service: A Universal and Scalable Mechanism for Constructing Multicast Acknowledgment Trees
Christian Maihöfer..201

Index..229

Contributors

Célio Albuquerque   *celio@ics.uci.edu*
University of California, Irvine, California, USA.

Ronald L. Boring   *rlboring@ccs.carleton.ca*
Computer User Research and Evaluation Laboratory, Carleton University, Ottawa,
Ontario K1S 5B6, Canada.

Jeff Bos   *jeffbos@nortelnetworks.com*
Usability Design Group, Service Provider and Carrier Group, Nortel Networks,
Ottawa, Ontario K2C 0A7, Canada.

Eva Castro
Departamento de Ingeniería de Sistemas Telemáticos, Universidad Politécnica de
Madrid, Spain.

István Cselényi   *Istvan.I.Cselenyi@telia.se*
Department of Network Services, Telia Research AB, Vitsandsgatan 9, S-12386
Farsta, Sweden.

Jan deMeer
GMD Research Institute for Open Communication Systems, Kaiserin-Augusta-
Allee 31, D-10589 Berlin, Germany.

Richard F. Dillon   *ddillon@ccs.carleton.ca*
Computer User Research and Evaluation Laboratory, Carleton University, Ottawa,
Ontario K1S 5B6, Canada.

Armin Eberlein
University of Calgary, Department of Electrical & Computer Engineering, 2500 University Drive NW, Calgary, Alberta T2N 1N4, Canada.

Steffen Egner
University of Maastricht, Maastricht, Netherlands.

Gábor Fehér   *feher@ttt-atm.ttt.bme.hu*
High Speed Network Laboratory, Dept. of Telecommunications and Telematics, Technical University of Budapest, Pázmány Péter sétány 1/D, H-1111 Budapest, Hungary.

Scott Gallacher   *d.s.gallacher@sms.ed.ac.uk*
Research Centre for Social Sciences, University of Edinburgh, High School Yards, Edinburgh EH1 1LZ, UK.

Alexei P. Galitsky   *aga@free.net*
Center for Computer Assistance to Chemical Research, N.D. Zelinsky Institute of Organic Chemistry of the Russian Academy of Sciences, 47 Leninskii Prospekt, Moscow, 117913 Russia.

Klaus Goldhammer   *Klaus.goldhammer@goldmedia.de*
Goldhammer Media Consultancy, Media Research, Oranienburger Str. 90, 10178 Berlin, Germany.

Gabriel Huecas
Departamento de Ingeniería de Sistemas Telemáticos, Universidad Politécnica de Madrid, Spain.

Jae-Young Kim   *jaekim@sejong.ac.kr*
Department of Communication Art, Sejong University, Seoul, Korea.

Dave Lawrence   *dave7@mdx.ac.uk*
Multimedia Informatics and Telematics Research Group, School of Computing Science, Middlesex University, Trent Park, London N14 4YZ, UK.

Christian Maihöfer   *maihoefer@informatik.uni-stuttgart.de*
Institute of Parallel and Distributed High-Performance Systems (IPVR), University of Stuttgart, Breitwiesenstr. 20-22, 70565 Stuttgart, Germany.

Andy McKinlay   *a.mckinlay@ed.ac.uk*
Department of Psychology, University of Edinburgh, Edinburgh EH8 9JZ, UK.

Andrei S. Mendkovich *asm@free.net*
Center for Computer Assistance to Chemical Research, N.D. Zelinsky Institute of
Organic Chemistry of the Russian Academy of Sciences, 47 Leninskii Prospekt,
Moscow, 117913 Russia.

Tomás de Miguel
Departamento de Ingeniería de Sistemas Telemáticos, Universidad Politécnica de
Madrid, Spain.

Evgeny V. Mironov *em@free.net*
Center for Computer Assistance to Chemical Research, N.D. Zelinsky Institute of
Organic Chemistry of the Russian Academy of Sciences, 47 Leninskii Prospekt,
Moscow, 117913 Russia.

Santiago Pavón
Departamento de Ingeniería de Sistemas Telemáticos, Universidad Politécnica de
Madrid, Spain.

Manuel Petit
Departamento de Ingeniería de Sistemas Telemáticos, Universidad Politécnica de
Madrid, Spain.

Rob Procter *rnp@dai.ed.ac.uk*
Institute for Communicating and Collaborative Systems, Division of Informatics,
University of Edinburgh, Edinburgh EH1 1HN, UK.

Tomás Robles *trobles@dit.upm.es*
Departamento de Ingeniería de Sistemas Telemáticos, Universidad Politécnica de
Madrid, Spain.

Juan Quemada
Departamento de Ingeniería de Sistemas Telemáticos, Universidad Politécnica de
Madrid, Spain.

Joaquín Salvachúa
Departamento de Ingeniería de Sistemas Telemáticos, Universidad Politécnica de
Madrid, Spain.

Christian Scheier
California Institute of Technology, Pasadena, California, USA.

Dmitri I. Sidelnikov *sid@free.net*
Center for Computer Assistance to Chemical Research, N.D. Zelinsky Institute of
Organic Chemistry of the Russian Academy of Sciences, 47 Leninskii Prospekt,
Moscow, 117913 Russia.

Andy Sloane *Andy.Sloane@computer.org*
CoNTACT Research Group, School of Computing and IT, University of Wolverhampton, Lichfield Street, Wolverhampton WV1 1SB, UK.

Tatsuya Suda *suda@ics.uci.edu*
University of California, Irvine, California, USA.

Hector L. Velayos
Departamento de Ingeniería de Sistemas Telemáticos, Universidad Politécnica de Madrid, Spain.

Robert L. West *rlwest@ccs.carleton.ca*
Computer User Research and Evaluation Laboratory, Carleton University, Ottawa, Ontario K1S 5B6, Canada.

Brett J. Vickers *bvickers@cs.rutgers.edu*
Rutgers University, USA.

Balz Wyss
Real Networks, Seattle, Washington, USA.

Chapter 1

Human–Computer Interaction, Quality of Service, and Multimedia Internet Broadcasting

Robert L. West, Ronald L. Boring, Richard F. Dillon and Jeff Bos

1.1 Introduction

At first glance, the usability issues related to streaming video or audio over the Internet seem minor. The user simply clicks on a link, a multimedia viewer opens automatically, some buffering occurs, and the show begins. Furthermore, the system is easy to manipulate and easy to learn, as most people are already familiar with similar controls on VCRs, CD players, and tape recorders. However, unlike these other methods for delivering multimedia content, multimedia Internet broadcasting (MIB) has the added dimension of variable bandwidth to contend with. Currently, bandwidth is limited over the Internet. In the future this may be less of a concern [1], but it will be some time before everyone has unlimited access to enough bandwidth to stream the highest quality video (i.e., sufficient to operate a large, high definition screen). However, in the near future people should be able to make bandwidth choices through quality of service (QoS) contracts that will allow viewers to reserve a particular level of bandwidth, in exchange for a fee [2–4].

Negotiating a QoS contract involves two parties—the broadcaster and the viewer. To start the process, the broadcaster must first decide what type of options to make available. These options and the rationale for choosing between them must then be communicated to the viewer, who will evaluate the options and compare them with options offered by other broadcasters. Thus, there are two sides to the QoS usability issue: (1) the tools and methods available to the broadcaster to create the options, and (2) the tools and methods available to the viewer to evaluate the options. For the broadcaster the goal is to be able to offer options that attract viewers. For viewers the goal is to get the highest QoS, given their budget. Over the past year, we have begun to examine the usability issues associated with negotiating QoS contracts. In this chapter, we present an overview of what we have learned so far. Our goal, at this point, is not to prescribe definitive solutions, but to illustrate some of the areas in which usability plays an important role.

1.2 The Problem Space

Typically, software packages for compiling MIB material allow us to choose different compression algorithms and different compression rates for video and audio, as well as different frame rates for video. Initially, it seems straightforward to create a set of bandwidth options (e.g., several different videos designed to operate at different bandwidths), but this task is not as simple as it seems. For example, assume for the moment that a broadcaster has made a decision as to which compression algorithms to use. Given a certain bandwidth they still need to decide how to allocate the resources between providing higher image quality (i.e., the video compression rate), higher audio quality, and higher frame rates. If we allow three settings (high, medium, and low) for each dimension, the result is 27 different options per bandwidth level. If we include choices as to compression algorithms and spatial resolution (i.e., the video display size) the number of choices goes even higher. Figure 1.1 illustrates a multidimensional space representing the choices faced by broadcasters. As the diagram indicates, decisions concerning the relative amount of bandwidth to devote to audio quality, image quality, and frame rate are nested within decisions concerning the amount of bandwidth and the specific auditory and video compression algorithms used. Note that, to simplify the figure, we assume that spatial resolution has already been decided. Our omission of spatial resolution also reflects the fact that we have not yet examined this issue and therefore do not discuss it in this article.

1.3 Scale Linearity

Another issue to be aware of is whether or not the scales used to navigate through the space described in Figure 1.1 are linear to human perception. For example, most users naively assume that the settings for video compression (often presented on a 100-point scale) map linearly onto the perception of video quality. Thus, when creating options, a broadcaster could easily be led to choose points equidistant along the scale to create equally spaced quality options. For example, when Bos [5] wanted to create five equally spaced video quality settings using the Sorenson codec [6], he chose compression settings of 0%, 25%, 50%, 75%, and 100%. The result was a scale with extremely minor differences at the top end and major differences at

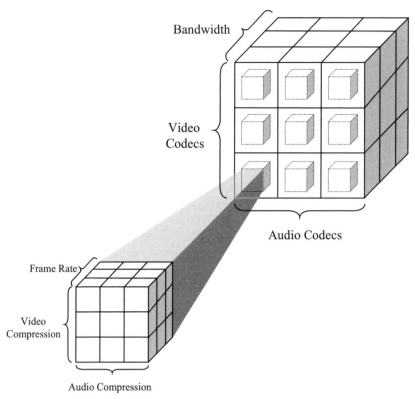

Figure 1.1 A representation of the choices confronting the broadcaster of multimedia Internet content.

the bottom end. For viewers interested in selecting a minimally acceptable, low QoS level, the scale would not allow a good range of choices.

To rectify this problem the quality settings interface could include a scale that reflects the human perception of quality. In psychophysics, the generally accepted method for developing such a scale is magnitude estimation [7]. In magnitude estimation, a stimulus is presented and an observer reports their subjective perception of the magnitude of a particular dimension of the stimulus [8]. Psychophysical studies indicate that, to a first order approximation, ratings of subjective judgements, such as quality, conform to a power law function [9],

$$R = KS^B, \tag{1.1}$$

where S is some physically measurable aspect of the stimulus, R is a number reflecting the observer's perception of subjective magnitude, K is a constant that represents the range of the R scale, and B represents the compression function used by the observer (people also use compression to save on bandwidth, e.g., [10]). This function is quite useful since by taking the logarithm of both sides we get

$$\log R = B \cdot \log S + \log K. \tag{1.2}$$

Plotting this equation gives a straight line with the slope equal to the compression function and the intercept equal to the scaling constant. From this, the parameter B can be used to transform a physically based scale to a perceptually based scale.

We performed a magnitude estimation experiment [11] in which we asked observers to estimate the smoothness of videos presented at different frame rates. Using a regression analysis, we obtained a value of 0.68 ($R^2 = 0.915$) for B (see Figure 1.2), indicating that the relationship between frame rate and the perception of smoothness can be described by a power function with an exponent of approximately this value. We plan to do further studies to confirm this value, but based on this study we can say that converting frame rate by raising it to the power of 0.68 should produce a more natural scale. Currently, we are in the process of performing the same type of experiment for video compression rates. However, unlike frame rate, the results of these experiments will be specific to the particular compression algorithm used. Also, we should not necessarily expect to get a power function since compression settings do not directly reflect a physical continuum.

1.4 Content Types

Another important issue is the interaction between content types and QoS settings. Apteker, Fisher, Kisimov, and Neishlos [12] found that people prefer different QoS settings for video depending on the nature of the content. However, the reason for

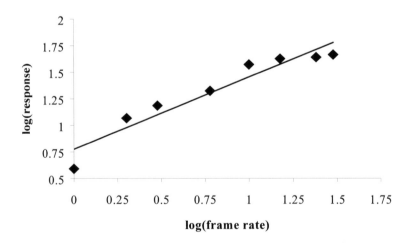

Figure 1.2 Magnitude estimation results describing the relationship between frame rate and the perception of smoothness.

such preferences could be perceptually based, or based on the viewer's purpose or goal. Take frame rate, for example. A philosophy student watching a lecture might choose a low frame rate since the movements of the lecturer are not so important, whereas a dance student watching a performance might want a high frame rate because the movements are important. In such cases, content would be associated with certain QoS choices, because it is somewhat predictive of who is watching and why. To be clear, we will refer to such cases as being influenced by the viewer's goals rather than by the content.

Note, though, that content could still have a perceptual effect on frame rate. For example, when the frame rate is lowered for fast action video the discrepancy between two frames will be greater than for slow action video. To illustrate this, imagine two videos, one of a person running, the other of a person walking. The effect of lowering the frame rate is to create gaps in the motion, but these gaps will be larger for the running person than for the walking person, and thus more noticeable. Because of this, people may be more sensitive to frame rate changes for fast action content than for slow action content.

To examine this question, we included a magnitude-matching experiment within the magnitude estimation experiment reported above. Magnitude matching involves having viewers make judgements of different stimulus types within the same experiment [13]. In the experiment we alternated fast content (footage of a football game) with slow content (a scene from a movie of two people talking). The responses to the fast content were then plotted against the responses to the slow content for each frame rate level. Figure 1.3 shows the graph. A regression analysis

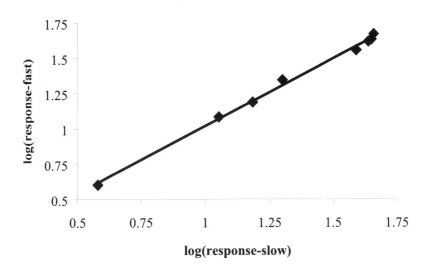

Figure 1.3 Magnitude matching results comparing the effect of frame rate on perceived smoothness for fast and slow action videos.

indicated that the slope of the fitted function was 1.04 ($R^2 = 0.997$), suggesting that speed of movement does not affect people's ability to judge frame rate.

The issues for video compression are more complex than for frame rate, since we know that different content will actually produce different results. For example, scenes with less movement will often be rendered with more detail than scenes with more movement. Because of this, broadcasters should be aware that they may need to adjust the compression level based on content. Possibly, guidelines describing the effect of content on quality could be developed, but they would need to be specific to the different types of compression algorithms. To examine this issue, we plan to include different content types in our magnitude estimation experiments on different video compression algorithms.

1.5 Scaling Quality

Scale values are used to communicate the broadcaster's evaluation of quality to the user, so it is important that the scale values accurately reflect the quality of the product. For example, if a broadcaster offers three options—high quality, medium quality, and low quality—the viewer will expect these categories to conform, approximately, to their expectations for high, medium, and low quality.

As Watson and Sasse [14] point out, there are serious problems with the International Telecommunications Union (ITU) recommended scales for measuring audiovisual quality [15–17]. The ITU approach is to use 5-point scales with labels describing each point (e.g., the image quality labels are: excellent, good, fair, poor, bad). One problem with this is that the labels may not reflect the same magnitude of quality when they are translated into different languages. While it is possible to address this issue to some degree (e.g., [18]), there is another serious problem. Reviews of psychophysical scaling techniques have found that there are relatively large individual differences in the way that individuals use scales to report subjective impressions of magnitude [19–22]. The reason this is a problem is that QoS agreements are made between a broadcaster and an *individual* viewer. Therefore, the broadcaster needs to understand what individuals intend when they communicate their desired QoS level.

To understand the implications of this it is important to distinguish between what people perceive and what they report. The whole process can be described as a function,

$$R = b(f(S)) \tag{1.3}$$

where S is the stimulus magnitude, R is the reported magnitude, f is the function describing how S is transformed into a perceptual experience, and b is the function describing how $f(S)$ is transformed to a scale value. The problem is that people have different b functions. One might also ask to what degree people have different f functions for subjective QoS judgements, such as video quality, video smoothness, video clarity, audio clarity, etc. The answer to this is that we can't tell, because we have very little control over the b function. However, anecdotally, we know that people are generally able to agree on judgements of audio and visual quality at a coarse grain level (e.g., this is very good, this is OK, this is terrible). So, it seems there is some common factor.

To address this problem, we have been working on a new approach called *constrained scaling* [23]. Our argument is that people are similar to measuring instruments that have not been calibrated. More specifically, we believe that when faced with a scaling task, people mentally construct the b function by a process containing ad hoc decisions. To avoid this, our approach is to calibrate people to a standard mapping before beginning the scaling task. This is done by teaching people a scale relating numbers to a stable perceptual dimension, such as loudness or darkness on a gray scale. Assuming their f functions are similar, this means they should all learn the same b function. Once a standard mapping is established, the stimuli of interest are presented. Initial results show that this technique considerably diminishes individual differences, indicating that the observers continue to use the learned b function [23].

Currently we are working on a PC-based version of constrained scaling that can be used to judge video quality. Our interest in this is twofold. First we want to conduct basic research to determine how similar judgments of quality are across observers. This is important to know as it sets an upper boundary on our ability to communicate quality through the use of ratings. Our second goal is to create a version of the constrained scaling technique that is easy to use for both the broadcaster and the viewer. This would involve creating a standardised scale that is very quick and easy to learn. Such a scale would significantly increase the ability of broadcasters and viewers to communicate about levels of quality.

1.6 Presenting the Options

In terms of presenting options, the broadcaster has several choices. The simplest form of presentation would be simply to offer the viewer different levels of quality. However, as outlined above, there are several important issues to address.

1. As noted above, what constitutes good quality will depend on the viewer's goals. These can be broken down into understanding the relative importance of audio quality, picture quality, and frame rate for the task in which the viewer is engaged. Essentially the issue is how to lower the bandwidth with a minimal loss of quality. Also, there should be some attention paid to identifying the highest and lowest quality settings that would be of use to the viewer. There is no point offering quality settings that are too low to be useful or that use up extra bandwidth without creating an appreciable increase in perceived quality.

2. The effect of content on quality also has to be considered. If it is deemed to be a significant factor, the quality ratings for different content types may need to be adjusted to compensate for the effect of content. For example,

using the same video compression setting, fast action content may appear as lower quality than slow action content at first glance.

3. The linearity of the quality options is also an issue. Unless there is some compelling reason to do otherwise, the different quality settings should seem to be equally spaced when viewed by the user.

4. Finally, the labelling of the quality categories should convey to the user a roughly accurate idea of the quality they should expect.

Thus, it is important for a broadcaster to understand the needs of their audience. To do this, they need to take a user-centred approach. This could involve getting comments on the options they intend to offer through interviews or focus groups, or through detailed studies of the users engaged in tasks along with psychophysical measurements of the different dimensions related to perceptions of quality. The latter course is more likely to come up with information that is broadly applicable (i.e., standards for specific tasks), but it is probably too labour intensive for the small broadcaster.

There are also other ways to structure quality options. For viewers with more expertise, one way is to provide an indication of the actual quality settings instead of an overall quality rating. The easiest way to do this would be to list the actual audio compression rate, video compression rate, and frame rate. However, as noted above, this can be misleading. A different approach would be to list each quality parameter according to a rating corrected to be linear to the human perception of that quality dimension.

1.7 Comparing Samples

The user must select between different broadcasters as well as between different quality options. In addition to issues such as cost and content selection, viewers should be favourable toward broadcasters that prove themselves reliable in terms of delivering the quality they promise. A broadcaster can go a long way to meeting this goal by paying attention to the issues outlined above, but it is possible to go further by supplying samples of the quality options (e.g. short downloaded video clips). Done right, such samples should make the level of quality for a particular option clear to the viewer and should also allow the viewer to evaluate the quality of the product they receive. Of course, this does not negate the need for attention to the issues outlined above. Providing well-balanced choices that are useful to the viewer is still critical. Good labelling also remains important, as the viewer should ideally be able to narrow their search for the best QoS level before viewing samples.

We have done usability testing on a number of different prototypes for comparing video samples and found that the process of comparing samples is not as simple as it might seem. The testing involved having viewers perform specific comparisons between video samples, as well as a more naturalistic task in which they selected the minimum acceptable quality from a group of video samples. The viewers were asked pre-prepared questions while they performed the task and were given a questionnaire at the end of the task (we used 10 users per usability test). The results are described below.

1.8 Design of a QoS Interface Prototype

There are many ways to offer options to a viewer, so we could not test all of them. However, we were particularly interested in creating an interface that would provide the viewer with a high degree of control over the different dimensions of quality. Therefore, we chose to provide an indication of the individual quality settings (i.e., audio compression rate, video compression rate, and frame rate) instead of an overall quality rating. Under these conditions, one is immediately faced with the problem that this amount of information is difficult for the user to organise and keep track of. To solve this problem, we developed a prototype that used three sliders to control the three quality dimensions. The user could set each slider to one of four settings and the corresponding sample would play. With four settings for each dimension, the prototype required 64 samples (all 64 samples contained the same content to facilitate comparisons). The implementation idea behind the prototype was that a broadcaster would supply the samples, plus a viewer for comparing them, in order to allow the user to explore and understand the range of choices and their implication for quality and cost (each sample would have a corresponding cost that would reflect the required bandwidth).

Another important design issue is that there are multiple ways to set up a comparison process. In particular, samples can be presented in serial or in parallel. For a single-screen process there are two options: (1) the user needs to load each sample to play it, creating a delay between viewings and causing extra steps, and (2) the user can switch between samples, both of which are running. This can be done within a single step (e.g., a button press) and involves no delay. For the parallel-screens process, the samples run on two video windows and can be compared directly. Since having two video windows running in parallel allows the most careful comparison, we adopted this strategy for our initial prototype. To further facilitate comparisons, we set up the system so that the two video windows always played the videos in sync.

1.9 Procedures and Affordances

Our initial approach to designing the interface involved supporting a specific procedure for comparing samples, which was explained to the users before testing. The interface is illustrated in Figure 1.4. The video window on the right showed the sample that represented the level of quality recommended by the broadcaster (i.e. the level deemed appropriate for the average user). The sliders at the bottom showed the quality dimension settings for that sample. However, if moved, the new quality settings would be displayed on the left video window, and the original slider settings would be marked with a different coloured indicator. When a new quality level was decided on, clicking on the "Accept" button moved the new sample to the right

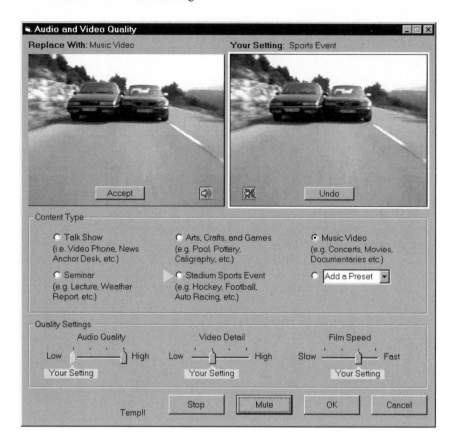

Figure 1.4. Our first QoS interface prototype.

video window, replacing the old sample. This process could then be iterated to fine-tune the user's quality settings until the video window on the right represented the minimum acceptable quality (note, we also used this interface to examine the idea of using preset quality values for certain content types, but we do not, as yet, have any significant findings in this area).

Testing revealed that the users found the comparison process to be difficult and confusing, both when asked to make specific comparisons and when asked to find the sample that provided the minimum acceptable quality. Based on our observations from the usability evaluation, we redesigned the interface from a different perspective. Whereas before we had relied on the users understanding a specific procedure, the second version was designed to present *affordances* [24] for understanding how to use the interface to make comparisons. Affordances, in this context, can be considered as structures in the environment that suggest certain actions. For example, a chair affords sitting because of the size and height of the seat and because it provides a surface to lean your back against.

We called our affordance-based design the *two-TVs model*. Instead of presenting the viewer with a specific procedure for making comparisons, we presented them

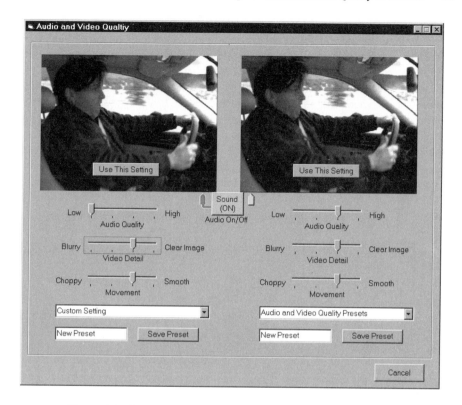

Figure 1.5 The two-TVs model, our second QoS interface prototype.

with two video windows, side by side, each with their own set of quality controls (see Figure 1.5). As the name indicates, this is similar to placing two TVs side by side as you might see in a store selling TVs. The set-up naturally affords the process of comparing the quality on one TV with the quality on the other.

A second round of usability testing revealed that the users found it much easier to make specific comparisons using this interface, but most still found it confusing to use the interface to determine a minimally acceptable quality level. Although this approach did not clear up all the problems, it did result in a clear improvement. We also identified two reasons for the persistent problem of finding a minimally acceptable quality level, which are discussed in Sections 1.10 and 1.11.

1.10 Auditory Issues

One problem with the two-TVs model was that the auditory component did not fit with our affordance model very well. To deal with the problem that you can only have one auditory track running at a time, we created the interface so that when the user changed the auditory quality control associated with one of the video windows, the system would switch to the newly selected sound track. In addition we included a control that sat between the two video windows and could be used to switch back and forth between the sound tracks associated with each video. The control also had an indicator to indicate which video window the sound track was coming from. Overall, users found the audio controls less intuitive than the visual controls.

The problem was also compounded by the presence of visual capture. Visual capture occurs when a sound and a visual event occur at the same time (e.g., when a tone and a light come on simultaneously) [25]. Generally speaking, when this occurs, the visual event will capture the auditory event so that the auditory event is perceived to emanate from the location of the visual event, even though its actual source is elsewhere. During the comparison process, we found that high quality video captured high quality sound. The result was that when viewers compared a sample that was high quality video and low quality sound with a sample that was low quality video and high quality sound, the high quality sound would seem to be coming from the high quality video. We found that users could easily be misled by this phenomenon. Based on this, our recommendation is that the sound be turned off when comparing two video images.

1.11 Problem Solving Issues

As a backdrop to this section, it is important to consider the user's attitude toward the task. Over all, we found users to have a strong expectation that the task would be easy and straightforward. However, this is not the case. The user must select a subset of comparisons from the relatively large number of possible comparisons and be able to derive the best choice from the results of these comparisons. While the affordance-based prototype made the controls much easier to use for creating specific comparisons, as in the first version it offered no help in terms of which comparisons to make.

This issue was addressed in a third usability study in which we asked users to compare three prototypes:

1. The two-TVs prototype with the auditory component removed (i.e., the user could manipulate video compression and frame rate only).
2. A one-TV prototype that was identical to Prototype 1 except that there was only one video window and one set of controls.
3. A one-TV prototype that required the user to change the settings then press a button to bring up a screen with the appropriate sample. To change samples, the video had to be stopped first before selecting the next sample and playing it (for Prototypes 1 and 2 the controls were online, so any change would immediately be visible on screen).

The user's task was to use each system to find the sample corresponding to their minimal acceptable level of quality. Due to the time delay, Prototype 3 made it very difficult to make comparisons and was rated as poor. Prototype 2 made it easy to make comparisons that involved changing one slider by one position setting, because the change was instantly visible. However, Prototype 2 was not much better than Prototype 1 for making other comparisons. Despite this, Prototype 2 was, on average, preferred to Prototype 1. The reason for this can be seen by comparing the procedures employed by the users who disliked Prototype 1 with the procedures employed by the users who liked Prototype 1. Those who liked Prototype 1 were systematic and proceeded by using one video as a reference. In most cases they initially set both video windows to either the lowest or the highest settings. The strategy was then to systematically degrade or upgrade one video and make comparisons with the other, which served as a reference. Once they had identified the video they thought would be the lowest acceptable quality, they used it as a reference and made further comparisons to verify that it was the lowest acceptable quality.

In contrast, the users who disliked Prototype 1 were unsystematic and found that Prototype 1 offered too many choices. Prototype 2 allowed them to receive feedback while exploring different settings and also *afforded* a particular strategy. Specifically, the way Prototype 2 was configured encouraged users to degrade the video along one dimension until it was at the lowest acceptable level, then to degrade it along the other dimension. Prototype 1 did not afford a comparison strategy but instead relied on the user to create an efficient, rational process for making comparisons. Because of this only the users who took this approach rated Prototype 1 positively.

To further investigate the role of affordances, we created a new two-TVs prototype that has two video windows, one with no controls that always plays the highest quality sample, and the other with controls for adjusting quality. Initial testing of this prototype suggests that it affords the strategy of degrading the video until it is unacceptably lower than the highest quality setting. However, this appears to be useful only for evaluating high end quality settings. An interesting issue for future research is the degree to which affordances can be used to direct the user's comparison strategies and how this affects the user's QoS choices.

1.12 Conclusions

When creating a QoS contract, it is important that both broadcasters and users are clear about the level of quality that is expected. In this chapter, we have tried to show how usability plays an important role in this process and to illustrate this with some of our findings. From our discussion, it should be clear that there are many usability issues that need to be addressed.

References

[1]   Hinden, R.M. (1996) "IP Next Generation", Communications of the ACM, 39(6), 61–71
[2]   QoS Forum. (1999) "White Paper—QoS Protocols & Architectures", Stardust.com Inc., Campbell, California.

[3]   Hafid, A., v. Bochmann, G., and Dssouli, R. (1995) "Models for quality of service negotiation in distributed multimedia applications", presented at the Second International Workshop on Protocols for Multimedia Systems, Salzburg, Austria.

[4]   Fishburn, P.C., and Odlyzko, A.M. (1998) "Dynamic behavior of differential pricing and quality of service options for the Internet", in "Proceedings of ICE 98", 128–139.

[5]   Bos, J. (2000) "A User Interface for Negotiating Quality of Service for Digital Video", Master's Thesis, Department of Psychology, Carleton University, Ottawa, Canada.

[6]   Sorenson Vision, Inc. (1997) "Sorenson Technology White Paper", Sorenson Vision Inc., Salt Lake City, Utah.

[7]   Bolanowski, S. J., and Gescheider, G. A. (1991) "Ratio Scaling of Psychological Magnitude: In Honor of the Memory of S. S. Stevens", Lawrence Erlbaum, Hillsdale, New Jersey.

[8]   Stevens, S.S. (1957) "On the psychophysical law", Psychological Review, 64, 153-181.

[9]   Stevens, S. S. (1975) "Psychophysics: Introduction to its Perceptual, Neural and Social Prospects", Wiley Interscience, New York.

[10] Olshausen, B.A., and Field, D.J. (2000) "Vision and coding of natural images", American Scientist, 88(3), 238–245.

[11] Boring, R.L., West, R.L., and Dillon, R.F. (2000) "Evaluation of frame rate quality for different video content types", presented at the CITO Digital Media Research Review, Toronto, Canada.

[12] Apteker, R.T., Fisher, J.A., Kisimov, V.S., and Neishlos, H. (1995) "Video acceptability and frame rate", IEEE Multimedia, 2(3), 32–40.

[13] Marks, L.E., Stevens, J.C., Bartoshuk, L.M., Gent, J.G., Rifkin, B., and Stone, V.K. (1988) "Magnitude matching: The measurement of taste and smell", Chemical-Senses, 13, 63–87.

[14] Watson, A., and Sasse, M.A. (1998) "Measuring perceived quality of speech and video in multimedia conferencing applications", in "Proceedings of the 6th ACM International Conference on Multimedia", 55–60.

[15] ITU-T P.800 "Methods for Subjective Determination of Transmission Quality", International Telecommunications Union, Geneva.

[16] ITU-T P.920 "Interactive Test Methods for Audiovisual Communications", International Telecommunications Union, Geneva.

[17] ITU-R BT.500-7 "Methodology for the Subjective Assessment of the Quality of Television Pictures", International Telecommunications Union, Geneva.

[18] Narita, N. (1993) "Graphic scaling and validity of Japanese descriptive terms used in subjective-evaluation tests", SMPTE Journal, 103, 616–622.

[19] Algom, D., and Marks, L. E. (1984) "Individual differences in loudness processing and loudness scales", Journal of Experimental Psychology: General, 113, 571–593.

[20] Logue, A. W. (1976) "Individual differences in magnitude estimation of loudness", Perception & Psychophysics, 19, 279–280.

[21] Luce, D. R., and Mo, S. S. (1965) "Magnitude estimation of heaviness and loudness by individual observers: A test of a probabilistic response theory", The British Journal of Mathematical and Statistical Psychology, 18, 159–174.

[22] Teghtsoonian, M., and Teghtsoonian, R. (1983) "Consistency of individual exponents in cross-modal matching", Perception & Psychophysics, 33, 203–214.

[23] West, R. L., Ward, L. M., and Khosla, R. (2000) "Constrained scaling: The effect of learned psychophysical scales on idiosyncratic response bias", Perception & Psychophysics, 62, 137–151.

[24] Gibson, J.J. (1979) "The Ecological Approach to Visual Perception", Houghton Mifflin, Boston.

[25] Coren, S., Ward, L.M., and Enns, J.T. (1999) "Sensation and Perception", Fifth Edition, Harcourt Brace, Toronto.

Chapter 2

Advanced Digital User Behaviour Analysis (ADUBA)

Balz Wyss, Christian Scheier and Steffen Egner

2.1 Introduction

The analysis of user behaviour is becoming more relevant in the Internet space. One may ask for the motivation underlying the analysis of Internet users and what types of studies are being conducted. Generally speaking, two main areas with different motivations can be identified:

1. *Scientific Research.* Many of the early studies about the behaviour of Internet usage have their origin in academic science. The Internet affects many areas of our being. As for other mass media such as radio and television, the global network has become a fundamental part of the communication and interaction of individuals in modern society. It is in the very nature of science to understand new phenomena such as the Internet and find explanations of how such phenomena are integrated in our everyday life.

2. *Commercial Research.* The Internet is developing towards a marketplace of increasing importance to the overall economy of post-modern societies. Within a short period of time the Internet has captured a significant share of the Gross Domestic Product (GDP) of many developed nations. The growing amount of business done via the Internet generates a need for commercial market research.

The general goal of scientific research is to better understand the behaviour of human beings. The commercial research goes a step further. Researching the behaviour of users helps businesses not only to better understand the needs of their customers, but also to improve the sales of products and services.

While the ultimate goals of commercial market research might be somewhat different from the goals of scientific research, their areas of interest and tools are often similar. The following three main types of research can be distinguished in terms of Internet user behaviour:

a.   *User Studies.* User studies are focused on the behaviour of people. The intention is to analyse how surfers use the Internet. Psychological and sociological questions are at the centre of this type of studies.

b.   *Product Studies.* The goal of product studies is to understand how a particular application or service is perceived and used by Internet surfers. Application or service specific questions are the main focus of this area of research.

c.   *Media Studies.* Media studies are geared towards the analysis of the tools which Internet surfer use. The focus is on analysing technical specifications with which users are confronted when using the Internet.

The topics of these types of studies often relate to each other, and various aspects and levels of perspectives overlap. This is particularly true in cases where rather complex topics are researched. For example, the question "How does the Internet impact the use of other media and the interaction between people?" relates to study type a. (User Studies) and c. (Media Studies). And the question "What are the socio-demographic characteristics of users who frequently consume streaming media?" relates to a. (User Studies) and b. (Product Studies).

Complex multilevel studies are not new to mass media research [1]. The complexity of the design and structure of studies is a mere representation of the complexity of life in modern societies.

2.2 Brief History of Internet Usage Behaviour Studies

Considering the very young age of the Internet as a mass medium, the analysis of Internet users has come a long way. It can be said that Internet user behaviour research has been adopted much faster than with other mass media such as radio and TV [2]. The fast adoption rate of user analysis within the Internet space is partly due to the very nature of the new technology. The Internet as a sophisticated technical network leads to new means of tracking and analysing the behaviour of users.

While the adoption rate of user behaviour analysis is phenomenal, we are still at the very beginning of what could be called a sophisticated research field. Until the beginning of the new millennium, the traditional online market research was mainly focused on relatively simple quantitative data gathering methods such as server and domain statistical studies, log file analysis, data mining [3] and click-through tracking. In the earlier 1990s, the publicly available studies were focused on the use of the technical infrastructure. The first studies focused on user behaviour analysis were mostly done in-house by commercial enterprises. They were often rather unsystematic snapshots and were rarely made publicly available. The main purpose of these studies was simply to better understand the data volume generated in order to determine the necessary bandwidth and server capacities. Also, general web site usage was analysed which helped companies to get a better sense as to which parts of a web site were popular and which not.

By the middle of the 1990s the first systematic user studies took place. One of the ideas was to track socio-demographic data of users. The data could then be put in relation to certain behavioural patterns, user values and opinions. The user surveys conducted by the GVU of Georgia Tech are a good example for this type of study [4]. Users had to fill out an online questionnaire where they were asked questions such as how often they access the Internet, if security was an important issue, or which browser they were using.

The GVU studies of Georgia, which were started in 1994, and similar projects were helpful in order to understand the characteristics of the earlier Internet audience and gave insights in the basic behavioural trends of the audience. The studies filled a void in the generation of data about the quickly growing Internet user base. The main problem of this type of study was that the respondents did not necessarily represent the real socio-demographic picture of the Internet audience. The results were based on a biased, non-randomised set of users.

Towards the second half of the 1990s, market research companies such as Nielsen Media Research, MediaMetrix, and NPD started regular surveys with representative and/or adjusted user samples[5]. Initially these studies mainly focused on basic ratings such as number of web pages viewed per user or unique monthly visitors to a web site (also called "reach"). Over time some of the rating studies included more in-depth analysis of user behaviour. At the same time desk market research studies also became more popular. Companies such as Forrester or Jupiter Communications introduced studies focused on trend forecasts such as Internet adoption rate and online consumer spending behaviour trends [6].

By the end of the 1990s the Internet evolved to a global commercial market place of unseen competitive challenges and new application and interaction potentials for users. Financial and marketing issues have become increasingly important to many Internet businesses. With the Internet becoming a more mature industry, more sophisticated user behaviour tracking tools became available, e.g. tracking marketing campaigns, click-through paths or even return of investments (ROI).

Not only has the scope of user behaviour studies broadened, but there seems to be a trend toward merging between the traditional offline market research industry and the online research services. Today's studies cover a broad range of topics geared towards user behaviour analysis such as:

- User motivation
- User perception
- User values and opinions

The tools and methods applied in today's user behaviour research in the digital network space are by no means comprehensive. As a matter of fact, there seems to be a considerable lack of concise and consistent tools and methods. Similar to the traditional market research, there are many discussions and disputes going on as to the validity and reliability of various methods and tools. Due to the incredible pace of new developments in the Internet area, these discussions will most likely continue.

2.3 User Behaviour Analysis in a Multimedia Internet Environment

The pace of new development of technical applications such as wireless, multimedia, and virtual 3D worlds as well as the constant flow of new web services constitutes a considerable challenge to the research community – in science as well as commerce. New developments in the digital space increase the need for more sophisticated user behaviour analysis tools and methods.

Advanced Digital User Behaviour Analysis (ADUBA) is an area of research, which addresses the need for more sophisticated user behaviour analysis tools and methods. Two main lines of research provide the foundation of ADUBA. First, results and methods from perception and cognition research are used to investigate and better understand user interactions with web content. For example, with the advent of 3D web content new challenges have to be met with regard to guiding the user through, say, a 3D-ecommerce site. How should 3D content be designed to be intuitive to users? How do customers use the mouse to navigate through 3D content? Other issues arise in the context of multi-modal perception. The web is increasingly becoming a provider of multi- and cross-modal content. Visual information is complemented and enhanced with audio, and possibly tactile feedback material. How should visual and auditory information be integrated for the content to be optimally perceived by users? What are the rules the brain uses to integrate such information? These are among the questions addressed by ADUBA.

The second line of research used in ADUBA is artificial intelligence. Instead of trying to *analyse* user behaviour, one may also try to *synthesise* and thus emulate it. For example, if one knew how users perceived web pages, one could build an expert system with which a large amount of pages can be analysed without resorting to laborious user behaviour analyses. Artificial Intelligence, in particular its latest developments [7], provides the tools to simulate human behaviour. This ranges from models of perception, attention and memory, to complete agent architectures that simulate users' behaviour on entire web sites (e.g. which ads are being looked at, which links are clicked, etc.).

The focus of ADUBA is thus threefold:

- *Next generation Internet research.* ADUBA provides tools and methods to analyse user behaviour with regards to new digital applications and web services such as multimedia streams, online games, 3D interfaces or audio chats [8].
- *Improvement of first generation Internet research.* ADUBA tools and methods go beyond basic quantitative data gathering such as rating studies or click-through analysis. ADUBA tools capture various types of user interaction such as eye tracking and mouse-clicks, etc. Qualitative aspects of user behaviour such as verbal responses are put in relation with other forms of human interactions.
- *Re-introduction to traditional research.* ADUBA tools and methods can be applied to traditional research such as cognitive science, clinical psychology, and market research.

There have been various tools and services that have grown out of the ADUBA research field. Interestingly, most of the leading ADUBA projects have either been initiated by academic research institutions or developed by them. This is true for projects undertaken by providers such as MediaAnalyzer/NetExpert (CalTech), Eyetracking (San Diego State University), and Eyetools (Stanford) [9]. Other providers such as Noldus Information Technology often highlight their close ties to academic research.

2.4 ADUBA Tools

In this section we shall discuss some core methods and features of ADUBA tools. These features represent just the tip of the iceberg. It can be expected that more features and applications will soon be available in the field of ADUBA.

2.4.1 Investigative Tools

Investigative tools are the first type of application to be discussed in this chapter. This type of tool covers the measurement and analysis of a wide range of user behaviours. The tools generally accept a variety of data formats as input—from general HTML web sites to common digital movie formats and streamed video.

At the core of most of the tools is a set of sophisticated tools with which behaviours such as eye or head movements that were filmed with a digital camera can be analysed. The analysis can range from simple reaction time measures to complete spatial analyses of eye movement data. In order to perform such analyses, test subjects will be confronted with a stimulus such as a web site or a video stream. The next step involves using the manual and automatic tracking aspect of the tools. In manual tracking, the user can insert visual markers that designate temporal and/or spatial events by using the mouse. A typical example for a temporal marker is "Inspection Start", i.e., the point at which a web user has started to inspect a web page. Spatial markers typically correspond to the resting location of the eyes and aspects of head position. The tools typically contain a large set of image processing mechanisms with which

a. eye movements and other user behaviour responses can be automatically tracked, and
b. raw eye movement data can be mapped onto the stimulus material.

This latter process is called "calibration", and in most eye trackers constitutes a notorious problem. This is because calibration is strongly affected by head movements. Ideally, the subject should not move the head at all. In reality, head movements are common. Some tools such as MediaAnalyzer solve the problem of head movements by allowing for relative calibration (other tools use different methods, or ignore head movements). Relative calibration takes tracked head movement data as the frame of reference, instead of some arbitrary frame during calibration. This new approach, while simple in principle, yields very accurate and robust results.

Some of the tools allow implementers to perform the entire analysis process on the stimuli input itself. In the case of MediaAnalyzer, results are, for example, directly superimposed on the video, thereby allowing the test subject to have complete visual control on the accuracy of the tracking.

The ultimate goal is to study how people perceive various types of digital content. Specifically, most tools allow the analysis of one or more of the following content:

a. static web page layout and compositions
b. static and animated advertising
c. dynamic, interactive multimedia streams (videos, movies, SMIL presentations).

For example, advertising agencies want to evaluate and compare various story boards of a video ad spot before going into full production. The goal is to find out which story people prefer, and what makes an ad spot particularly attractive to different audiences. This is in order to be able to go back to the pre-production stage and change the content of the ad spot based on the findings of the test.

The ad spot is provided to a sample of test users. During the presentation mouse clicks and eye movements of each single user are tracked. In addition to measuring the perception flow, users' opinions (e.g. like/dislike) about the ad spot are recorded. The end result is a set of data which helps to select the best and most effective ad story. This in turn will help to increase sell-through and customer satisfaction.

2.4.2 Predictive Tools

While analytical tools are used to analyse content based on user feedback, predictive tools help to predict behaviour by using artificial intelligence methods as used in cognitive science. The artificial intelligence methods simulate users' interaction.

There are several advantages of applying artificial intelligence, one of which is typically the lower cost of research because computer algorithms are used to analyse digital content instead of test users. Some of the ADUBA tools mentioned above such as MediaAnalyzer/NetExpert include artificial intelligence features.

Artificial intelligence can be used for many research purposes in the ADUBA field. For example, artificial intelligence features can be used to predict the saliency of web sites. Click-through rates, stickiness of web sites, and/or customer conversion and retention rates can be improved by knowing how to distinguish salient from non-salient parts of a web site. It is known, for example, that visual attention is shifted towards the most salient parts of a visual scene. For example, a red dot on a blue homogenous surface will immediately attract attention through a so-called pop-out process.

Saliency can be determined across different dimensions. Typical dimensions are colour, shape or motion on a web page. In NetExpert, for example, saliency for different feature dimensions is computed separately, yielding a saliency "map" for each feature dimension. These saliency maps are then integrated to result in an overall saliency or conspicuity map. This map indicates locations of the visual scene (e.g. web page) that stick out, and thus attract user attention.[1]

In order for these computations to work, ADUBA tools navigate to the indicated web page where a screenshot of the web page is taken. The page is subsequently analysed in terms of saliency. In addition, some tools download the HTML code to analyse, if available, the size and location of images and text.

The analysis of static web sites for users' behaviour prediction is a relatively simple task compared with analysis of multi-mode applications such as a SMIL stream in which sound, video, images and text are simultaneously displayed. The interaction between the various modalities can be very complex. The ability to analyse multi-modal situations is key. In real life, users are commonly exposed to situations where more than one modality is involved. Currently only a few ADUBA tools include complex multi-modal analysis features which allow reliable prediction of user behaviour relating to multi-modal content/situations. NetExpert is one of the tools that offers multi-modal features. If NetExpert encounters auditory information on a web page, it will try to integrate it, in terms of saliency, with the visual data. The main result of these cross-modal processes will be predictions as to how sound on a web page (or other multimedia content) will modulate visual responsiveness in users.

Learning features are another component of predictive ADUBA tools. Research in artificial intelligence shows that general-purpose expert systems without learning features typically fail to adapt to different situations as they are not flexible enough

---

[1] There exist a wide range of models of how the brain shifts visual attention to a certain region in space (e.g., a part of a web page). Tools such as NetExpert currently simulates users' shifts of attention to locations on multimedia content such as web pages or video streams; for more information see http://goethe.klab.caltech.edu/~itti/attention/ index.html.

to adapt to specific conditions.[2] Learning features allow more reliable forecasts since the systems are better adapted to different situations, particularly complex and quickly changing situations.

Some ADUBA tools are equipped with learning features by means of neural networks. It is possible to quite reliably predict users' perception of complex applications such as flash animations or rotating ads with ADUBA tools that come with learning features. One way in which learning features are implemented in ADUBA tools is by training the tools to pay attention to idiosyncratic features of the digital content. This can be done by either hard-coding preferences, or by employing reinforcement learning algorithms. The latter works analogously to training a dog, for example, by rewarding good choices or actions (in NetExpert, good or useful predictions of where users shift their attention), and by punishing bad ones.

A further extension of ADUBA tools is behavioural responses in terms of navigational processes. Currently, most tools analyse the perceptual content of one single static web page, and generate predictions about the most salient parts thereof. A logical next step is to include simple means to navigate through multiple web pages or a set of entire web sites based on these perceptual results. Specifically, ADUBA tools will determine which link on a page is in a high-saliency region. Once determined, it will "click" this link and navigate to the resulting page. At this point the process starts again, i.e., NetExpert starts with analysing the visual and auditory content of the new page. The main results of this entire process are

a.   predictions as to what parts of individual pages users will pay attention to, and what parts they will neglect entirely

b.   which pages on a site users will visit as a result of the perceptual content of pages.

2.5 ADUBA Show Cases

Sophisticated ADUBA tools such as MediaAnalyzer and NetExpert can be used to analyse simple "flat" HTML pages as well as dynamic streams such as a movie clip or multi-source SMIL presentations. In this section we present a couple of selected show cases.

2.5.1 HTML Page

Figure 2.1 is a snapshot of a static web page, with eye movements of users superimposed (indicated as black circles in the figure). These data were obtained with MediaAnalyzer. In this figure the upper-middle part of the page is attended most often. This is a general rule that we have found. This is consistent with recent research showing that the top parts of objects and scenes are attended more often,

---

[2] One of the main reasons for the lack of flexibility is that intelligent systems, such as animals or humans, are adapted to a particular ecological niche. For example, humans cannot perceive infrared light.

compared with the bottom parts. In addition to a bias to the upper parts of web pages, we also have found a bias to the left, in particular in the top third of web pages.

The results may originate from our reading experience, and/or from the fact that on most pages, the navigational buttons are located on the left. Such judgements about parts and/or entire web pages are typical results of ADUBA studies. In addition to measuring eye movements, mouse events (e.g., mouse clicks, mouse moves) can also be tracked. For example, it is of interest how long it takes, on average, a user to click a link. This kind of reaction time measure, while very simple in principle, can be very informative, in particular when compared across pages and user groups. It becomes even more relevant in the case of 3D content.

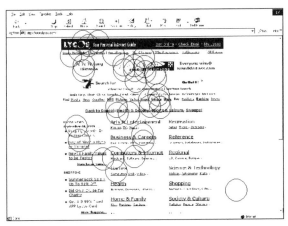

Figure 2.1 Eye movements on a static web page.

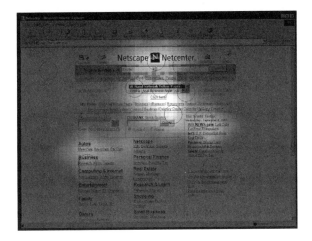

Figure 2.2 Heatmap of user's eye movements.

Another way of representing results is illustrated by the screenshot in Figure 2.2. The figure represents a so-called "see-through" heatmap. This heatmap spares only those parts of web pages and stream frames that have been attended to. Heatmaps thus provide a view on a page through the user's "mind" or eye. In the example shown in Figure 2.2, again the top third part was attended most, with a bias to the middle.

2.5.2 Simple Streams

ADUBA tools are particularly well suited to track user behaviour of multimedia streams such as music clips and movie trailers. Figure 2.3 shows a music video clip of the pop star Jennifer Lopez. In this instance, the user's attention is focused on the hand of the singer, indicated by the circular symbol.

2.5.3 Dynamic SMIL Presentations

SMIL is a language similar to HTML that synchronises various types of data such as flash, video, audio and text into one single layout. ADUBA tools such as MediaAnalzyer and NetExpert are used to measure the quality of the SMIL presentation. The example in Figure 2.4 shows a SMIL presentation that includes live stock charts, a rolling stock ticker, a video window, audio and rotating ads at the bottom. In Figure 2.4 the attention of the examined users is on the video window on

Figure 2.3 Representation of user's attention during a video

the right top corner of the SMIL presentation. In Figure 2.5 the user's attention is on the left side of the rotating advertisement at the bottom. A comparison of Figures 2.4 and 2.5 seems to indicate that the moving images within the video window are more attractive in terms of users' perception than rotating movements of the advertisement.

Figure 2.4 User's attention on a SMIL presentation (1).

Figure 2.5 User's attention on a SMIL presentation (2).

Figure 2.6 Child's eye movement.

Figure 2.7 Adult's eye movement.

As indicated in the early part of this chapter, ADUBA tools such as MediaAnalzyer and NetExpert can be used for various purposes. The SMIL presentation showcase in the previous paragraph is an example of how to analyse various layouts of multimedia content. In the next three sections there are more showcases, which illustrate the potential of ADUBA tools to analyse various other situations in digital media research.

2.5.4 Content Analysis

Many issues of scientific and commercial research are centred around content analysis. In particular researchers study the influence of demographics on the perception of content. Figures 2.6 and 2.7 show how a particular situation in the comics movie "Bugslife" is perceived by people of different age groups. Figure 2.6 represents the eye movements of an eight-year-old child. The attention is on the face of the creature on the right side. The same situation is perceived quite differently by a 35-year-old adult. Figure 2.7 shows that the adult is focused on the writing on the top left corner of the frame.

Identifying differences of perception between various demographic user groups is just one research application of ADUBA tools. Other ADUBA research projects centre around questions such as "Do users understand the content?", "Does the audience like what they see?", "What do users like, what do they dislike?" Answers to these question can be used in many ways, e.g. to make sure the narrative of a movie is well structured before the movie is released to a broader audience or to develop educational multimedia material, which provide high attention spans and effective learning results.

Figure 2.8 Attention on words in an advertisement.

2.5.5 Ad Spot

Similar to content analysis, ADUBA tools such as MediaAnalyzer and NetExpert are particularly well suited for the analysis of commercials. The tools can be used for pre- or post-test. The example in Figures 2.8 and 2.9 is a post-test of a pre-roll Buick ad. Pre-roll ads are placed in front of the actual content file (as opposed to in-

Figure 2.9 Attention focussed on colour contrasts and shapes.

stream ads which appear during a content stream and as opposed to interstitial ads which are shown between two content sets).

Figure 2.8 indicates that the user's attention is on the title words rather than on the Buick itself. Figure 2.9 shows that users often tend to focus their attention around a combination of colour contrasts and distinguished shapes of objects.

2.5.6 Product Placement

ADUBA tools such as MediaAnalyzer and NetExpert can be used for very complex

Figure 2.10 User perception starts at the front wheel...

Figure 2.11 ....moves to the front of the car...

Figure 2.12 ...and to the driver.

perception analysis projects. The example above shows the perception of a BMW product placement in the James Bond movie "The World Is Not Enough". Figures 2.10, 2.11, and 2.12 show the flow of user perception from the right front wheel to the front of the car with the BMW sign and to the driver. The results indicate that the users perceive the BMW sign. Further analysis such as written and/or verbal interviews of the test persons will help to confirm the results of the eye-tracking.

All the above showcases represent a selection of application areas of ADUBA tools. ADUBA tools can be flexibly used for a broad variety of study objects and designs in order to find answers to many different questions.

2.6 Conclusions and Outlook

Researchers in science and commerce have come to rely on user analysis tools in order to better understand the user behaviour of surfers. Web service managers and producers benefit from the very same user behaviour analysis in order to make digital content more attractive and consumer friendly, which in turn helps to increase overall customer satisfaction.

As the Internet continues to mature and as broadband is becoming more popular, new applications and web services will be developed [10]. The user behaviour research will have to adopt and improve its tools and methods to the new applications. ADUBA is one approach to provide more sophisticated tools and methods in order to analyse complex user behaviour in the digital space.

While various ADUBA studies show promising results, further validation of the tools and methods is needed. This is particularly true for the analysis of causes and effects between user behaviour on one side and new technical applications and new web services on the other side. ADUBA is not a self-explaining expert system. Assumptions and conclusions of research projects have to be handled carefully. This in order to avoid misinterpretations as they happen all too often in the field of traditional and digital media behavioural research [11,12]. Also, it has to be noted that ADUBA has its limits in term of the areas it can be applied to. ADUBA is only relevant to a selected set of user behaviour analysis.

There are many important milestones along the way of the research of human interaction with media technology. From the rudimentary mass media research in the 17th and 18th centuries to the well-established mass media research service industry in the 20th century to the digital research of the Internet era, many research projects and many findings can be found that are of key relevance to society [13]. The sophisticated tools and methods introduced in the field of ADUBA are significantly contributing to the better understanding of human behaviour.

References

[1]   Pan, Z. & McLeod, J. M. (1991). Multilevel Analysis in Mass Communication Research. Communication Research, Vol. 18, Nr. 2, S. 140-173.

[2]   McQuail, D. (1978). The Historicity of Mass Media Science. In: Wilhoit, G. C. (1980). Mass Communication. Review Yearbook. Vol. 1. Beverly Hills: Sage.

[3]   Wyss, B. (1999). Reading Consumers' Minds: Instant Data Mining on the Internet. Media Trend Journal, No 3, p. 48–50 (text in German).

[4]   http://www.cc.gatech.edu/gvu/user_surveys/

[5]   http://www.nielsenmedia.com/;   http://www.netratings.com/;   http://www.npd.com/; http://www.mediametrix.com/

[6]   http://www.forrester.com/; http://jup.com/

[7]   Pfeifer, R. & Scheier, C. (1999). Understanding Intelligence. Boston: MIT Press.

[8]   Levy, M. R. & Windahl, S. (1985). The Concept of Audience Activity. In: Rosengren, K. E., Wenner, L. A. & Palmgreen, Ph. (1985). Media Gratification Research. Current Perspectives. Beverly Hills: Sage.

[9]   http://www.mediaanalyzer.com, http://www.eyetracking.com, http://www.noldus.com
       http://www.eyetools.com/

[10]   Wyss, B. (1999). The Digital Entertainment Paradise. Radio/TV Gets Real With
       Capacity Expansion. Media Trend Journal, No 7/8, 46–48 (text in German).

[11]   McLeod, J. M., Kosicki, G. M. & Pan, Z. (1991). On Understanding and
       Misunderstanding Media Effects. In: Curran, J. & Gurevitch, M. (1991). Mass Media
       and Society. London: Arnold.

[12]   Hanson, J. (1987). Video Games: Competing with Machines. In: Thomas, S. (1987).
       Culture and Communication: Methodology, Behaviour, Artifacts, and Institutions.
       Norwood (NJ): Ablex.

[13]   Lowery, S & DeFleur, M. L. (1983). Milestones in Mass Communication Research.
       New York: Longman.

Chapter 3

The Influence of Network Quality of Service Factors on the Usability and Effectiveness of Multimedia Internet Broadcasting

Andy McKinlay, Rob Procter and Scott Gallacher

3.1 Introduction

We report here the results of two experimental studies in which we evaluated the usability of multimedia internet broadcasting in a training application and investigated the effects of network quality of service (QoS) on subjects' capacity to assimilate the factual and emotional content.[1]

Many companies are now becoming interested in the use of multimedia, internet-based broadcasting as a staff training and general information aid. With Web-based presentation tools, text, graphics, audio and video can be easily combined to serve a diverse range of business communication applications and content. The use of such media has already demonstrated its worth in distance learning and related applications [12]. For corporate network managers, however, the spread of these applications represents an additional—and as yet largely unquantified—load on company intranets that are typically expected to support a wide variety of communications services. It would simply be unacceptable for new traffic to

---

[1] An earlier, shorter account of this work was published in [9].

degrade other services; equally, if it is necessary to add extra network capacity, then the question is how much, and would the investment deliver the desired results? It is essential to consider, therefore, what combinations of media content may provide the most effective solutions to business communications needs, and to characterise their network QoS requirements. In turn, this may involve examining how factors such as network bandwidth effect users' perceptions of multimedia Internet broadcast quality and acceptability, and its effectiveness for specific applications.

The problems inherent in the use of public, packet-switched communications networks for real-time data transmission are, of course, well known [2]. They give rise to numerous effects that may influence the "watchability" of multimedia Internet broadcasting. These include the delay or loss of frames, audio clarity, lip synchronisation during speech, and a general perturbation of the relationship between the visual and auditory components [1]. Little is known, however, of how the impact of these effects is perceived by users [4,7]. Previous studies have suggested that different types of video information may have different requirements [1]. Part of our aim in these studies was to investigate what influence the dynamic fluctuations in network bandwidth typical of shared packet-switched networks might have on usability, especially in relation to the visual and non-verbal, vocal communication channels.

An investigation of the usability of multimedia internet broadcasts and, in particular, the influence of network QoS on users' perceptions of quality will assist in informing minimum QoS requirements and in the drawing up of guidelines for multimedia content creation and selection. For example, it may be the case that multimedia materials created for a specific form of delivery such as broadcast TV are not as effective when delivered via the internet.

3.2 Affective Content and Communication

Social psychologists have claimed [3] that affective information is conveyed to a large extent by non-verbal information of the sort which is carried in the visual and non-verbal, vocal channels, where "affect" refers to temporary emotional states such as mood or more stable emotional states such as aspects of personality. When these channels are inhibited, or unavailable, interpersonal communication may become more problematic. For example, email communication between friends is susceptible to mis-judgements of mood due to the absence of non-verbal information that in an everyday conversation would alert the hearer to the speaker's intentions. Similarly, email communication between strangers may be susceptible to mis-judgements of more stable affective factors such as those deriving from personality. Such problems may explain, for example, the prevalence in email communication of the overt inclusion of extra content that helps clarify affective tone (e.g., smileys or ironic commentary).

The foregoing implies that even a relatively minor degradation of the visual channel may impact upon the extent to which people perceive affective information in interpersonal communication. Specifically, it can be hypothesised that the degradation of the visual channel will reduce non-verbal signals, which will, in turn, reduce the extent to which people are willing to ascribe emotional overtones to a scene.

Such effects may have significant implications for multimedia internet broadcasting in general, and for the design of usable multimedia materials intended for application in, for example, vicarious learning [6] and multimedia learning environments (MLEs) [11] in particular. Vicarious learning refers to the re-use of people's experiences as a learning aid for others. It exploits our capacity to learn by watching other people, e.g., the ways in which other people solve problems. In such circumstances, both factual and affective information may be important for the audience's understanding.

Vicarious learning seeks to allow the audience to share as much as possible of the original learning situation that they are observing. It follows that the audience needs to be able to understand fully the communicative background of the original learning setting which they are vicariously experiencing, including its affective aspects. However, if, for example, network QoS factors lead to the degraded transmission of affective information, this may adversely affect the audience's capacity to make affective judgements relevant to their understanding of the content. Consequently, combining vicarious learning approaches with network-based delivery may present new challenges, for both the design of the multimedia learning materials and for the network services employed in their transmission.

In addition from a more general usability evaluation, therefore, a particular aim of our study was to explore the effects of network QoS on an audience's comprehension of affective information carried in the visual channel.

3.3 Background

We are involved in a long-term study a number of multimedia projects (including video conferencing and WWW) within Scottish Bank,[2] a large UK bank. Our investigations are based around detailed case studies of the development and adoption of the technology [10]. One area of great interest for the bank at the present time lies in the delivery of training materials to staff over the bank's internal digital network.

Currently, much of the bank's staff training and more general briefing activities are carried out using the bank's own internal TV network. Presentation formats commonly used include full screen captions with voice-overs and short video segments of presenters. The bank's Learning Technologies Group, who are responsible for meeting the bank's training requirements, were keen to discover whether training materials could be delivered in a usable form over the bank's digital network. If this is feasible, then the options available for the style and management of training become significantly increased. Scottish Bank's network managers and IT strategists, on the other hand, were equally keen to discover to

---

[2] The names of people and companies have been anonymised.

what extent this new application would require additional investment in network technologies and infrastructure.

In order to begin to answer these questions, we devised an experimental study of the influence of media content and network QoS on subjects' recall and comprehension of the contents of multimedia Internet broadcasts. Having considered the issues discussed in the previous section, we decided to focus in particular on the effects of QoS on affective information uptake.

The limitations of laboratory studies as a technique for investigating users' requirements for IT systems are now widely known and acknowledged. User requirements must be contextualised to be properly understood; they also cannot be assumed to be fixed, but are subject to change as users learn and adapt to new technologies and their specific affordances. We argue, however, that laboratory studies have a role to play in helping formatively to map out the design space and to assess the potential impact of design options.

3.4 Network Simulation

The goal of the network simulation was to allow for setting different levels of packet loss. The simulation topology was chosen to duplicate Scottish Bank's intranet characteristics as far as was reasonably possible. This was imperative if the experimental results were to have a direct relevance for the bank's network managers, but, as we see below, did lead to some problems in generating controllable QoS effects.

The simulation consisted of two 4 Mbps token rings connected by a router. A Windows NT Server was connected to one token ring and two client workstations were connected to the other so that packets transmitted by the server had to pass through the router before being received by the clients. In addition to the multimedia broadcast server and client workstations, there were two background traffic generators that could be configured to generate arbitrary loads on the network. One load generator was connected to the same token ring on which the multimedia server was located; the other was connected to the router through a 10 Mbs Ethernet. All token ring stations were set to operate without priority. The simulation network is shown in Figure 3.1.

To investigate the effect of network congestion on multimedia internet broadcast service usability it was necessary to be able to simulate traffic conditions such that total bandwidth demands exceeded network capacity, thus constraining the multimedia broadcasts to work under less than optimal bandwidth conditions. In such circumstances, where a network service is operating under a real-time transmission protocol with no re-transmission, a loss of packets would be inevitable, leading to a lower overall end-to-end QoS. The behaviour of token ring networks complicates the achievement of such controllable bandwidth conditions, however. A fundamental characteristic of the token ring is fairness, so it is difficult to manipulate traffic conditions such that unfairness results. The consequence is an

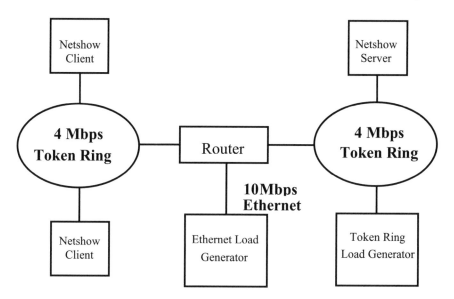

Figure 3.1 Simulation network topology.

unstable operating characteristic that is difficult to control and a QoS that tends to degrade very quickly as overall network traffic increases.

It was necessary to devote some considerable time to experimenting with different configurations before we were able to achieve a satisfactory outcome: a level of background load that resulted in significant loss of multimedia broadcast packets, but without causing the network to collapse altogether. The selected load was typical of a "small request—large reply" scenario. The token ring load generator was configured to create a background load of 40% of the token ring network bandwidth, and the Ethernet load generator was configured to create a load of 61% of token ring bandwidth. Under these background load conditions, the overall packet loss from the multimedia broadcast server averaged between 30 to 40%. This packet loss was not uniformly distributed in time, but was "bursty" in character, varying between zero and 100%.

3.5 The Experiments

Two experiments were designed to gather subjects' assessments of session quality and usability, and to measure their capacity to assimilate the content of the materials under different network conditions. Two different network traffic conditions were used:

1. *No-load*: delivery under "perfect" network conditions, i.e., with no other traffic on the network, and
2. *Load*: delivery under "real" network conditions, i.e., with simulated background traffic on the network.

When the level of background traffic was sufficiently high, it induced short, pseudo-random reductions in bandwidth available to the real-time multimedia broadcast server. The objective effect of the load was to cause a loss of audio and video packets, which, in turn, resulted in the dropping of video frames and short segments of audio. Subjectively, the effect was a degradation of quality – brief periods of jerky motion, reduced audio clarity and lapses in audio–video synchronisation—in a way that appeared to be random in time.

The software used to implement the multimedia broadcast server was Microsoft NetShow 2.0. This is a streaming multimedia system capable of providing either on-demand or multicast services. For the experiments, the latter option was chosen. The client workstations were 333 MHz Pentium PCs with 17 inch, high resolution, colour monitors, Creative Labs Sound Blaster 16 bit sound cards and headphones. The multimedia material was presented on the client workstations using Microsoft's Internet Explorer (version 4) browser with a Windows Media Player plugin (see Figure 3.2). Client buffering of incoming packets was turned off.

Various combinations of type of multimedia content of the information and training materials were available from the bank, including:

1. audio only
2. audio with captions
3. audio with captions and video.

Figure 3.2 The client user interface

The materials finally chosen for use were two company videos, each containing mixed sequences of captions with voice-over and speakers appearing on camera. These were prepared for transmission by the multimedia broadcast server by being digitised and converted to Advanced Streaming Format (ASF) using the ALEP.net codec (16 KHz sampling) for audio and MPEG-4 v2 Video codec (15 fps and 320×240 size) for images. Further details of the multimedia content used in each experiment are given below.

Forty-eight subjects were all recruited from administrative staff at the University of Edinburgh. This group was selected as being broadly similar to Scottish Bank's target audience in terms of age range and occupation. The group consisted of males and females, with ages ranging from 18 to 61. Figure 3.3 shows the subject group sex and age profile. The subjects were paid £5. They varied in computer experience from "novice" (less than one year) to "expert" (more than ten years). The average subject spent over 10 hours per week using a computer in their work, of which between 4 and 10 hours per week was spent using multimedia applications, had at least 6 months experience of Internet use, and spent between 1 to 10 hours using the Internet per week.

3.6 Experiment One

The objective of this experiment was to investigate the effects of network QoS on subjects' assessment of session quality and to measure their assimilation of factual information.

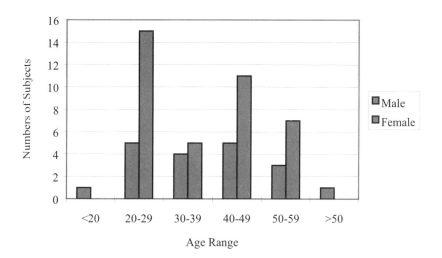

Figure 3.3 Subject sex and age profiles.

Hypothesis: Where information content is purely factual, there will be no differences between the two conditions in people's capacity to assimilate it.

3.6.1 Method

Paid groups of subjects were asked to view and listen to a six-minute video consisting of a mix of captions and short video segments of speakers. Two subjects at a time sat at individual client workstations, which were arranged in a typical desktop configuration. To eliminate the possibility of distractions, each workstation was screened off from the surroundings. The subjects were given brief instructions on the use of Internet Explorer and the Media Player and shown how to adjust the monitor and headphone sound volume. A short test sequence was then played to allow subjects to check for picture quality and sound level and the session was then started.

The topic of the video was a report of the bank's half-yearly results. The emphasis throughout was on the putting over of factual information and this was done in the style of an extended TV news item. The content consisted of an on-camera presenter linking three individual presentations to camera by senior bank executives. Important items of information (e.g., profit figures) were summarised using full screen captions and voice-over.

Immediately following the session, the subjects were asked to complete two questionnaires. The first concerned their assessment of the session. Using a five-point scale, ranging from 1 (very poor) to 5 (very good), subjects were asked to evaluate the session in terms of the overall quality, with respect to a number of more specific quality measures, how interesting they found the material, and to choose from a list of factors those which they thought had impaired quality. They were also asked to evaluate the usability of the system in the context of regular use on the same scale. Subjects could add free-form comments if they wished to do so. The second questionnaire was a short test of subjects' comprehension of the material based upon their recall of its factual content. Twenty-four subjects in total took part in this experiment, with twelve subjects in each condition, in a between-subjects design.

3.6.2 Results

The mean subject scores for the two conditions of session quality measures,

Table 3.1 Mean subject scores for overall session quality, quality factors and usability.

	No-load		Load	
	Mean	**SD**	**Mean**	**SD**
Overall quality	2.75	0.97	1.75	0.75
Comparison with live sessions	2.46	1.23	1.60	0.76
Ease of understanding presenters	3.42	1.24	1.17	0.39
Technical quality	2.66	1.15	1.58	0.79
Usability	3.33	1.07	1.70	0.86

usability and for factors impairing the session, are shown in Tables 3.1 and 3.2 respectively.

3.6.2.1 Quality

Subjects rated the quality higher in the *No-load* condition than in the *Load* condition (see Table 3.1). A two-way mixed ANOVA showed that there was a significant two-way interaction, $F(4,88) = 2.84$, $p < 0.05$. Post-hoc tests showed that there were four significant simple effects. *Overall quality, Ease of understanding, Technical quality* of the session and *Usability* were all rated more highly in the *No-load* condition than in the *Load* condition.

3.6.2.2 Factors Impairing Quality

Table 3.2 shows the summed scores for factors cited as impairing the session. It can be seen that in the *No-load* condition, *Audio-Video synchronisation* and *Video quality* were the most frequently cited factors mentioned (10/12 and 5/12 respectively). In the *Load* condition, five of the six factors are cited more frequently than in the *No-load* condition, but it was *Audio quality* which was cited most often by subjects (10/12).

3.6.2.3 Factual Recall

Comparisons were made between the two conditions using an independent samples t-Test. There was no significant difference in the extent to which subjects were able to display correct factual information uptake between the two conditions. The mean score for the *Load* condition on the information scale was 34.5 and for the *No-load* condition, 33.2. The hypothesis that there would be no difference in factual recall between the two conditions was therefore confirmed.

3.6.3 Discussion

The results show that the reduction of network QoS caused by the high background load had no significant effect on subjects' factual recall. However, it did have a significant effect on subjects' evaluation of quality as measured by *Overall quality, Ease of understanding presenters* and *Technical quality* and on their evaluation of *Usability*. It is also clear from the summed scores of factors cited as impairing the session that subjects perceived the effect of the background load in a consistent and

Table 3.2 Summed scores for factors cited by subjects as impairing the session.

	No-load	Load
Caption quality	0	2
Audio quality	1	10
Video quality	5	8
Audio–Video synchronisation	10	9
Transmission gaps	1	9

general way. The only factor not comparably cited in the *Load* condition was that of *Caption quality*. This result is in line with expectations as this part of the multimedia content is the least dynamic and so least likely to be affected by fluctuations in transmission bandwidth.

We suggest that the reduction in quality may influence users' information uptake in several ways. For example, if it is very severe (e.g., loss of extended segments of speech and/or video), it may lead to overall information loss; if less severe, it may still be enough to cause distraction and so inhibit uptake through disruption of users' concentration. Our results show that the threshold for the former effect may be quite high—perhaps because the natural information redundancy in audio/video communication is typically high enough to compensate for all but the most severe cases of information loss.

The results also show that whilst the reduction in quality was too low to disturb subjects' concentration, it was sufficiently high to be apparent. In real situations of use, the margin between quality loss being apparent and being distracting may be quite small, and so we would argue that the former should be taken as the threshold for end-user acceptance.

Finally, it is important to note that in the *Overall quality, Comparison with live presentations* and *Usability* measures, even the *No-load* condition scored relatively poorly with means of 2.75, 2.46 and 3.33 respectively. The conclusion that the system falls short of usability requirements—even under ideal load conditions—is reinforced by the fact that several subjects commented that the system was "unusable".

3.7 Experiment Two

The impact of adverse network load conditions on the visual channel may be to reduce the extent to which people perceive affective information. Specifically, it may be that degradation of the visual channel will reduce non-verbal signals, which will, in turn, reduce the extent to which people are willing to ascribe emotional overtones to a scene. Where information content is purely factual, there will be no differences in people's capacity to assimilate it.

> *Hypothesis*: Following Brown [3], it was assumed that information about matters of fact would be carried by the verbal channel via audio signals while emotional information would be carried by the non-verbal channel via visual signals. In line with the argument outlined above, it was predicted that there would be a difference between the *No-load* and *Load* conditions in terms of the extent to which emotional overtones are ascribed to a scene, with people in the *Load* condition being less likely to ascribe emotional overtones. It was also hypothesised that there would be no difference between the two conditions in terms of the extent to which subjects were able to display correct factual information uptake.

3.7.1 Method

Paid groups of subjects, none of whom had taken part in the first experiment, were asked to view and listen to an eight-minute video describing company policy with respect to a specific workplace issue. Two subjects at a time were sat individually at the client workstations, which were arranged in a typical desktop configuration. The subjects were given brief instructions on the use of Internet Explorer and the Media Player and shown how to adjust the monitor and headphone sound volume. A short test sequence was then played to allow subjects to check for picture quality and sound level and the session was then started.

The material consisted of captions with voice-over and short segments of between 2 to 3 minutes of dramatised scenes from a workplace. The latter were designed to illustrate and emphasise the main theme of the video, which was harassment in the workplace. The dramatised segments showed, in the style of a TV play, actors portraying incidents of harassment in which characters were shown displaying some typical behaviours that might engender feelings of harassment in

---

Scene: Open plan office; several people seated; male figure in background walking towards seated foreground male figure, carrying documents; he puts down documents on latter's desk with a flourish and begins talking.
Manager: Exactly what is this Alan?
[Cut to close up of Alan; Alan turns to the manager]
Alan: It's my paper on communicating best practice.
Manager: No it's not, it's crap, that's what it is, sheer unadulterated crap.
[Cut to woman in office; she turns to look in direction of conversation; she looks dismayed]
Alan: I don't think ...
Manager: Alan!
[Cut to Alan, manager and woman in background] Do you realise that I have to present these ideas at a 3 o'clock meeting today to three senior ...
[Cut to close up of manager; he is angry] managers and a director! I can't show them this rubbish.
[Cut to Alan] It isn't even what I asked for.
Alan: [Cut to Alan, manager, woman in background] I have the memo that you sent me just yesterday about it (picks up piece of paper) and I've definitely covered the salient points ...
Manager: [Cut to Alan, manager] It's too long, it doesn't make any sense ...
[Cut to view of colleague on phone] If you carry on producing work like this ...
[Cut to manager, Alan in background, woman and male colleagues in foreground] (bangs table) your days here are numbered, mate!
[Cut to Alan, manager, woman in background] You've got 2 hours to re-write it. Turns and leaves. [Fade to black]

Figure 3.4 Extract of the transcript from a segment of the content of the audio–video material used in the second experiment.

another. In each scene, an actor portrayed the effect that these behaviours had on the harassment victim, thereby enabling the audience to vicariously experience these feelings.

In summary, the contents consisted of factual information about company policy and affective information, i.e., information representing the feelings of people portrayed in the dramatised segments. It is reasonable to assume that, by making the distressing effects of harassment very clear, this latter content is as important to understanding the overall "message" as the former.

By way of illustrating the style of the content, Figure 3.4 is an extract from the transcript of one of the segments.

Immediately following the session, the subjects were then asked to complete two questionnaires. The first concerned their assessment of the session. Using a five-point scale, ranging from 1 (very poor) to 5 (very good), subjects were asked to evaluate the session in terms of the overall quality, with respect to a number of more specific quality measures, how interesting they found the material, and to choose from a list of factors those which they thought had impaired quality. They were also asked to evaluate the usability of the system in the context of regular use on the same scale. Subjects could add free-form comments if they wished to do so. The second questionnaire was a short test of subjects' comprehension of the material based upon their recall of its contents. Subjects were asked to: (a) answer factual questions, (b) comment on what they thought was happening in the dramatised video segments, i.e., to judge the emotional state of people portrayed in the dramatised segments, and (c) specify their confidence in their answers (for an example of (b) and (c), see Figure 3.5). There were two conditions, distinguished by the background network load: *No-load* and *Load*.

Twenty-four subjects took part, with twelve subjects in each condition, in a between-subjects design.

3.7.2 Results

The mean subject scores of quality measures, usability and factors impairing the session for the two conditions are shown in Tables 3.3 and 3.4 respectively.

Record your assessment of the manager's behaviour towards his subordinate by choosing a point on the scale below between the following pairs of opposites. In each case, also record your confidence in your assessment.													
							Confidence						
Anxious	1	2	3	4	5	Composed	Very	1	2	3	4	5	Not very
Impatient	1	2	3	4	5	Patient	Very	1	2	3	4	5	Not very
Constructive	1	2	3	4	5	Unconstructive	Very	1	2	3	4	5	Not very

Figure 3.5 A sample question measuring subject affective information content perception and confidence.

Table 3.3 Mean subject scores for overall session quality, quality factors and usability.

	No-load		Load	
	Mean	**SD**	**Mean**	**SD**
Overall quality	3.58	0.90	2.08	0.67
Comparison with live sessions	2.54	1.37	1.42	0.79
Ease of understanding presenters	3.92	1.38	1.67	0.65
Technical quality	3.17	1.03	2.08	1.16
Usability	4.00	0.85	1.83	0.72

3.7.2.1 Quality

Subjects rated the quality higher in the *No-load* condition than in the *Load* condition (see Table 3.3). A two-way mixed ANOVA showed that there was a significant two-way interaction, $F(4,88) = 2.94$, $p < 0.05$. Post-hoc tests showed that there were four significant simple effects. *Overall quality*, *Ease of understanding* and *Technical quality* of the session and *Usability* were all rated more highly in the *No-load* condition than in the *Load* condition.

3.7.2.2 Factors Impairing Session

Table 3.4 shows the summed scores for factors cited by subjects as impairing the session. It can be seen that in the *No-load* condition, audio quality, audio/video synchronisation and video quality were the factors most frequently mentioned as impairing the session (3/12, 5/12 and 3/12 respectively). In the *Load* condition all of the five factors were cited more frequently than in the *No-load* condition, with *audio quality*, *video quality* and *audio/video synchronisation* tying for first place and *transmission gaps* a close second (9/12, 9/12 and 8/12 respectively).

3.7.3 Factual and Affective Recall

In order to compare differences between factual information uptake and perception of emotion, two scale scores were computed. The first scale score, measuring

Table 3.4 Summed scores for factors cited by subjects as impairing the session.

	No-load	Load
Caption quality	2	3
Audio quality	3	9
Video quality	5	9
Audio–Video synchronisation	3	9
Transmission gaps	1	8

information uptake, summed responses to those questions dealing with matters of fact, with smaller scores representing fewer mistakes. The second scale score, measuring the extent to which emotional features were ascribed to the scene, summed responses to those questions dealing with emotions, with smaller scores representing a greater willingness to ascribe emotionality to the scene.

Comparisons were made between the two conditions using an independent samples t-Test. There was no significant difference in the extent to which subjects were able to display correct factual information uptake between the two conditions. The mean score for the *Load* condition on the information scale was 20.8 and for the *No-load* condition, 19.8.

There was a significant difference in the extent to which subjects ascribed emotional overtones to the scene, with $t(22) = 3.35, p < 0.01$. The mean score for the *Load* condition on the emotion scale was 24.0 and for the *No-load* condition, 16.8. Both hypotheses were therefore confirmed. There was no significant difference, however, in subjects' confidence levels between the two conditions.

3.7.4 Discussion

As in the previous experiment, the results show that fluctuations in network QoS did not effect factual information uptake or subjects' interest in the material, but did effect their perceptions of quality as measured by *Overall quality*, *Ease of understanding presenters* and *Technical quality* and their evaluation of *Usability*. These results also show that loss of information did influence the extent to which people are willing to ascribe emotional overtones to a scene. The results for factors cited as impairing the assimilation of affective content are broadly consistent with those from the first experiment.

The results also show that loss of quality does influence the extent to which people are willing to ascribe emotional overtones to some kinds of content. The suggestion here is that this is a consequence of the differential effects of fluctuations in network QoS on audio and visual signals where audio signals carry the verbal information channel and the visual signals carry the non-verbal information channel. Non-verbal information, as represented by affective content, is degraded by reductions in QoS in a way that factual informational content is not. This is pointed up by the fact that in this second experiment there is a significant simple effect for *Content* in which subjects evaluated this factor more positively in the *No-load* than in the *Load* condition.

One possible explanation for this may lie in the fact that people perceive spoken verbal material in a way that makes subtle disruptions in audio signals unimportant [5]. Previous research has shown that high-quality audio is more important than video in many computer-supported co-operative work settings [8]. Our results are interesting in that they do not conform to these earlier findings. Rather, they suggest that in some task performance settings, the order of importance of audio and video may be reversed.

Finally, in the *Overall quality* and *Usability* measures (though not *Comparison with live presentations*), the *No-load* condition scored relatively well, with means of

3.58 and 4 respectively. These results are higher than those obtained in the first experiment and suggest that under ideal load conditions (though again, not under adverse load conditions), the system would probably meet usability requirements. It is possible, however, that these higher ratings for *Overall quality* and *Usability* are due to subjects being more engaged by the material used in the second experiment. Subjects rated their *Level of interest* in the material more highly in this experiment than in the first. Table 3.5 shows the *Level of interest* scores for the two experiments.

A two-way ANOVA showed that the differences in *Level of interest* were significant, $F(1,44) = 8.37$, $p < 0.01$. These results are consistent with an intuitive comparison of the contents of the two materials. That the *Level of interest* declined in the *Load* condition in both experiments is not surprising either, but does underline the importance of the network QoS on subjects' responses.

Table 3.5 Mean subject scores for subjects' *Level of interest* for the two experiments.

	No-load	Load
Experiment One	2.50	1.50
Experiment Two	4.17	3.25

3.8 Summary and Conclusions

In the first experiment, we found that there was no difference in subject recall of factual information between the two conditions, but there was a clear preference for the *No-load* condition. There were significant differences in subjects' evaluation of *Overall quality*, *Ease of understanding*, *Technical quality* and *Usability* between the two load conditions. In the second experiment, we found that loss of quality impaired subjects' uptake of affective information content and there was a clear preference for the *No-load* condition. Again, we found that there were significant differences in subjects' evaluation of *Overall quality*, *Ease of understanding*, *Technical quality* and *Usability* between the two load conditions. Comparing the data from the two experiments, we also found a significant difference in subjects' *Level of interest* across both the network load conditions and the material content.

We acknowledge the problems of extrapolating from these experimental results to "real world" use situations. Our users were only subjects, and the results can only be taken as snapshots of their impressions, reactions and performance: habitual use by real users in their working environments might yield different conclusions. We do not contend that experimental evaluations are sufficient in themselves, but we do believe that they have a role to play when used formatively to explore user requirements, the trade-offs between, for example, choice of media and nature of the application, and usability under realistic network traffic conditions. These are important issues for the take-up of multimedia internet broadcasting in corporate environments. We argue that experimental investigations should be seen as part of a repertoire of evaluation techniques that would include, *inter alia*, small-scale pilot studies. As such, they can be a useful tool for corporate decision-makers, a conclusion corroborated by feedback from our collaborators within Scottish Bank.

In this particular study, there are issues regarding what level of generalisation may be made, given the network simulation's particular packet-loss characteristics. It may be that this is a factor in subjects' responses as well as the overall bandwidth loss itself. Other factors such as the video codec employed may also have some impact on results. Despite these qualifications, we argue that the results do have a wider validity, and raise some interesting issues for multimedia internet broadcast applications.

First, current debates about QoS in network management tend to focus on objective parameters of quality and tend to ignore users' opinions. Our study suggests that this is a mistake, while also providing the foundation for a more systematic exploration of network QoS issues as experienced by users. The implications of poor usability for the uptake of multimedia internet broadcasting services are fairly clear. Indeed, even though we did not find any differences in factual assimilation between the network load conditions, we would argue that in real situations of use, poor usability would inevitably have an impact on effectiveness as measured by information uptake; over time, users' lack of tolerance of a service which they perceive as poor will be reflected in learning outcomes.

Second, the differences that we observed in learning outcomes for factual and affective information recall in the second experiment has some interesting implications. Interest is growing in MLEs and related approaches such as vicarious learning: learning not through direct participation, but through observing others [6]. Multimedia materials such as the package used in the second experiment implicitly rely upon vicarious learning, and the presumption that the audience will be able to register the emotional impact of the behaviour that they observe being acted out [11]. Our results indicate that the network QoS requirements for affective information are higher than for factual information. In addition, they suggest that creators of multimedia content should pay attention to the mode of its delivery; content designed for one mode of delivery may not be suited to another.

Third, the implications of our results are not limited to the use of pre-recorded multimedia. By extension, we may also conclude that the QoS requirements of any multimedia internet broadcasting service in which affective information plays an important role in outcomes will be higher. Some obvious – and rather important – examples would include video conferencing. Our results are consistent with those of other studies that have shown that low video quality inhibits non-verbal communication in video conferencing (e.g., [7,13]). For example, Monk and Watts found that low quality video caused speech between participants to be more formal [7].

Having established that network QoS can affect outcomes in multimedia internet broadcasting applications, we need now to investigate a wider range of network topologies and load conditions to identify where such QoS effects start to become significant. Although our results have direct applicability for the chosen network topology (and hence the bank), different network topologies may exhibit different load and QoS characteristics.

Finally, we plan to consider more fully how the results may serve to help define guidelines for MLE material selection and design and to establish QoS criteria for multimedia internet broadcast networks which are more relevant to users' needs.

References

[1]   Apteker, R., Fisher, J., Kisimov, V. and Neishlos, H. (1995) "Video Acceptability and Frame Rate", *IEEE Multimedia*, 2(3), 32–40.
[2]   Brebner, G. (1997) *Computers in Communication*. McGraw-Hill, London.
[3]   Brown, R. (1986) *Social Psychology*: The Second Edition. Free Press, New York.
[4]   Karlsson, G. (1995) "Asynchronous Transfer of Video", Swedish Institute for Computer Science Research Report No. R95-14.
[5]   Kellog, R. (1995) *Cognitive Psychology*. Sage, London.
[6]   McKendree, J., Stenning, K., Mayes, T., Lee, J. and Cox, R. (1998) "Why observing a dialogue may benefit learning", Journal of Computer Assisted Learning, 14(2), 110–119.
[7]   Monk, A. and Watts, L. A (1995) "Quality Video Link Affects Speech But Not Gaze", in Proceedings of the ACM Conference on Human Factors in Computing Systems, (Denver CO, May), ACM Press, 274–75.
[8]   Olson, J., Olson, G. and Meacher, D. (1995) "What Mix of Video and Audio is Useful for Small Groups Doing Remote Real-time Design Work?" in Proceedings of the ACM Conference on Human Factors in Computing Systems, (Denver CO, May), ACM Press, 362–8.
[9]   R. Procter, A. McKinlay and S. Gallacher (1999) "An Investigation of the Influence of Variable Network Load on the Effectiveness of Multimedia Presentations". In Simone, C. and Weisband, S. (Eds.) Proceedings of Group'99, the International Conference on Supporting Group Work (Phoenix Arizona, November), ACM Press, 160–168.
[10]   Procter, R., Williams, R., and Cashin, L. (1996) "Social Learning and Innovations in Multimedia-based CSCW", ACM SIGOIS Bulletin, December. ACM Press, 73–76.
[11]   Rogers, T. (1999) "Transforming perspectives with interactive drama". http://caiia-star.soc.plym.ac.uk/starproductions/tomwww/index.html
[12]   Sloane, A. (1996) Multimedia Communication. McGraw-Hill, London.
[13]   Whittaker, S. (1995) "Rethinking video as a technology for interpersonal communications: theory and design implications", International Journal of Human-Computer Studies, 42, 501–529.

Chapter 4

Distributed Global Conferences over Heterogeneous Networks

Tomás Robles, Juan Quemada, Tomás de Miguel, Santiago Pavón, Joaquín Salvachúa, Manuel Petit, Gabriel Huecas, Hector L. Velayos and Eva Castro

4.1 Introduction

Many multimedia applications have been developed during the past years for supporting co-operative work, tele-teaching and many other activities involving groups of persons distributed at different locations and communicating by means of telecommunication networks. Most of this effort has been devoted, till now, to deal with technical problems: network design and network interconnection, applications, etc. It is now becoming increasingly important to tackle the problems related to the organisation of these activities as distributed events, involving sophisticated equipment and the users of the system. It will be shown that the organisation of a distributed event is qualitatively different from the organisation of a similar event in a single place and during a specific period of time.

Using multimedia applications we may organise a large number of distributed activities [1,2,3]: videoconferences, co-operative work, courses and conferences involving a large number of auditoriums located at different cities. This chapter describes the material and the activities required for the organisation and management of a distributed conference using a service creation platform (ISABEL [5,15]) and supported by current broad and wide band communication networks.

World coverage implies the usage of long-distance communication, with the problems inherent to protocol interconnection. This produces co-ordination problems such as time differences, cultural diversity (language is one of them, but not the most important) and various problems related to the organisation and management of spread groups.

The set-up of a distributed event requires coverage of the following sub-objectives: to build a network able to support the interchange of multimedia and control information during the event; to use a suitable tool for providing a service that fulfils the requirements of the event we are organising; and to use tools and organisation methods to deal with the problems of origination related to the planning, management and realisation of the event.

Services bases on ISABEL offer a set of facilities that make them especially suitable for developing global communication services in areas where international co-operation is required:

1. It offers a scalable architecture that may support the coverage of large geographic areas and connect a large number of sites.
2. It offers the capacity to perform the global management of the event from a single point. It allows the effective and user-friendly design of strategies and services for management.
3. It allows the definition of new services or the adaptation and tuning/parameterisation of already defined services.
4. It works over heterogeneous networks, providing a uniform Quality of Service (QoS) over them, by the use of a special adaptation agent called IROUTER [4].

The most complex event that may currently be organised is a distributed conference. It involves the participation of several auditoriums, from where speakers make presentations and people attend local or remote presentations. The resulting event is a combination of a real-time TV programme with several studios, and a standard conference. The difficulty is increased by the difficulties related to the use of advanced communication networks, which are still not at a commercial stage. During a conference, all the activities occur during a few consecutive days (usually two or three days), without time for recovering lost sessions and with few opportunities for making relevant modifications.

4.2 ISABEL: A Platform for Service Provision

ISABEL [10] is a computer-supported co-operative work (CSCW) application designed within the European broadband programs RACE and ACTS to support the creation of innovative remote collaboration services in the area of synchronous group-collaboration. By group-collaboration we mean interconnection of people located in auditoriums or various kinds of rooms, using a workstation-based CSCW application, whose display is shared by all site attendants (projected on a large screen if there are a number of them). The service platforms created using ISABEL have supported the realisation of any group synchronous collaboration model [11].

4.2.1 The ISABEL Service Model

An ISABEL Event is the realization of a concrete group collaboration service modelled as an activity [8,9,12]. ISABEL provides a framework for the creation of new services. Figure 4.1 shows the steps during event realisation:

1. We start installing the ISABEL software and customising already defined services or defining new ones from scratch. Examples of ISABEL services are: teleconference, tele-meeting, tele-working, etc. The creation of

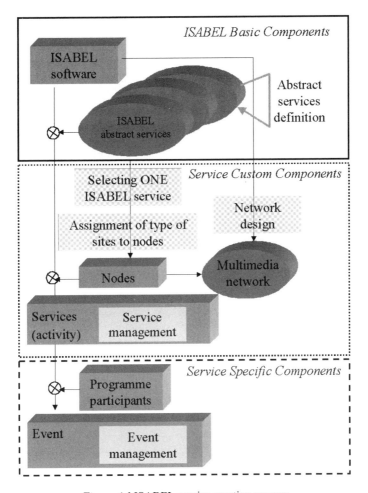

Figure 4.1 ISABEL service creation process.

ISABEL services requires definition of the attendant's site, the interaction modes and the roles that each person will play.

2. During a second phase, once the service we want to provide has been identified (tele-class, working sessions, etc.) we set up a service that may be used for the realisation of several events. We need to assign to each node involved on the service one of the types defined by ISABEL, specifying which roles it will play during each mode. Combining the application characteristics and the participating nodes, we will define the multimedia network that will support the service.

Specific ISABEL services are defined by modifying one of the predefined abstract services (or just creating a completely new one) with the specific information or the service we will set-up:

- Participant sites: number, location, classification and main characteristics.
- Network nodes and links, including QoS parameters.
- Expected/possible quality of the event.

3. Finally, combining a service with content information, we carry out the event.

Multimedia network definition, and the configuration and activity file are the two main products of this phase.

The last phase uses an existing activity to complete a distributed event. Information about the programme (timetable, location of speakers, scheduling of presentations and parallel sessions, etc.) is provided in this phase. This information is specific for each ISABEL event (each execution of the service). Content provision and distribution is the last step in this final process.

An ISABEL event involves a list of participating sites. A site is an access point to the virtual workspace for one or more attendants located in a room or a big auditorium.

An ISABEL site is a place from which anybody attends/participates in the conference. Several types of sites can be differentiated [11]. Those sites are also nodes of the service. The sites that will participate in the conference may be classified as follows:

- *Interactive Site (IS):* from which attendants may interact (send and receive audio, video and data) with other sites. ISs are associated with maximum interaction functionality and standard interaction control permissions. Most of the interaction modes apply to ISs because event attendants are distributed over all connected ISs. We defined an Open Event when any ISABEL site is free to connect with the event, whereas a Closed Event allows only the connection of a reduced set of sites given during event definition. Two special kinds of IS may be classified for organisation and management:

- *Main Interactive Site (MIS):* a special IS, where there is an audience, and the *speakers* will make presentations. A MIS has the functionality of any IS but some interaction modes provide them with special configurations: its video is bigger than the rest or it is allowed to make a presentation. This is because usually they should provide a more reliable network access. It is also highly recommended that they offer failure recovery facilities with back-up networks and equipment.

- *Control Site (CS):* the most important site of the event, as it is devoted to the start and control of the whole conference, performing also remote control of the ISs. A CS is an interactive site, which is the first site connected to the event. (Sometimes the master site is not an interactive site. It is possible to configure a site as a dispatcher of ISABEL conferences. For example, when a Web Server is used to co-ordinate the connection phase.) When an IS wants to be involved in an event it contacts the master site to be authenticated, check its participation permissions and receive the event description. After the connection phase, the site is included in the event group as an IS with a particular set of roles assigned. The CS may be located at one of the MIS, or may be an independent place with neither public nor speakers.

- *Watch Point (WP):* a site able to receive event information, however it is not included in the event group and it is not able to send information to the rest of the participants. In video-on-demand services, attendants use a WP to receive the programme. Equipment and technical conditions of connections and equipments will not interfere with the conference's core.

Site behaviour is defined by the assignment of roles. Each event identifies one set of roles defined in the activity. One role must be assigned to each site for each

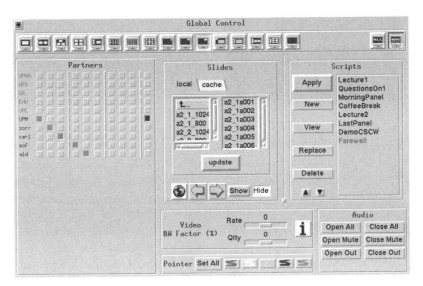

Figure 4.2 Operator's control interface.

interaction mode (ISABEL mode). There are roles common to many activities. When a more dynamic and flexible interaction is required, conference operators may use the advanced control interface (Figure 4.2), that allows on-the-fly assignation of role to each site.

Figure 4.3 User control panel.

In many services, all the participant sites have the same view of the conference, and may use the same services and applications. A simple user control panel (Figure 4.3) shows services available at each site.

The ISABEL mode creates groups of capabilities, and its parameters that will be

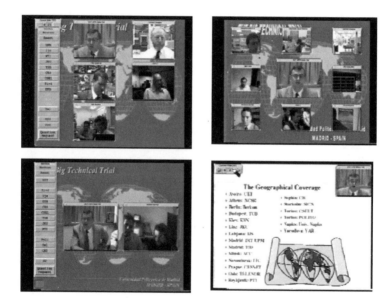

Figure 4.4 ISABEL modes at work.

used together under certain circumstances. Those capabilities include: audio, video, display sharing, presentation capabilities, etc. Figure 4.4 shows a schema of the most typical ISABEL modes: panels, discussions, questions and presentations.

ISABEL also provides tools for recording events. The ISABEL grabber (IG) is a special kind of site, similar to a WP, devoted to record all information received during an event and store it in a server. After the event, users can play back the event from the events server, connecting its workstation as a WP.

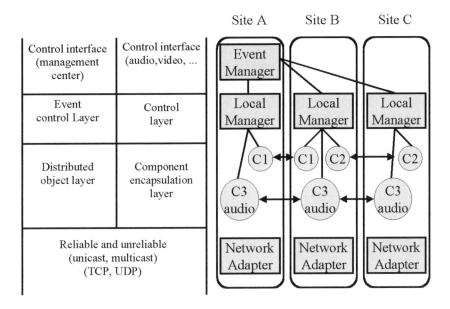

Figure 4.5 ISABEL layered architecture.

ISABEL has been designed using a layered approach with the goal of being modular and easily updateable, as shown in the left part of Figure 4.5. ISABEL provides two different parts in each layer, a control related part and a shared media part. The system is structured in three basic layers: the user interface, the conference control and the distributed object layer. These layers have been constructed over a standard TCP/IP service [12].

The right-hand part of Figure 4.5 provides a more detailed view of the interaction between the control stack and the media stack. A general conference manager is devoted to set-up the event and takes care of sites' group management. It implements the management policy of a given service controlling the local managers. The communication between the media components is always performed through the local managers.

The *user interface layer* defines the interaction control between the user and all the application elements. It has been implemented using TCL-TK. The ISABEL interface changes depending on the ISABEL being used. The interface of the control part provides access to the management capabilities, either globally or locally. Single ISABEL components may also contribute to the use interface with their specific user interface elements.

The *conference control layer* is the real ISABEL kernel. It is a distributed object mainly devoted to provide real-time conference control. It also enables the communication of the user interface with the ISABEL components located at the *distributed object layer*.

The *component layer* provides access to the individual media component managers. This layer is responsible for establishing the different multimedia streams. The media components are dynamically configurable according to the interaction modes defined for each ISABEL service.

Finally, the *communications layer* is a transport network that provides stream multiplexing over standard IP protocols. Conferences with many participants can only make effective use of bandwidth by using multicast facilities. This layer allocates the different information streams to specific characteristics of the underlying access network, depending on bandwidth and QoS demands.

The data traffic generated by ISABEL is therefore generated by many independent and variable rate sources (Figure 4.6). Single sources of traffic will send traffic data to a network agent called the ISABEL Network Adapter (INA) [13,14]. It combines all the data streams into a single data stream and routes them through the underlying access network adapting ISABEL QoS requirements to the requirements of the traffic network service available. The overall traffic generated has a complex pattern and shape, and is not well suited for transmission across existing networks. INA generates a single output data flow combining all the data received from single components. The resulting traffic is adapted to the requirements of the network service available.

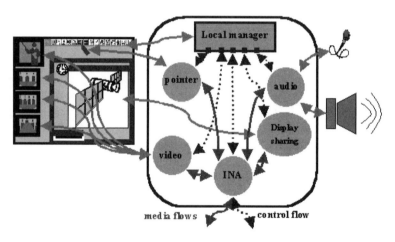

Figure 4.6 Data traffic and network traffic.

ISABEL architecture provides a very flexible framework, which allows the building of different kinds of distributed CSCW configurations. This architecture has been implemented on a SUN WS with UNIX. The X window interface has been used. Special hardware boards providing ATM connection and video compression are also used. ISABEL has been ported to Silicon Graphics and recently to LINUX.

4.2.2 Service Set-Up over Heterogeneous Networks

ISABEL is based on TCP/IP. It has been designed to support site interconnection through heterogeneous networks, from narrowband (such as ISDN or standard Internet) to broadband networks (such as ATM or asymmetric satellite connections) and from unicast point-to-point to multicast multi-point connections [16].

The INA is the transport agent for the ISABEL application providing an additional layer in the software structure of the application. None of the ISABEL components sends its data directly to the network. Instead, they all rely on having the INA do it for them.

ISABEL isolates data transportation (devoted to INA) from processing. The INA is mainly focused on data flow information providing the following functions:

1. Application level traffic shaping to fit a given bit rate. This feature improves the usage of bandwidth drastically and decreases the amount of packet drops. It transforms VBR into CBR-like at application level. Therefore, it eliminates the buffering required in the network to cope with traffic bursts. It also sorts out application traffic to reduce the jitter of the most time-sensitive media.

2. It supports a wide range of bit rates: from very low (128 Kb/s) to very high (10 Mb/s and more). It allows working with the most-used network profiles.

3. It enables inter-working among users connected through multicast and users connected through any unicast network. This service is used when dealing with satellite and ISDN networks.

4. It supports flexible data service pattern specification. Service differentiation for each component: priority and required packet discarding policies, fragmentation, etc. Packet scheduling is developed according to the specified service pattern of each component data stream and to preserving the negotiated bandwidth. Packet scheduling is performed through an intelligent packet discard that allows the reduction of bandwidth of a high-quality multimedia data flow by a given factor by dropping lower priority packets. This operation is performed preserving the integrity of the application; e.g. reducing the performance of secondary components (keeping the functionality) to prevent the degradation of primary ones (usually the audio stream).

5. It can work as an autonomous application flow distribution. ISABEL Network Node (INN) has become a complex application router to connect certain remote users with special network characteristics with the rest of meeting users. It minimises copies when a group should be linked from one site and multicast is not available.

6. It supports intelligent multiplexing of several sources into a single stream. In case of overloading of the output circuit, it enables a selective intelligent traffic shaping at application level. The primary adaptation is audio streams. Different audio codecs are mixed simultaneously (G.711, G.721, etc) into a single audio stream, so that audio can be sent/received at

multiple qualities according to available bandwidth without compromising the performance of other components.

7.   It supports internal signalling, used to simplify the set-up of a virtual ISABEL interconnection network between ISABEL sites.

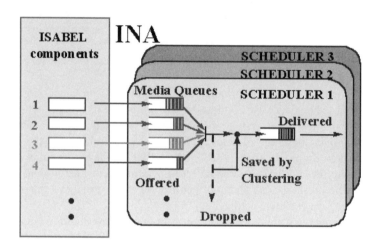

Figure 4.7 The INA architecture.

The INA driving principle is that multimedia data generated by a distributed interactive application is short lived: data not delivered in time will not be delivered at all. A packet that will not be delivered in time can cause either the full media flow to stop and re-synchronise (insert buffering in the application) or a waste of bandwidth. Packets delivered out of time will be discarded by ISABEL components and overload applications and network performance.

An essential element of the INA component is the scheduler. It decides which packets cannot be delivered within a time limit (the liveness of the information in that packet). Consequently, INA will drop packets that are out of time. Strategies for managing packets may be selected by each ISABEL component, resulting in an intelligent traffic management policy that combines the requirements of each single component and is intended to use all the services provided by the underlying access network.

The INA internal architecture is made of input and output queues. Output queues have an associated bandwidth and for each type of data traffic a relative priority value is defined. Each multimedia data flow accesses INA by one input queue. Each scheduler takes input information trying to output from the delivered queue. All information is delivered, if output bandwidth is enough. The intelligent packet discard mechanism is activated, if output bandwidth is less than all the input information.

It is important to note that typically each information unit can be distributed across several packets. The loss of one single packet converts to useless information of the same unit transmitted in another packet. This is the case of big documents, images or video frames. Each component should specify to INA its clustering structure: which packets are parts of the same semantic unit and other related QoS requirements. The priority in combination with clustering information is taken into account by the INA when generating a packet scheduler, so that information is discarded in clusters and the whole cluster selection is considered when accepting traffic from the component.

Figure 4.7 shows the INA internal structure, where traffic from the input queues are subject to analysis by INA and discarded or accepted applying different strategies for each media packet information. Some packets, which would be initially discarded, are otherwise accepted because of the clustering of packets. The information on which packets have been saved by clustering is continuously used as feedback information for the scheduler, which tries to generate an optimal traffic schedule associated with a network and application constraints.

INA implementation comprises several schedulers. There is typically one scheduler per link (i.e. one scheduler per ISDN call), although two or more remote sites, which in fact share the link, can also share the scheduler. The INA also contains a traffic schedule, which tries to balance the available bandwidth and provide a fair share of the bandwidth between the remote applications.

For each media the application defines an access gate over which the media traffic is going to be delivered. At a typical user workstation each media within INA will have two gates: one connected to the local application component and one bound to the network transport layer to send and receive the media data to the rest of the sites. In a typical scenario, there is not much difference between the INA set-up and having the components directly using unicast or multicast sockets to send or receive media data.

This architecture is fully scalable, and this is its main advantage. For instance, within a multicast conference a new gate from a workstation connected by a unicast link, can be accommodated. This gate is connected with other gates in the INA remote client workstation (see Figure 4.8).

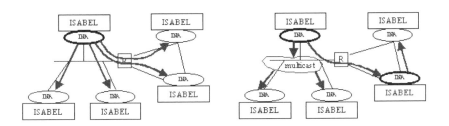

Figure 4.8 Interconnection architectures: unicast mesh and flow concentrator.

The new user could forward the traffic to another user or even to another segment of multicast users. Application components are kept isolated from network issues. The application may switch from standard multicast set-up to unicast copies if required by underlying neworks. ISABEL components always see the same INA as the network service. How this is performed is of no concern to the application.

Another important functionality of INA is the capability of performing flow adaptation for users connected through lower bandwidth connections. A high performance conference in ISABEL typically runs at an aggregated bandwidth of 2 Mb/s (2 active audio sources and several video streams from all participants), or even 6 Mb/s in certain configurations. However, some users may want to participate in the conference and cannot afford such a high bandwidth (for example a low bandwidth ISDN link). In this case we have an ISABEL *flow server* configured to forward all traffic from the network to some application filters which perform the bandwidth adaptation, and then forward the output from filters to the user(s) with limited bandwidth capabilities. In this way, it is also possible that the user requests the application to send more data than the data channel available. INA is configured to filter the excess before transmitting to the network.

Transformation of audio flows requires the combination of all the sources into a single flow. When it is imposed by networks characteristics it is also possible to perform transformations from ISABEL standard audio formats (16 bits, 16 kHz) to more restricted format (G711, G723 or GSM). When dealing with video it is not possible to perform the same type of transformations, but channel selection, frame resizing and degradation of frame rate is done. This way of providing support to lower bandwidth users is aligned with the Internet Engineering Task Force (IETF) proposal of application bridges in the Real-Time Protocol (RTP) specification.

4.3 Preparation of the Distributed Conference

The management of a standard conference implies the co-ordination of two groups of people that will work in parallel: the contents group and the infrastructure group. The management of the contents of the conference is in charge of the conference diffusion, organising the call for papers, paper review and selection, chairman identification, and the design of a programme to organise the presentations of the selected papers. The infrastructure group will reserve rooms and auditoriums, allocate the secretariat of the conference, manage audio-visual equipment of the auditoriums, edit the proceedings, manage inscriptions, select auxiliary personnel, manage publicity of the conference, etc.

A distributed conference organised with ISABEL is organised in two parallel planes:

- *Contents plane*, which includes all the elements related to the information that participants will interchange during the conference. Management of this plane is similar to a standard single-venue conference. Special attention must be paid to geographical distribution of the participants and provide mechanisms for a prior collection of presentations that need to be distributed to all the participating sites.
- *Technical organisation plane,* which includes all the problems related with the distributed organisation of the conference. It includes the use of a large

communication network, the usage of a sophisticated application (ISABEL) and accurate co-ordination before and during the conference realisation.

Co-ordination between the two planes is realised by the co-ordination plane. The persons involved in this group will be in charge of the *global process co-ordination*, defining and maintaining links between the contents plane and the technical organisation plane. Their main objective is that the use of such a sophisticated technology is as transparent as possible.

The organisation of one event of such a size and complexity requires very precise co-ordination. One of the first tasks to be accomplished is the assignation of roles to each person that will participate.

The complexity of a distributed conference requires careful planning, and the realisation of tests and rehearsals to minimise the number of incidences and problems during the realisation of the conference. The following elements must be planned and tested:

— *Set-up of the event in the web server.* It will provide basic support for configuration and operation of the communication network; installation and operation of ISABEL; identification of the auxiliary equipment required for the auditoriums; scheduling and execution of tests and rehearsals; co-ordination of speakers and chairmen. An e-mail list is used for the co-ordination of the previously identified planes of control.

— *Network definition.* Allocating the required networks resources, and configuring them to co-operate with ISABEL network features to provide the required QoS.

— *Programme definition and contents provision.* This is the central element for defining the content, scheduling and organisation of a conference. It is especially important in a distributed conference, when presentations must be co-ordinated from several sites. It is very important that all the persons involved in the organisation (contents, technique and management) have a deep understanding of the detailed programme to ensure good co-ordination of all of them. How ISABEL helps to deal with a detailed programme is described in detail in Section 4.3.2.

— *Testing plan.* A testing plan must also be scheduled to integrate the large number of human and equipment resources involved in these kinds of large events. The testing plan must also take into account:

  – Testing interconnections and the access network
  – Individual testing plans for each site
  – Interconnection and interoperability testing among main sites
  – Interconnection and interoperability testing among main and interactive sites
  – Tests and rehearsals for special and/or complex sessions.

4.3.1 Network Definition

Three elements must be analysed and combined when building the ISABEL network: network links, network nodes and ISABEL sites.

4.3.1.1 Network Links

ISABEL is ready to work over a large variety of network technologies: optical fibre ATM links, satellite links, ISDN public lines (multiplexing several B-channels), etc. All these subnetworks should be interconnected building one IP network. ISABEL will run over such an IP network adapting multimedia flows to the provided QoS.

The ISABEL QoS definition is based on the QoS perceived by end-users (participants in the conference), not in network parameters such as cell loss rate, delay jitters, etc. ISABEL provides software that converts network QoS to multimedia QoS. In this way, conference designers will deal with video quality (frames per second, image resolution and compression algorithm) and audio quality (sample rate, sample size and coding) instead of packet drop or end-to-end delay.

Availability of network links with the associated bandwidth and QoS parameters provides basic information to:

–   Characterise global conference quality
–   Identify required network nodes for QoS adaptation.

4.3.1.2 Network Nodes

Network nodes provide services for QoS adaptation between sub-networks and/or combination/replications of multimedia traffic for several ISABEL sites in order to save bandwidth.

Figure 4.9 shows the global picture of one possible ISABEL multimedia network.

4.3.1.3 ISABEL Sites

These will be connected to the leaves of the network. Information about number, location, type and main characteristics of ISABEL sites will provide information for:
–   Identification of new network nodes which will deal with the combination and replication of multimedia traffic for saving network bandwidth.
–   Classification of sites.

One of the ISABEL site categories will be assigned to each site, depending on its relevance. The levels of relevance have been identified as:

1.   The core of the conference, composed of CS and MIS. The disconnection of any IS allows the rest of the ISs to go ahead with the conference. Contingency plans must be scheduled to deal with problems at CS and/or MIS.

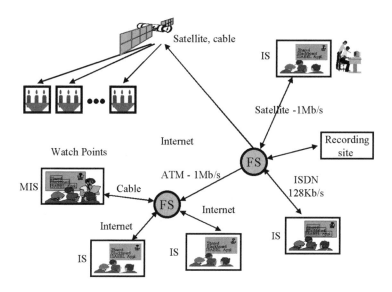

Figure 4.9 Multimedia network.

2. ISABEL allows that any IS assumes the role of CS, immediately and without disturbing the conference development.

3. The ISs have relevance because they usually collect a large number of attendants that will participate in questions and discussions. Individual problems of the IS are not relevant problems for the global conference, but ISs with frequent problems may jeopardise the development of the conference.

4. Finally, watchpoints are passive receptors of the distributed information. Their number, performance and quality do not interfere at any time with the core of the conference.

4.3.2 Programme and Contents

The main input for the content organisation is the programme of the conference. It has been defined as a process to produce information suitable for the ISABEL application starting from the general programme of the conference. At present, this process is done mainly by hand, it is under development as a CSCW web-based application that will automate the process.

Combining participant information with the general programme, the detailed programme is produced. It summarises all the information required during the realisation of the event to control the conference.

The conference manager starts the process by creating the general programme (the conference programme itself). From this programme, one form is produced for each single activity during the conference (paper presentation, panel discussion, tutorial, etc.). These forms are completed by participants (mainly speakers and

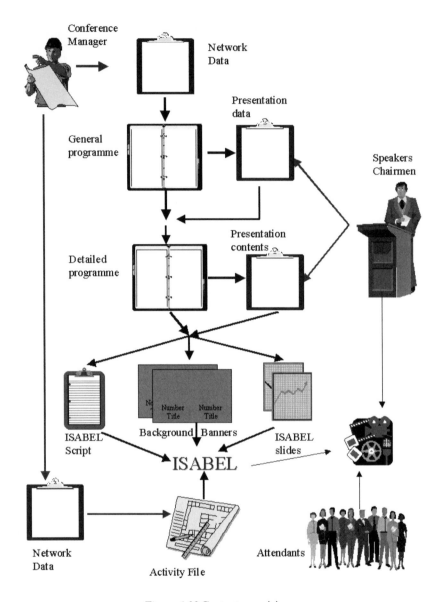

Figure 4.10 Contents provision.

chairmen) providing information such as: name and other data of speakers and chairmen, their location during the presentations, content material provided/required during the presentation, etc.

Before the start of the event, participants must provide content (typically slides), that, combined with the detailed programme, will produce:

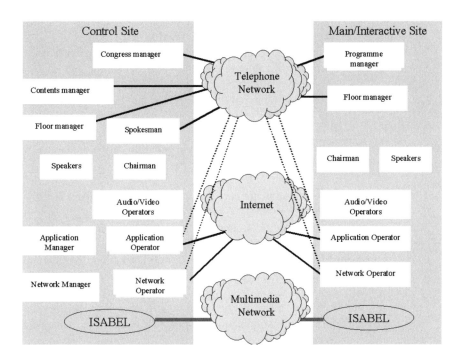

Figure 4.11 Communications during the event

- ISABEL scripts files that control systematically the distributed conference from the CS
- Backgrounds and banners with names and other data about participants
- Slides converted to ISABEL format.

This information and the corresponding activity file are loaded by the ISABEL application. Then the event will start with the participation of speakers, chairmen, attendants, etc., and under the control of ISABEL operators. This process is outlined in Figure 4.10

4.4 Realisation of the Distributed Conference

Service operation is fully based on Internet communications. Service operation features are centralised in a Web Server currently located at http://isabel.dit.upm.es. This server offers capabilities for: event description and creation, network definition and configuration, program creation and transformation, contents collection and transformation, test and rehearsal scheduling, co-ordination of infrastructure management, co-ordinates of content managers and co-ordinates of speakers and chairman.

ISABEL allows also the control of the whole conference from a single point using a graphic interface:

- Selection and/or adaptation of one of the predefined ISABEL modes
- Selection of the sources of video and audio to be distributed to the conference
- Selection of sound, control of volumes, control of echo cancelling, etc.
- Selection of backgrounds and slides to be used
- Loading of the detailed programme of the session and application of each step.

The first element to define is the communication infrastructure that the organisation will use. Figure 4.11 describes the main communication media that will be used during the conference:

- The multimedia communication network that connects the sites that will support the conference.
- The application and network operators will use the standard Internet communication mechanisms. IRC (Internet Relay Chat) has proved to be very useful as a private communication mechanism for co-ordination, notification of incidences, etc. If the Internet connection fails, telephone will be used to connect the MIS with the CS.
- For large and complex events, one audio-conference service has been successfully used for co-ordination sessions among the conference manager, the programme managers of each site, speakers, and eventually the contents manager.

Although detailed, a programme is loaded in the application, and it will drive the application's behaviour during the event. It is also possible to have full control of the application and manually configure the application directly, in real-time, during the event, by the use of a graphic interface.

4.4.1 Monitoring

In order to reduce the number of problems perceived by attendants during the conference, we must continuously monitor three elements:

- *The network:* to anticipate any problem that may impact the QoS requirements that allow the application to offer good quality to the attendants. In this kind of situation it is always better to apply preventive actions introducing, when required, breaks or changes on the programme while the network is fixed, than wait till these problems produce a malfunction of the application.
- *The application:* may also suffer local problems, or problems that are more general if they affect the control site. Special attention must be paid to the sites with repeated and continuous problems. Sites with very frequent problems will dramatically degrade the behaviour of the application, and jeopardise the evolution of the distributed conference. In this situation the conference manager may decide to disconnect some sites for some time, until they have solved the problems.

- *The contents:* problems, usually considered as minor problems during standard conferences, like the late arrival of one of the speakers, the long duration of a welcome speech, etc., are in this context specially relevant. It is important that all the sites receive precise and timely information about such incidences, their causes (if they are known), duration (if foreseen), and what will be the next step.

4.5 Conclusions

The organisation and development of a distributed conference using multimedia applications and networks suitable for supporting multimedia traffic requires a wide usage of human and material resources. The technological problems related to the network's bandwidth and coverage, and the creation and usage of new and powerful tools for services creation (ISABEL), being solved in part, organisation problems start to be the main problem. Facilities and tools for helping in the management of such services and event must be part of the applications that will be used in the organisation of this kind of distributed event. These requirements affect the network support management, the interchange of multimedia flows or whatever element that is part of the organisation. The information and its management must be considered an important element in every management organisation, even more when there are groups of persons involved who are spread around the world. Good information management, using the most advanced technologies and tools available, will be one of the keys to success.

Good preparation, including tests and rehearsals of real situations that will happen during the event, is the best way to ensure that everyone will know what to do during the real event. Motivation and implication of persons involved in the organisation, including the participants in the content, and the speakers, is an essential element to having a successful conference. The organisation must be supported by a wide communication platform that allows fast decision agreement with the best information possible during the duration of the event.

Even when the organisation is at its best, some major problems may happen in the days or even hours before the event start. Back-up plans must be defined and alternatives sought for dealing with problems such as general failure of communication networks, unavailability of one or more MIS, etc.

With enough experience in the organisation of this kind of complex event, and applications such as ISABEL have a sufficient degree of maturity, it becomes necessary to develop applications specially dedicated to the organisation, management and co-ordination of events. This is part of the work currently being done around ISABEL. In a short time, it is planned to produce a workflow tool that will be integrated with ISABEL providing support for the management of the events.

Finally, the main objective of this is to provide mature organisational procedures and tools to permit the use of such new technologies in a simple way as we do today with programs such as document editors, Internet web browsers, etc.

References

[1]   Wilson (1991) "Computer Supported Cooperative Work". Computer Networks and ISDN Systems, pp 91–95, volume 23.

[2]   D. Marca and G. Bock (1992) "Groupware: software for computer-supported cooperative work". IEEE Press, 1992.

[3]   L. Lindop, T. Relph-Knight, K. Taylor, A. Eager, G. Einon, K. Joyce, A. Stevens (1995) "Groupware : Let's work Together". PC Magazine, August 1995.

[4]   T.P. de Miguel, S. Pavón, J. Salvachúa, J. Quemada, P.L. Chas, J. Fernandez-Amigo, C. Acuña, L. Rodríguez, V. Lagarto, J. Bastos (1994) "ISABEL - Experimental Distributed Cooperative Work Application over Broadband Networks", pp. 353–362, Springer-Verlag - Lecture Notes in Computer Science, Volume 868.

[5]   A. Azcorra, T.P. de Miguel, M. Petit, L. Rodríguez, C. Acuña, P.L. Chas, V. Lagarto, J. Bastos (1995) "Multicast IP support for distributed conferencing over ATM". Networld+Interop 95, pp. 9, March 1995. Las Vegas (USA).

[6]   J. Nunamaker (1999) "Collaborative Computing: The next milennium". IEEE Computer, Vol. 32, n. 9, pp. 66–71.

[7]   F. Fluckiger (1995) "Understanding Networked Multimedia", Prentice Hall, 1995.

[8]   J. Quemada, T.P. Miguel, A. Azcorra, S. Pavón, J. Salvachúa, M. Petit, J. I. Moreno, P. L. Chas, C. Acuña, L. Rodríguez, V. Lagarto, J. Bastos, J. Fontes, J. Domingues (1995) "Tele-education Experiences with the ISABEL Application", High Performance Networking for Tele-teaching - IDC´95, Madeira, November 1995.

[9]   The TECODIS Project home page: http://www.dit.upm.es/~tecodis

[10] ISABEL Application home page: http://isabel.dit.upm.es/

[11] J. Quemada, T.P. de Miguel A. Azcorra, S. Pavón, J. Salvachúa, M. Petit, D. Larrabeiti, T. Robles, G. Huecas, D. Rodríguez, F. Echevarrieta, E. Castro (1998) "Teleservice creation with ISABEL in heterogeneous network environments", Interoperability of Networks for Interoperable Services, ISSN 1385 9501, Ottawa, July 1998.

[12] J. Quemada, T.P. de Miguel, A. Azcorra, S. Pavón, J. Salvachúa, M. Petit, D. Larrabeiti T. Robles, G. Huecas (1996) ISABEL: "A CSCW application for the distribution of events. Multimedia Telecommunications and Applications", Ed: G. Ventre, J. Domingo, A. Danthine. Springer-Verlag, - LNCS 1185, ISSN 0302-9743.

[13] M. Petit, T.P. de Miguel (1996) Distribution of Multimedia Information Experiences over Broadband Networks. EUNICE '96 Summer School, Lausane, September 1996.

[14] M. Petit, T.P. de Miguel (1996) Flexible Support for Advanced CSCW Conferences: the ISABEL irouter. PROMS'96: Protocols for Multimedia Systems, Madrid, October 1996.

[15] S. Pavón, T.P. de Miguel, M. Petit, J. Salvachúa, J. Quemada, L. Rodríguez, P.L. Chas, C. Acuna, V. Lagarto, J. Bastos (1994) "Integracion de Componentes en la Aplicacion de Trabajo Cooperativo ISABEL", Jornadas Telecom 94, Noviembre, 1994.

[16] A. Azcorra, T. Miguel, J. Quemada, S. Pavón, P. Chas, C. Acuña, P. Aranda, V. Lagarto, J. Bastos, J. Domingues (1994): "Distance Learning: Networks and Applications for RACE Summer School '94", Centro de Etudos de Telecomunicacoes, The ATM Forum Newsletter September, 1994 - Volume 2 Issue 3.

[17] D. Larrabeiti, M.C. Agúndez, A. Azcorra, C. García, J. Quemada, T.P. de Miguel, M. Petit (1997) "Towards the integrated configuration and management of multicast teleconferences based on IP over ATM", HP Openview University Association Workshop, Madrid, April 1997.

Chapter 5

Global360/NICE Video Conference Model

Andrei S. Mendkovich, Alexei P. Galitsky, Evgeny V. Mironov and Dmitri I. Sidelnikov

5.1 Introduction

The term "videoconference" which is used to define an event with remote interactive users who communicate by technical means for video and audio broadcasting is rather vague, as it is equally applicable to the events that differ radically in both technology and structure.

The year 1964 may be considered as the beginning of the videoconferencing epoch when AT&T was the first to exhibit a video telecommunication system Picturephone at the World Fair. Despite high public interest in the system, its extensive deployment failed as it called for special, not widely available and rather expensive communication channels. At that time, capacities of communication channels were 3 orders of magnitude less than was necessary for Picturephone functioning. Its usage also required a preliminary order of dedicated communication channels and hence dramatically lowered the system's consumer attractiveness. The Picturephone sales and production were shut down in 1973.

Further efforts by the companies engaged in R&D of videoconference systems focused on cutting down technical and operational costs. This reduction was rather slow.

The system developed by Compression Labs, Inc. appeared on the market in 1982. Its price amounted to 250 000 USD, and it used channels to be leased for about 1000 USD per hour. In 1986 PictureTel Corporation proposed a much more economical system for 80 000 USD which used 100 USD per hour channels. Only 5 years later this company managed to reduce the equipment set price to 20 000 USD and communications costs to 30 USD per hour and made the system affordable for a broad range of corporate users [5].

Anyhow, it was as late as the 1990s when videoconferences entered the accessible service pool. It was achieved due to the expansion and globalisation of the data transmission network infrastructure (primarily the Internet), breakthroughs in digital audio and video signal compression technologies, and reduction of data unit transmission rates in public networks. In addition, the progressing advancement in computer equipment and emergence of desktop videoconference systems based on home PCs were accompanied by relevant hardware and software cost reduction of by around 30% a year [3]. Amongst the key factors responsible for the cost reduction was a switchover to mass production of standardised hardware and software. The latter, in its turn, was a result the adoption of two important standard series by ITU-T (International Telecommunication Union – Telecommunication Standard Section), namely H.320 in 1990 and H.323 in 1996–1998, and T.120 in 1993–1996. The compatibility of various manufacturers' systems was thereby achieved.

Meanwhile, structural changes in the videoconferencing market were taking place. In particular, its sector related to sales of systems demanding a specially equipped room (Conference Room) that had comprised 60% in 1993 featured a 10-fold decrease by 1997. Meanwhile the sectors involved in sales of systems for small groups and home PC-based desktops increased from 10% to 40% and from 16% to 38%, respectively [16], for the same period. Not the least reason for such a violent growth of the above market sectors was likely to be a fast promotion of ISDN with its sales, e.g. in the USA, reaching 85% by 1995 [3].

Therefore, the first phase of the videoconference technologies evolution was complete by 1996–1997. It resulted in videoconferencing becoming a standard and accessible service. This chapter deals with a review of the specifics and main trends inherent to the second phase of the evolution of this service.

5.2 New Phase of the Videoconference Revolution

At the beginning of the second phase, a broadband telecommunication infrastructure became available to a wide range of corporate and individual users in both technical and economic respects. In 1998, 78% of US small businesses were active Internet users with 14% of them leasing T1/DS-1 channels, which quite recently had been leased only by large companies [18]. According to the latest Strategic Group researches [19], at the end of 1999, nearly 1.9 million households subscribed to high-speed access via a cable modem, digital subscriber line (DSL), direct broadcast satellite or wireless broadband. That represented a 185% increase over 1998 totals, which is higher growth than household Internet adoption in general.

The use of a broadband network infrastructure let videoconferencing reach a so-called "business quality" or even "near-TV quality" and made it a routine tool in business activities. The outputs of the surveys [21] done by Wainhouse Research in the USA in 1999 bear witness to the expansion of diverse videoconferencing practices among corporate users. Only a small portion (below 10%) did not display interest to this service and did not intend to use it in the near future (Table 5.1). Specifically, as it is apparent from Table 5.1, videoconferencing communication systems ranked about the same as audioconferencing systems in popularity.

Table 5.1 USA companies' position with respect to videoconferencing (1999) [21].

Videoconferencing system	Use now	Plan to deploy in 2000	Plan to test in 2000	No plan to deploy
Group	82%	9%	2%	6%
Personal	56%	15%	20%	9%
Audio	80%	6%	4%	6%
Real-time streaming broadcast	35%	26%	25%	9%

Another important feature of this period was the fact that the Internet began claiming the role of a universal communications medium. That was reflected in the revision of ideas about optimal telecommunication network architecture. It resulted in the concept of Optical Internet [1,2] – a network focused on IP-traffic transport. Among the first implementations of this concept was the Canadian research and education network CA*net3 launched in 1998 [6]. Experience in designing and operating CA*net3 showed that this architecture was capable of dramatically cutting down high-speed Internet service cost in the near future [7] and, hence, the cost of the use of various multimedia applications over IP, including videoconferences. Also, in the late 1990s there was a clear tendency for various services to migrate to the IP platform, e.g. IP-telephony [4,12], broadcasting over IP [13], etc.

It is therefore not surprising that videoconference users started to prefer H.323 systems based on IP protocol. As revealed by the research [21], in 1999, 29% of companies operated systems of that type and 32% planned to start using them in 2000. Moreover, 56% of businesses with experience in the systems' operation believed that those systems fully meet all their requirements, and 68% even plan to extend their use over the next 12 months.

According to the experts' assessment [22], the segment of the videoconferencing market related to the use of IP technologies will grow at a 57% rate, and the revenue of the manufacturers will reach 235 000 000 USD in 2004. For ISDN-based systems, the growth rate will make up only 7.7%, and the peak value of gross returns will not exceed 170 000 000 USD. The same period is anticipated to be marked with a gradual setback in the production and use of dual mode ISDN/IP software and hardware [23].

The popularisation of videoconferences involved a great change in the range of users. The videoconference systems operating in the 1980s served mostly top business managers and governmental officers. By the mid-1990s, the pattern had changed and another group, formed by research and educational community members, was among the most extensive system users. Moreover, in some countries, including Russia, this group has been dominating not only by its activity but also by its relative size.

As a whole, the high participation level of this category of users is quite justified, as workshops, meetings, symposiums, etc. are a traditional and important form of professional information exchange. The predominance of these users in Russia is governed by a number of features specific to this country: great distances between research and educational centres, lack of funding for an adequate level of customary scientific co-operation forms, e.g. national and international meetings, scientific tourism, etc.

Changes in the kinds of videoconference users effected dramatically the requirements of those systems and, as a consequence, their evolution trends. In particular, the appearance of research and educational community members among the system users accounted for a number of specific requirements, which had not been characteristic of the first phase of the systems evolution when a "video meeting" involving a few small local groups with prevailing oral information exchange used to be the basic form of videoconferencing. The following specific requirements are worth noting:

–   scalability, with respect to both the local audience number and the total amount;
–   high quality video and audio to provide distant users with an adequate image of the demonstrated object;
–   efficient support for both audio–video and data;
–   co-operative use of applications;
–   mature integrated management system for both technical and content components of a videoconference.

Additionally, videoconferences are currently considered as a part of the computer-supported co-operative work (CSCW) of distributed groups rather than as an isolated service.

Targeted and consolidated efforts focused on meeting those requirements were undertaken in 1996–1998 under the NICE and EXPERT projects of the ACTS (Advanced Communications Technologies) Program [8] within the 4th Framework program of the European Commission. The outputs of the NICE/ACTS project [11] deserve detailed consideration in this chapter since they finally resulted in the formulation of a new model of a distributed network event. Three Russian agencies were official partners of the NICE/ACTS project consortium:

–   Zelinsky Institute of Organic Chemistry RAS (IOC RAS) (Network Operations Center of the academic and research network FREEnet), Moscow;
–   Yaroslavl State University (University Internet Center), Yaroslavl; and
–   International Telecommunications Center, Novosibirsk.

Russian participation in the consortium contributed to the introduction of broadband distributed applications in this country and secured Russia's involvement in a train of international actions in 1997—1998 conducted with the use of the above technologies.

The implementation of the Russian part of the project was supported by the Russian Foundation for Basic Research as an important component in the development of computer-supported technologies for CSCW of distributed research teams [20].

5.3 NICE Project

The key objective of the NICE project was to investigate the issues associated with the implementation of broadband distributed applications using an ATM infrastructure. Distributed network events (videoconferences) and broadband asynchronous services were chosen as basic application types.

Table 5.2 NICE/ACTS Project consortium.

No:	Institution	Country
1	Belgacom NV	Belgium
2	Alcatel Bell Telephone	Belgium
3	CSC Ploenzke AG, Broadcast and Communication	Germany
4	Portugal Telecom CET Centro Estudos Telecomunicacoes	Portugal
5	Centro Studi e Laboratori Telecomunicazioni S p A	Italy
6	Politecnico di Torino	Italy
7	Universita di Napoli Federico II	Italy
8	Deutsche Telekom Berkom GmbH	Germany
9	Swiss Telecom PTT	Germany
10	Telefonica de Espana S A	Spain
11	Universidad Politecnica de Madrid	Spain
12	North West Labs Ltd	Ireland
13	Koninklijke PTT Nederland NV KPN Research	Netherlands
14	National Centre for Scientific Research Demokritos	Greece
15	NTUA Institute of Communications and Computer Systems	Greece
16	Thesa Ltd	Greece
17	EUTELSAT	France
18	France Telecom CNET	France
19	Telenor AS	Norway
20	Post and Telecom Iceland	Iceland
21	University of Newcastle	UK
22	CESNET, Association of Legal Entities	Czech Republic
23	Center for Informatics and Computer Technology	Bulgaria
24	System Investment Telecommunications Limited	Hungary
25	Institute Jozef Stefan	Slovenia
26	Ukrainian Office of the International Science Foundation	Ukraine
27	Analytical Computer Centre of the Ministry of Education and Science of Belarus	Belarus

No:	Institution	Country
28	Yaroslavl State University	Russia
29	Novosibirsk International Telecommunications Center	Russia
30	International Telecommunications Centre KSNet	Ukraine
31	N.D.Zelinsky Institute of Organic Chemistry	Russia
32	Swedish Institute of Computer Science	Sweden
33	Johannes Kepler University, Linz	Austria
34	Bureau for International Research and Technology Co-operation	Austria
35	Technical University of Budapest and MATAV PKI	Hungary

The NICE project was characteristic of a complex approach to the development of videoconferencing systems that provided for the improvement of both different technological components and relevant organisational and technical models. It is worth noting that the field testing of the results was performed during on-going large-scale international distributed events. The complex character of the project to a great extent dictated the identification of the project consortium partners. As seen from Table 5.2, along with research institutions, it involved leading European telecom operators.

5.3.1 Technology

As mentioned above, applications for distributed network events with the use of a broadband communication environment were the research subject of the NICE project. A demand for scalability of the designed standard configurations determined their heterogeneity at channel and application levels. Only in this manner was it possible to reach the desired popularity and participation of audiences in various geographical regions, where the readily available telecom infrastructure differed greatly.

5.3.1.1 Physical and Channel Levels

For the above reason, the global dedicated networks created to carry out planned experiments, field trials and public demonstrations actually covered all main telecommunication media on a physical level, including both satellite links and terrestrial channels (optical fibre, copper and radio) [10]. At the channel level they were:

- ATM;
- ATM with UPC;
- ATM Cadenza adapters (for satellite channels);
- ATM with ATMA;
- ISDN; and
- Ethernet.

5.3.1.2 Network and Applications Software Levels

The core protocol used at the network level was IPv4. The applied videoconferencing software was represented by several tools from different companies, in particular, MMC [9] (Deutsche Telecom Berkom), BETEUS [24] (France Telecom), ISABEL (see Chapter 4 and [17]) (Universidad Politecnica de Madrid), and Mbone [15]. It fell into two categories: commercial and pilot products.

Table 5.3 International trials and public demonstrations by the NICE EXPERT projects.

Date	Name of international event	Sites	Applications package	Status
7.3.96	International teleconference	8	ISABEL	Trial
9–12. 7. 96	4th Advanced Broadband Communications Summer School (ABC96)	25	ISABEL	Major trial and public demonstration
13.12.96	G7 GIBN editorial working group	4	MMC	Trial
21.1.97	CEE/NIS workshop	10	ISABEL	Trial
6.03.97	USINACTS Seminar	4	ISABEL	Major trial and public demonstration
16–18.6.97	Global360	21	ISABEL	Major trial and public demonstration
8–12.9.97	Smart Communities	3	BETEUS	Major trial and public demonstration
17.10.97	Big Technical Trial	18	ISABEL	Trial
12–13.11.97	CEE/NIS Event	15	ISABEL	Major trial and public demonstration
26–27.11.97	Kiev–Torino trial	2	ISABEL	Trial
26–27.3.98	East–West Telematics Congress, Vienna	4	ISABEL	Major trial and public demonstration
25–26.9.98	IDC98, Lisbon	20	ISABEL	Major trial and public demonstration
30.11.98 – 2.12.98	IST98/Global360	19	ISABEL	Major trial and public

Date	Name of international event	Sites	Applications package	Status
16–17.06.99	Russian–British Digital Workshop	5	Mbone	demonstration Regular event. (Not trial)
22–24.11.99	IST99–Russia	8	Mbone	Regular event. (Not trial)

Most attention was paid to the testing, adaptation and tuning of the ISABEL software which had been used for most of the distributed network events under the NICE project (Table 5.3). This was because a few specific features make it highly suitable for running large videoconferences. Among them are:

– control centre system;
– both multicast and unicast capabilities within a dedicated network, which enable one to use eventually any desirable network topology at minimal cost;
– flow servers converting multicast flow to unicast flows and enable the use of various capacity channels within a dedicated network;
– watch points where the audience have a chance to follow the conference using a broad scope of technologies, both symmetric (e.g. ISDN) and asymmetric (e.g. ADSL and DirectPC technologies);
– facilities for selective quality control of individual broadcast components and services (e.g. video, audio, control, and asynchronous services) operated within the available data transmission speed;
– ISABEL/Mbone gateways enable one to use other than ISABEL applications (e.g. VIC/VAT, IP-TV) for receiving and broadcasting, and provide the possibility of broadcasting the conference outside of the dedicated network to a wide scope of Internet users;
– possibility to work with shared applications.

ISABEL provides a wide scope of other videoconferencing capabilities, e.g. a demonstration of lecturers' graphic materials, operative exchange of files in the background mode, use of "whiteboard"-type graphic applications, management of remote users' turns in question sessions, etc.

It is also worth pointing out that ISABEL has an open interface that makes it possible for developers of other applications to create gateways to ISABEL.

Table 5.4 lists the core functional elements of a dedicated network for running an ISABEL-supported distributed event. As a detailed consideration of hardware and software configurations of those elements is outside this chapter's concerns, let us give a brief description needed for discussing a new model of a distributed event developed within the NICE project.

The *main site* incorporates:

–   ISABEL station;
–   conference hall or meeting room equipped with audio and video facilities, and in some cases with special light system;
–   local network and local cable system;
–   system for technical staff communication with the control centre; and
–   screen and projection equipment.

Table 5.4 Main functional elements of a dedicated network for carrying out a distributed event.

Element	Function	Configuration
Network node	Aggregation of data streams and multicast broadcasting	ISABEL-router
Main site	Integration of a local event into the distributed event	ISABEL interactive site
Interactive site	Broadening the circle of active participants of the distributed event	ISABEL interactive site
Watch point	Demonstration of the programme of the distributed event to remote audiences	ISABEL watch point
Control centre	Remote control of the ISABEL applications configuration at the sites	ISABEL server
Central studio	Channel (program) organisational control	ISABEL interactive site

Main sites should be arranged in places of local events (involving normally from several dozens to several hundreds of participants) to integrate them into a global distributed event. That is why technical facilities in use should ensure high quality of transmitted and received audio and video signals, a capability of receiving questions from distant participants of a distributed event to speakers in the main site, and interaction of attendees in this auditorium with speakers at other main sites and their participation in discussions. Figures 5.1 and 5.2 present the schemes of the main site core systems set up at the Zelinsky Institute for conducting the distributed Global360 Congress in 1997 [14].

A *main site* is the key element of a distributed event. Its functioning on both technical and organisational level should be efficiently co-ordinated with the control centre, which is, as a rule, located separately. In the NICE and EXPERT events, the system for technical staff communication with the control centre included a phone conference and IRC teleconference.

Conducting large-scale international conferences, including distributed ones, normally calls for the use of several languages and synchronous interpretation facilities. Relative to a distributed network teleconference, the latter implies not only management issues but also a technical challenge, as it increases the number of audio streams requiring operative commutation (Figure 5.3).

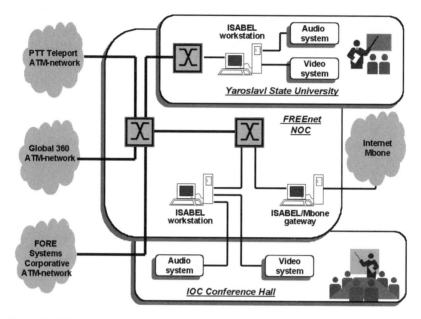

Figure 5.1 ATM-networks of main site (IOC) and interactive site (Yaroslavl State University) of Global360 Conference (1997).

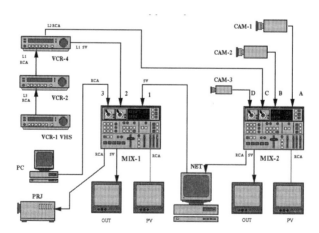

Figure 5.2 Main site video system (IOC). Distributed conference Global360 (1997).

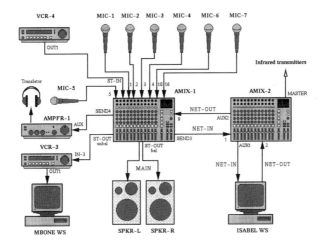

Figure 5.3 Main site audio system (IOC). Distributed conference Global360 (1997).

An *interactive site* is generally similar to a *main site* mentioned above, except it focuses on a smaller number of users (about a few dozen) and does not imply servicing of a local event and its integration to a distributed event (Figures 5.1 and 5.4). Its complex facilities chiefly aim at giving local participants an opportunity to listen to presentations on the agenda, put questions to distant speakers and take part in the discussion, if it is scheduled.

The technical facilities of an *interactive site* do not usually incorporate audio and video mixing appliances (Figure 5.4), and a synchronous interpretation subsystem.

A *watch point* is the simplest technical element for demonstrating a distributed event programme to local viewers. The minimal configuration envisages a workstation with downloaded ISABEL software in the watch point configuration.

The *control centre* provides remote control of the configuration of all ISABEL applications running in all *interactive sites*. A centralised control function is an unique feature of ISABEL that enables to stage the whole conference by a unified script. From the control centre it is possible to adjust the levels of audio signals coming from each *interactive site*, to arrange and design the picture received at each site, including the order, positioning and size of windows on the screen, and demonstration of slides, logotypes, and other graphics. The demonstration capabilities afford a unified view of the picture at each *interactive site*.

A *network node* is a network infrastructure element that aggregates traffic from *interactive sites* (attached to it) for further transmission to the network's core elements. It also provides downstream multicasting from the centre to interactive sites. *Network nodes* enable to optimise traffic and mitigate capacity requirements of

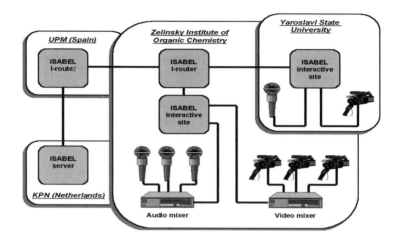

Figure 5.4 Logical schemes of main site (IOC) and interactive site (Yaroslavl State University) and their interconnections to international network of the distributed conference Global360 (1997).

involved channels. *Network nodes* should be positioned in topologically critical points of the network.

The above elements of the dedicated network secured both high scalability of the system and its adaptability to specific conditions. Therefore it became feasible under the NICE project to develop and implement a new, effective and flexible organisational and technical model for conducting large-scale distributed events.

5.4 Organisational and Technical Model

The development of a new distributed event model should be viewed as one of the major results of the NICE project and as a new phase in the advancement of technologies to support distributed groups.

Similar to other information technologies, the development of videoconferencing models represented an evolution step from imitation of traditional co-operative interaction forms to creation of new forms, which could not be in principle implemented earlier. At the first phase videoconferences were treated as a technical means designed to extend the scope of lecturers and audience of a traditional conference by including distant participants, whose attendance at the conference hall ceased to be obligatory. This model of a distributed event, usually called a "virtual conference hall", brought about certain benefits, though it actually did not involve any modifications of the agenda or preparation procedure, which generally retained their habitual forms. The changes were mostly of a quantitative character and did not

Publishers/Broadcasters   **Video conference managed facilities**   **Subscribers/Audiences**

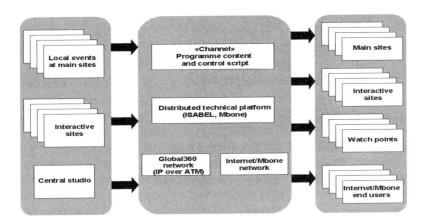

Figure 5.5 Relationship between content sources and audiences in Global 360 model.

affect the programme contents or qualitative membership of the audience that remained the same professional group as in a traditional conference. Hence, the "virtual conference hall" model persisted in the common shortcoming of a professional event, i.e. the presentations of interest to a much broader audience could acquire public awareness only as a short communication in mass media, if any.

The largest practical implementation of the "virtual conference hall" model was the 4th Advanced Broadband Communications Summer School (ABC96) (see Table 5.3) a distributed event set up by the NICE project consortium. There was an ISABEL-supported dedicated network and distribution to the global public Mbone.

Despite its obvious success, ABC96 clearly revealed that events on such a scale (several main sites, 13 interactive sites and 10 watch points) called for a considerable revision of the model.

The major requirement of the model demanded efficient (on both technical and organisational levels) integration of audio and video data incoming from multiple sources into a single homogeneous programme accessible, in real time mode, to a wide range of viewers. A television term "channel" was used to define the total of broadcast material. In line with the new model, a "publish-and-subscribe" scheme supported the interaction of data sources and the audience (see Figure 5.5).

This approach is especially attractive for the scientific community in Russia where during the last decade popular science and public awareness of scientific achievements have been dramatically degrading (e.g. fall in science publications, editions and TV shows). At the same time, the country is undergoing an extensive advancement of its computer network infrastructure and growth in the number of Internet users.

Relative to an event such as a conference, the channel formation needed integration of:

- programmes of a few large conferences held at main sites;
- materials to be broadcast from other interactive sites; and
- special materials for broadcasting from the control centre.

The implementation of this model called for new components, procedures and functions, such as:

- control script;
- special channel of operative communications with sites for technical co-ordination and programme control;
- professional design of background screen pictures and inscriptions;
- professional mixing and preparation of video materials; and
- professional moderator.

The core component of the model is a control script. It enables to use adequate technical tools for the presentation of materials on the channel programme and synchronise organisational and technical operations. The control script should be an electronic document containing the per minute channel agenda, digital code for each item of the programme, screen format, headlines, speakers' names, and other information depicted on the screen at broadcasting. Also, the script should include names of files with illustrative materials to be submitted to the control centre in advance for their conversion to the format appropriate for ISABEL (.GIF) and further full-screen presentation.

ISABEL converts a control script to a control file containing all necessary technical information on each programme item (screen format, background graphics, IP address of an interactive site, etc.). During the conference the control file is executed in real-time mode.

5.5 Model Testing

For the first time this model was used for running the distributed International Congress Global360 (see Table 5.3). It gave its name to the model. The Global360 network connected 25 interactive sites and watch points in 17 countries. Four large conferences were sources of materials to shape the contents of the Global360 channel, namely:

- Global Networking 97 (Calgary, Canada);
- 2nd International Distributed Conference on Network Interoperability (Madeira, Portugal);

- Broadband Communications for Research and Education (IOC RAS, Moscow, Russia);
- 21st Century – the Communications Age (European Parliament, Brussels, Belgium).

They were supplemented with videoconference materials from 11 local interactive sites in different countries.

The experience in management of this distributed event revealed that the model makes it possible for local interactive sites, where the event is not official and attendees are not high in number, to include their materials into the overall broadcasting programme and actively participate in distributed sessions, discussions and presentations.

The geographic spread of interactive sites covered a wide range of time zones (from GMT – 6 in Calgary to GMT + 7 in Novosibirsk). It accounted for a considerable duration of daily broadcasting (about 10 hours) and further highlighted the similarity of this event to a television channel and its distinction from a traditional conference.

This difference became even more pronounced due to the inclusion of a new element, "tele-demonstration", to complement traditional presentations. For example, there was performed a real-time demonstration of distributed systems developed under the research projects EXPERT, CASHMAN, VISTA and WATT with their elements located in Lozenge, Madeira and Calgary. The screen structure had three windows, in one of which the demonstration itself took place and the other two displayed speakers commenting on the picture and attendees asking questions.

Further development of the model associated with shifting from integration of individual local actions to integration of technologically heterogeneous distributed events. The model's evolution in this direction became a strong incentive for Russian participation in such events, and, accordingly, reasoned consideration of the Russian specifics. In particular, the Mbone technology was (and still is) most beneficial financially for Russian local interactive sites in distributed events.

In particular, IOC RAS, a NICE project consortium partner, deployed the multicast-capable network, FREEnet Mbone, in 1996. Since then, it has been extensively used for running videoconferences, audio/video broadcasts and joint sessions of distant distributed groups. The FREEnet Mbone covers five Russian regions and establishes a broadband ATM link with the national multicast traffic exchange point M9-MIX.

Over the period from February 1997 to July 1998, the FREEnet Mbone was linked to the global virtual network Mbone (via the German network ECRC). Thereby the research institutions connected to the FREEnet Mbone had access to various international conferences and were able to conduct audio- and videoconferences with their overseas colleagues (refer to http://www.free.net/NTL/).

Within the NICE project *Software ISABEL/Mbone Gateway* was developed. The gateway converts ISABEL-format packets to packets appropriate for the Mbone freeware VIC/VAT. Another kind of the gateway, *Analog ISABEL/Mbone Gateway*, was also used in the NICE project (see Figure 5.1). In this manner the integration of

Table 5.5 IST98/Global360 main participants

Code	Institution	City	Element supported	Time zone (vs. GMT)
CRC	Communications Research Centre	Ottawa	Main site	-5
ITR	Iceland Telecom	Reykjavik	Interactive site	0
UPM	Technical University of Madrid	Madrid	Interactive site	1
UPC	Technical University of Catalonia	Barcelona	Main site	1
CER	CERN	Geneva	Watch point	1
ASP	ACTRIS	Basel	Main site	1
DTB	Deutsche Telekom Berkom	Berlin	Main site	1
JKU	Johannes Kepler University	Linz	Control centre	1
GSL	G360 Studio	Linz	Central studio	1
CES	CESNET	Prague	Main site	1
BRN	Masaryk University	Brno	Main site	1
SNA	Slovenian National Assembly	Ljubljana	Interactive site	1
TEL	IST98 Teleconferencing Room	Vienna	Main site	1
DTV	IST98 Digital Theatre	Vienna	Main site	1
BUD	MATAV & Technical University of Budapest	Budapest	Main site	1
DEM	NCSR Demokritos	Athens	Main site	2
ACC	Analytical Computing Centre	Minsk	Interactive site	2
KSN	KSNet	Kiev	Main site	2
IOC	Institute of Organic Chemistry/FREEnet NOC	Moscow	Main site/ Control centre	3
YAR	Yaroslavl State University	Yaroslavl	Interactive site	3
CRL	Communications Research Laboratory	Tokyo	Main site	9

distributed events in technologically heterogeneous networks was carried out: ISABEL over the broadband dedicated ATM network and narrowband Mbone over the regular Internet.

Along with the project consortium partners listed in Table 5.2, the Russian Institute of the Information Society (IIS) contributed a notable share to the development and testing of this model version.

The first full-scale trial of this option of the model was carried out in September 1998 during the "International Distributed Conference" – IDC98 (see Table 5.3). The conference (main site in Lisbon) was conducted in the framework of EXPO98 and integrated with the distributed conference "Information Society and Modern City" (main site in Moscow) set up by IIS and supported by the Moscow Government and Moscow Duma (City Parliament).

In the course of the trial, organisational and technical aspects of integrating technologically heterogeneous distributed events, including the interaction of control centres and concurrence of control scripts, were finalised. In addition, a scheme with two simultaneous Mbone sessions, broadband (1 Mbps) and narrowband (256 Kbps), gatewayed to each other via video gateway (VGW) was successfully used.

Final upgrades and trials were accomplished in November 1998 during the preparation and running of the international congress and exhibition Information Society Technologies (IST98) organised by the EU in Vienna (see Tables 5.3 and 5.5).

The distributed event Global360 with the main site in Vienna represented an "extension" of the congress and integrated it with parallel events in Basel (local conference) and in Russia (distributed videoconference). The Global360 control centre was located in the University of Linz (Austria). The exhibition IST98 housed a special interactive site – Digital Theater. It was both a studio for the Global360 moderator and a broadcasting source for a number of G360 channel programmes. It also gave the exhibition visitors a chance to participate in interactive sessions. ISABEL v.3R3 was used as the basic software.

The total duration of the three-day Global360 broadcast was 29 hours. This included presentations from six parallel IST98 sessions as well as those from the parallel events and sites in Canada, Japan, Russia, and some European countries (Table 5.5).

The dedicated Global360 network (Figure 5.6 and Table 5.5) linked 19 interactive sites. From among them 17 sites acted as sources for broadcasting the materials covered by the overall programme of the G360 channel. In total there were 28 sources of materials to shape the channel programme.

The inter-regional distributed conference "Global-Russia" (main site in Moscow) was conducted in parallel with Global360. It was an extension to the conference Information Society Technologies – Russia (IST98-Russia) that took place in Moscow, at the Zelinsky Institute of Organic Chemistry RAS. The Global-Russia control centre was set up at the Network Operations Centre for the academic and research network FREEnet and carried out technical integration of this particular event with Global360 (Figure 5.6). The conference hall of the IOC RAS was simultaneously a main site and a broadcasting source for two channels: Global-Russia and Global360. The Global-Russia network comprised four interactive sites and five watch points in Kemerovo, Krasnodar, Moscow, Novgorod, Saint Petersburg, Saransk, and Yaroslavl.

The Global-Russia channel programme comprised IST98 presentations in the main site, presentations from the distant interactive sites and G360 channel materials that were of utmost interest for Russian participants. The G360 materials that had remained outside of the Global-Russia programme became available to the Russian participants due to a special parallel session where the G360 programme found its full coverage. The Conference opening ceremony started with a welcome greeting by the Deputy Chairman of the Russian Federation Government V. B. Bulgak to the IST98-Russia and IST98 participants and was simultaneously broadcast over the G360 and Global-Russia channels.

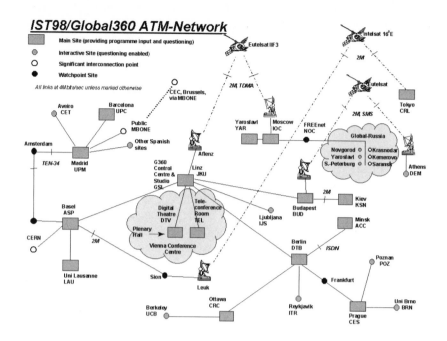

Figure 5.6 Dedicated IST98/Global360 network (for participants' codes see Table 5.5).

The success of this large-scale congress was a milestone to mark that the implementation of the technical platform and distributed network event model developed within the NICE project was not an experiment any more and could be recommended as a standard technical solution. The successful experience in the use of this model for conducting in 1999 two planned distributed international events (see Table 5.3), which were not experimental, proved this.

References

[1]   Arnaud B. (2000) "Overview of the Latest Developments in Optical Internets" (http://www.canet3.net)

[2]   Arnaud B., (2000) "Optical networks for the rest of us" (http://www.canet3.net)

[3]   Brandel M. (1995) "Videoconferencing slowly goes desktop", Computer World, Feb. 20, 81.

[4]   Brown D., (1999) "Deploying VoIP-Forklift or Migrate?", Network Computing, June 14 (http://www.nwc.com)

[5]   Bulkeley W. (1996) "Picture-Phone marketers target the home PC.", The Wall Street J., Feb.27, B1.

[6]   CANARIE CA*NET 3 News Archives (1999) (http://www.canet3.net)

[7]   Chung T., Coulter J., Fitchett J, Mokbel S., Arnaud B. (1999) "Architectural and Engineering Issues for Building an Optical Internet."(http://www.canet3.net)

[8]   a) European Commission, (1997) "ACTS97 – Advanced Communications and Services. Project Summaries" (Ref. No. AC971392-PS), 190-191;
        b) European Commission, (1997) "ACTS97 – Advanced Communications and Services. Practical Experimentation and Trials" (Ref. No. AC971392-T), 168-169.

[9]   a) (1999) ftp://www-ks.rus.uni-stuttgart.de/pub/mice/publications/bris95.ps.gz;
        b) (1999) http://www.uni-stuttgart.de/SONAH/2ndcall/download.html.

[10]   Galitsky A. (1998) "Network infrastructure for distributed videoconferencing as implemented under the NICE Project." Pre-Proceedings of the Russian National Research and Methodical Conference "Telematika-98", 86.

[11]   Hallan A. (1999) "Shaping the Virtual Conference Hall" in Pre-Proceeding of the Internet Workshop'99 (IWS'99) Osaka, 166–173.

[12]   Higgins K., (1999) "Voice Over IP: The Battle Heats Up", Network Computing, March 8 (http://www.nwc.com).

[13]   a) Jinzenji H., Hagishima K. (1997) "Real-Time Audio and Video Broadcasting of IEEE GLOBECOM '96 over the Internet Using New Software", IEEE Communication Magazine, 35, 4, 34–39;
        b) Rath K., Wanigasekara-Mohotti D., Wendorf R., Vermaz D. (1997) "Interactive Digital Video Networks: Lessons from a Commercial Deployment", IEEE Communication Magazine, 35, 6, 70–74.

[14]   Mironov E. (1998) "Experience in conducting distributed videoconferences." Pre-proceedings of Russian National Research and Methodical Conference "Telematika-98", 84–85.

[15]   a) Schulzrinne H., Casner S., Frederick R., Jacobson V. (1996) "RTP: A transport protocol for real-time applications." IETF, RFC 1889, January;
        b) Schulzrinne H. (1996) "RTP profile for audio and video conferences with minimal control." IETF, RFC 1890, January;
        c) Fenner W. (1997) "Internet group management protocol, version 2." The Internet Society, RFC 2236, November;
        d) Macedonia M., Brutzman D. (1994) "Mbone provides audio and video across the Internet." IEEE Computer, April;
        e) Armitage G., (1996) "Support for multicast over UNI3.0/3.1 based ATM networks." IETF Draft, February;
        f) Estrin D., Farinacci D., Helmy A., Thaler D., Deering S., Handley M., Jacobson V., Liu C., Sharma P., Wei L. (1998) "Protocol independent multicast-sparse mode (PIM-SM): protocol specification." The Internet Society, RFC 2362, June;
        g) Casner S., Jacobson V. (1999) "Compressing IP/UDP/RTP headers for low-speed serial links." The Internet Society, RFC 2508, February.

[16]   Sprey J. (1997) "Videoconferencing as a communication tool", Professional Comm., 40, 41–47.

[17]   a) Steinmetz R. (1994) "Multimedia: advanced teleservices and high-speed communication architectures." In Steinmetz R. (Ed.). "Lecture Notes in Computer Science", Volume 868, Springer-Verlag;
        b) De Miguel T., Pavón S., Salvachua J., Quemada J., Chas P.L., Fernandez-Amigo J., Acuña C., Rodriguez L., Lagarto V., Bastos J. (1994) "ISABEL – experimental distributed cooperative work application over broadband networks.", Lecture Notes in Computer Science, Volume 868, Springer-Verlag, 353–362;
        c) Azcorra A., Miguel T., Quemada J. et al. (1994) "Distance learning: networks and applications for RACE Summer School '94", The ATM Forum Newsletter, Volume 2, Issue 3;

d) Quemada J., Miguel T., Azcorra A. et al. (1995) "ABC 95: A tele-education case study. High Performance Networking for Tele-teaching", IDC'95, November, Madeira;
e) Quemada J., Miguel T., Azcorra A. et al. (1995) "Tele-education experiences with the ISABEL application. High Performance Networking for Tele-teaching", IDC'95, November, Madeira.

[18] The Strategis Group (1998) "Business Branding & Bundling Telecommunications Services: 1998." (http://www.strategisgroup.com/press/pubs/)

[19]   The Strategis Group (2000) Press Release, February 15 "Residential High-Speed Internet: Cable   Modems,   DSL,   and   Wireless   Broadband" (http://www.strategisgroup.com/press/pubs/)

[20] Volfengagen V.,. Kalinichenko L., Mendkovich A., Syuntyurenko O. (1998) "Informational systems and telecommunications in research", Herald of the RFBR, 4 (14), 4–50

[21] Wainhouse Research (1999) On-Line Survey, December, "Visual Collaboration Applications and Deployment Interest" (http://www.wainhouse.com)

[22] Wainhouse Research (1999) Publication No.901, October, "Teleconferencing Markets and Strategies: Multimedia Networking Infrastructure" (http://www.wainhouse.com)

[23] Wainhouse Research, (2000) March, "Teleconferencing Markets & Strategies Volume 2: Videoconferencing Endpoint Products Group and Personal Videoconferencing Systems" (http://www.wainhouse.com)

[24] a) Walter T., Brunner M., Loisel D. (1995) "The BETEUS communication platform". Proceedings of the First International Distributed Conference IDC'95, November, Madeira;
b) Blum C., Dubois P., Molva R.. (1995) "A semi-distributed platform for the support of CSCW applications". First International Distributed Conference, November, Madeira;
c) Besson M., Traore K., Dubois P. (1995) "Control and performance monitoring of a multimedia platform over the ATM pilot". First International Distributed Conference, November, Madeira.

Chapter 6

Towards an Advanced Quality of Service Architecture

Jan deMeer and Armin Eberlein

6.1 Introduction

This chapter addresses questions such as "What must a QoS-aware architecture look like?" or "What building blocks does a QoS-aware architecture consist of?" in the context of interactive multimedia applications (IMM). As an integrated part of QoS architectures, capabilities must exist which support management and control of functionality and performance of IMMs. For an architecture that is said to be QoS-aware, the IMM service quality provided must be controlled and, if necessary, adapted to previously agreed targets. QoS-awareness operations are to be placed in locations of interest of the considered architectural model that allow access to interfaces, provide negotiation, adaptation and tuning capabilities etc. For the design of QoS architectures there are two basic classes of requirements. The first class of requirements is derived from applications that benefit most from QoS architectures. Interactive multimedia services are the main representatives of this category of applications. The other class of requirements deals with constraints on how to construct a framework of QoS that provides the building blocks, i.e. the concepts, operations and tools, of QoS architectures. Consequently this chapter discusses first, the properties and features of IMM services which must be taken into account during the design of an architecture that is QoS-aware, as well as the middleware of a distributed system. Next, architectural building blocks are introduced and their technical aspects with respect to QoS are discussed. Then, recent architectural approaches are presented that claim to be QoS-aware. However, in order to find out whether an architecture is suited for QoS management and control, one needs a kind of conformity criteria. It is a definitive goal of this chapter to present a set of criteria that allows evaluation of architectures with respect to the derived set of QoS-conformity criteria. Hence, QoS-conformity comprises architectural concepts and features used to control and manage the quality of interactive multimedia services for the whole time the application is active. Whereas the latter set of criteria addresses *application sensitivity*, the former set addresses *architectural constructivity*.

Section 6.2 discusses IMM requirements representing application sensitivity. Section 6.3 deals with various views of QoS, as provided by the major standardisation bodies like ISO, ITU-T, ETSI and IETF. Section 6.4 contains the descriptions of the basic functions and mechanisms that are needed during the evolutionary phases of a QoS-controlled service. They comprise prediction, resource reservation, negotiation, monitoring, tuning and termination mechanisms. In order to evaluate the presented QoS architectures a new *QoS reference architecture* is introduced in Section 6.5, which identifies structures to deal with forward and backward controlling and which identifies locations or interfaces in the architecture at which QoS-related activities, like observations, tuning or resource actuating are to be done.

The architectural approaches presented in Section 6.6 include an ODP-conformant approach, the CORB-Architecture of the OMG, the Telecommunication Architecture TINA, the QoS-A approach from Lancaster University (UK), the HeiProjects of the IBM-Labs in Heidelberg (Germany), the Tenet architecture of the University of California in Berkeley and the Omega architecture of the University of Pennsylvania. The presented architectures are then evaluated against the collected criteria of QoS application-sensitivity and constructivity. From this evaluation an initial set of recommendations of QoS-conformity is derived. The concluding section discusses the benefits and drawbacks of the specified QoS-conformity evaluation criteria with respect to applications and architectural design.

6.2 Quality of Service Requirements of IMM services

Interactive multimedia services have not been in existence for very long. However, they have become of great importance in the last few years. Applications, such as video conferencing, video on demand (VoD), and interactive games [12] have been paid a lot of attention due to their potential to raise revenues. However, large-scale deployment of such services will impose very high constraints on virtually all system components, especially the network devices and end-systems. One of the key features of IMM is the vast amount of data that needs to be transmitted at high speed in order to provide a high-quality multimedia service. Depending on the quality of the video and the compression scheme, a single movie can require 25 GBytes of storage [6]. Very high transmission rates are required to deliver this data in time. Again depending on the quality and the compression scheme, transmission rates of

135 Mbps and more can be necessary. In fact, one of the hardest requirements of IMM services is the in-time delivery of data. A frame that arrives after its deadline is worthless and can drastically reduce the quality perceived by the user. Furthermore, IMM data of many applications has to be delivered as a continuous stream. If too much data is delivered, data will be lost due to buffer overflow; if too little data arrives at the receiver's side, the receiver will experience buffer starvation. It is therefore crucial to look for means that can guarantee a certain quality of service for multimedia services.

IMM applications have to meet certain properties, which have a great influence on the quality of interactive multimedia services:

1. Continuity, because streams of data are delivered to IMM applications
2. Capacity, because large amounts of data are transported by streams
3. Timeliness, because of real-time transportation constraints
4. Integrity, because of presentation constraints.

The resources used by IMM services, i.e. networks, switches, channel bandwidths or flow control mechanisms of protocols, must be capable of supporting selected QoS characteristics and mechanisms that help maintain the properties listed above. This means that certain characteristics and mechanisms which provide "continuity" are to be implemented at given system component interfaces in such a way that, for example, enough bandwidth will be made available during the whole transmission time in order to guarantee continuity of a stream of data. "Capacity" is a property that requires either space for buffering or bandwidth for transportation or a combination of both. To achieve "timeliness" resource control mechanisms must be implemented that avoid traffic jams. "Integrity" requires reliable transmission protocols. Loss or duplications of data (i.e. packets of a stream) must be detected and if possible be corrected. Hence, a critical issue of the design of QoS architectures is the deployment of various kinds of mechanisms to observe and to control stream continuity, buffer capacities, transmission delays and integrity of data.

6.3 Views on Quality of Service

The notion *Quality of Service (QoS)* is a widely used term in standardisation and research efforts. QoS originally emerged in communications to describe characteristics of data transmission. Especially in ATM, QoS is an important issue [19].

The definition introduced by the ODP description 11.2.2 of ISO/IEC IS 10746-2 [23] states:

> The notion QoS is a system or object property, and consists of a set of quality requirements on the collective behaviour of one or more objects... Note: QoS is concerned with such characteristics as the rate of information transfer, the latency,

the probability of a communication being disrupted, the probability of system failure, the probability of storage failure, etc

The European Telecommunications Standards Institute (ETSI) describes in its book *ETSI and the Information Society* [24] the QoS notion from the end-user's point of view. Methods for the evaluation of service or system usability and human factors are needed to improve the regular process of development.

It should be possible to evaluate the characteristics of a system or service as to its task performance. This should be done both qualitatively and quantitatively.

Together, the definitions of ISO and ETSI span the scope of QoS, i.e. comprising characteristics and functions of networks and applications.

The OSI Reference Model [23] describes QoS as being mainly related to speed and reliability of transmission, such as throughput, delay, delay variation (jitter), bit error rate (BER), cell loss rate, and connection establishment failure probability etc. An OSI (N)-QoS subsystem is equipped with three auxiliary QoS management functions, i.e. for policies, interaction constraints and QoS parameters, that allow filtering and observation of QoS characteristics of input and output data to and from the OSI (N)-subsystem. Because of these built-in auxiliary functions the exchange of QoS-related information with functional entities in a higher-layer (N)-subsystem is thus possible. For completeness, it shall be noted that the presented QoS extensions to the OSI RM are documented in a separate standard called *Quality of Service Framework* which was published as ISO International Standard No. 13236 [25] in 1997.

The *QoS Framework in ODP* [27] is an outcome of the standardisation work of recent years and was expected to become an international standard during the year 1999. This standard is more complete than the IS13236 in the sense that it is based on the object-oriented approach of ODP and can thus easily be applied to IMM

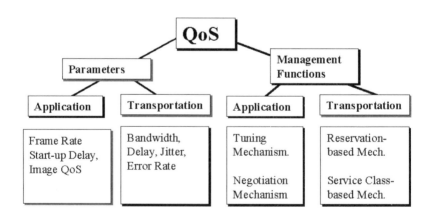

Figure 6.1 Quality of Service framework.

services. Straightforward notions like flow (stream), QoS contract and formal approaches to specify QoS constraints have been invented by this standard. The framework of QoS for ODP consists of an entity-relationship-like approach that invents a number of QoS concepts and combines them into certain QoS relationships. For example, QoS parameters contain the values of QoS limits, targets, thresholds or signals. The latter QoS values are to be understood as the quantification of the QoS characteristics. QoS parameters on the other hand are exchanged among QoS management agents that perform dedicated tasks such as monitoring, control or administration. Generally, the QoS management of a system is driven by the QoS characteristics that are specified as user requirements or system policies. A QoS characteristic itself represents on the one hand QoS aspects of the system, service or the resources, but on the other hand the actual behaviour of the application.

Figure 6.1 presents the QoS categories divided into parameters and management functions according to the QoS framework of ODP. Parameters and management functions apply to IMM services as well as to transportation services. The application-related parameters mainly describe presentation characteristics, for example, image size and resolution, frame rate, start-up delay etc. The transportation parameters describe the most common network characteristics, i.e. bandwidth, delay, jitter and transmission error rate. Compared with the parameters, the QoS management functions are less obvious but more important with respect to the anticipated QoS capabilities. Management functions used by applications differ from those that are used by transportation protocols. Transportation QoS management is principally not capable of exploiting the advantages of feed-back QoS control mechanisms for network-wide communications because transportation resources are normally shared by many applications. If there is no dedicated reservation possible, reservations will be done using statistical mean values. Hence peak rates might not violate QoS contracts, but will still lead to congestion and data loss. Transportation protocols react to congestion by applying forward control mechanisms like dropping of transportation units or by queueing remaining transportation requests. These mechanisms are called forward control mechanisms, because traffic control is only performed after congestion has been detected. Backward control mechanisms however are able to avoid congestion, *per se*. Hence applications can act prior to congestion. This is possible because application resources will not be shared with other applications as is the case for transportation resources which have to be shared by many users. Thus, on the application level, there is no statistical sharing of resources between several applications. In other words, forward control is performed in the direction of data flow, whereas backward control feeds information backwards, i.e. in the opposite direction to the flow of data. As outlined in more detail in Section 6.5, the combination of both control principles leads to a two-level QoS control architecture, i.e. the divison into an application and a networking layer.

Nevertheless, QoS management functions can be distinguished according to their policies. One policy is to establish control mechanisms along the transportation path or along the connection. Another policy is to establish control per message. All resource reservation mechanisms like those used by ATM or RSVP [9] fall into the first category. Message-based, sometimes also referred to as connection-less, control is provided by the so-called Differentiated Services [10]. Messages are uniquely identified during their flow through the network and handled according to the service class to which the message stream belongs. Each unique identifier contained in each message represents a certain service class. This control policy is therefore also referred to as being service class oriented.

Non-standardised but very useful categorisation frameworks of QoS have been provided by Guo [7], Nahrstedt [14,15] and Vogel [20]. Guo [7] distinguishes between application QoS and network QoS parameters. The application QoS parameters specify image quality and size, frame rate and startup delay. The network QoS addresses bandwidth, delay, jitter and error rates. A more comprehensive QoS framework is given by Nahrstedt [15]. It defines five different levels of QoS. The user QoS is the quality of the service as perceived by the user. The application QoS is specified in terms of media quality (e.g., data-unit rate and end-to-end delay) and media relations (such as synchronisation). The system QoS describes communication and operating system requirements, such as task processing time, ordered delivery of data, error-recovery mechanisms and scheduling mechanisms. *Network QoS* addresses issues such as latency, bandwidth and jitter. Device QoS parameters specify timing and throughput demands for media data units. Vogel [20] defines Quality of Service as

> ..the set of those quantitative and qualitative characteristics of a distributed multimedia system necessary to achieve the required functionality of an application.

There are five categories of QoS parameters:

- *performance-oriented parameters* are end-to-end delay and bit rate;
- *format-oriented parameters* are video resolution, frame rate, storage format and compression scheme;
- a *synchronisation-oriented QoS parameter* is, for example, the skew between the beginning of audio and video sequences;
- *cost-oriented parameters* are related to connection and data transmission charges and copyright fees;
- *user-oriented parameters* describe the subjective image and sound quality.

It can be said that standardised and non-standardised frameworks mainly concentrate on defining relationships between QoS parameters and on their classification. The dynamic co-operation that exists between network and application components for the control of various qualities of several multimedia services has been less intensively studied by current frameworks. This chapter is thus devoted to identifying mechanisms that handle end-to-end QoS constraints and that can be integrated into a unified architecture.

6.4 Quality of Service Management Functions

For the purpose of classifying QoS management functions, the QoS framework of ISO[25] has invented certain stages in the evolution of quality-controlled services. These phases describe the following service evolution activities:

1. a priori service seizing applies prediction mechanisms of expected QoS characteristics in order to establish a certain QoS context.
2. Preparation of service establishment requires resource reservation mechanisms for predicted QoS contexts.
3. Execution of service establishment requires negotiation mechanisms in order to agree upon QoS requirements.
4. Operation of services requires mechanisms that *honour* previously negotiated QoS agreements.
5. Termination of services requires mechanisms by which all reserved resources, services and connections are freed or reset.

In accordance with this phased approach, the QoS framework of ISO [25] provides guidelines for the specification of QoS. So-called specifiers consist of the unique name of QoS characteristics, their definition of purpose, their quantified parameter values, their derivation rules from non-quantified notions to quantified values, their specialisation rules from generic to specialised, as well as usable QoS and optional specifiers for further information.

This is suitable for users and their applications who need to be able to specify the QoS required to provide an interactive multimedia service with the desired quality. It is essential that the users can specify the QoS requirements using terms they can understand. A user can understand terms like resolution, image size, colour depth, but will find it difficult to specify jitter or cell-loss rate. However, the latter terms are very meaningful at the network level. This means that the user's QoS specification is declarative in nature, i.e. the specification merely states what is required rather than how this is to be achieved.

6.4.1 Prediction

By determining the actual system load and QoS limits, a QoS context is calculated by which the requested service can most probably be provided without degradation of quality. An example of a typical prediction mechanism is the admission control function. Admission control is responsible for comparing the QoS requirements arising from a new service request with the resources available in the system. The acceptance of a new request depends on the scheduling mechanisms, on the characteristics of the traffic and on the available resources. A set of tests is run to determine if the new service request can be supported without violating the guarantees given to already existing sessions.

6.4.2 Resource Reservation

Resource reservation and negotiation mechanisms are quite similar. The different notions are possibly due to their different context of application. Resource reservation is a notion used in the networking domain and allows the reservation of all resources that are necessary to achieve a compulsory QoS context (see explanations below). Negotiation on the other hand tries to reach agreement on application QoS characteristics. However, there is no agreement without resource reservation on the application and transportation layers.

Due to the stringent timing-constraints for the delivery of data in multimedia applications, resource reservation is commonly used to provide a compulsory QoS. A resource reservation protocol firstly establishes a path through the network and then reserves resources (e.g., CPU, memory, bandwidth, etc.). This can be done using two approaches. The pessimistic approach reserves resources based on the worst-case traffic, which means that the system is under-utilised, but a *guaranteed QoS* is provided with a very high probability. The optimistic approach allocates resources based on the average characteristics. This leads to high resource utilisation but overload situations can still occur. Hence compulsory services can never provide service guarantees.

6.4.3 Negotiation

Negotiation is a mechanism that interprets the complex semantics of the QoS parameters of the possible different participant's roles in an application. Roles of participants are called initiator, responder and arbiter. The arbiter role is played by the network that interconnects initiator and responder. QoS parameters and characteristics normally have an *m:n* relationship. Within this relationship negotiation must reach an agreement on, for example, the *highest quality attainable* (HQA) of an operating target with best effort QoS, or the *controlled highest quality* (CHQ) on an upper limit with compulsory QoS, or the *lowest quality acceptable* (LQA) on a lower limit with guaranteed QoS. Since for best effort QoS there is no assurance, no monitoring and no remedy activities, best effort service is only applicable when fixed parameter values of targets and thresholds do not exist. *Compulsory QoS* [25] on the contrary provides monitoring services but is not even able to provide a guaranteed QoS. However, when QoS degrades below an agreed minimum level, the service can be aborted or the messages transmitted can be dropped. In order to guarantee QoS, services are not allowed to be aborted because of QoS violations of other applications. Instead new resources must be added to the service to maintain the guaranteed level of QoS.

In the literature, compulsory or guaranteed services are sometimes also referred to as *predicted* or *deterministic* services respectively. The deterministic service offers hard QoS guarantees to all packets belonging to a stream. The predicted service that is based on statistical bounds provides weaker QoS guarantees than the deterministic service, but stronger ones than the best-effort service.

Negotiation also occurs between vertical architectural layers within one system. This kind of negotiation is called *QoS mapping* [6]. The lower layers need to support the QoS expected by the higher layers. This kind of negotiation takes place during call set-up. The mapping process, sometimes also referred to as QoS translation [7], will take place between several layers in a hierarchy. Each layer will request a certain QoS from its adjacent lower layer. However, it is to be expected that a one-to-one mapping is not always possible. If a direct mapping is not possible, the appropriate QoS parameters will need to be negotiated. This negotiation between two adjacent layers in one end system is sometimes referred to as layer-to-layer negotiation.

However, for already established calls, re-negotiation of the QoS parameters might become necessary as well. For instance, during a medical tele-consultation, the transmission of high-quality X-ray images requires a better QoS (e.g., higher bandwidth), which can result in network congestion unless initially negotiated QoS parameters of a less stringent application can be reduced after re-negotiation. This requires a system to continuously monitor the actual QoS and to use re-negotiation mechanisms to adapt the QoS parameters or resources to the user demands or to the actual network load. Re-negotiation of the initially agreed QoS context might be initiated by the user or the underlying system. Depending on the QoS context re-negotiation may allow the user to request a higher or lower level of quality. The user can, for example, ask for colour quality while the current session is in "black & white" mode, or can reduce the QoS requirements in order to save costs. System-initiated re-negotiation is usually caused by a severe lack of resources in cases when automatic QoS adaptation is not sufficient to resolve the problem.

Figure 6.2 presents the basic principles of a negotiation algorithm. It shows a 1:n-party negotiation algorithm, which is called multicasting negotiation. It shows

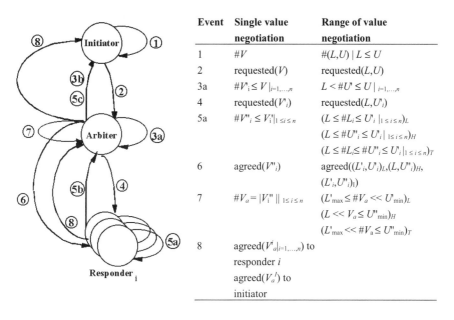

Event	Single value negotiation	Range of value negotiation
1	$\#V$	$\#(L,U) \mid L \leq U$
2	requested(V)	requested(L,U)
3a	$\#V'_i \leq V \mid_{i=1,\ldots,n}$	$L < \#U' \leq U \mid_{i=1,\ldots,n}$
4	requested(V'_i)	requested(L,U'_i)
5a	$\#V''_i \leq V'_i \mid_{1 \leq i \leq n}$	$(L \leq \#L_i \leq U'_i \mid_{1 \leq i \leq n})_L$
		$(L \leq \#U''_i \leq U'_i \mid_{1 \leq i \leq n})_H$
		$(L \leq \#L_i \leq \#U''_i \leq U'_i \mid_{1 \leq i \leq n})_T$
6	agreed(V''_i)	agreed($(L'_i,U'_i)_L,(L,U''_i)_H,$ $(L'_i,U''_i)_1$)
7	$\#V_a = \lvert V_i''\rvert \mid_{1 \leq i \leq n}$	$(L'_{max} \leq \#V_a \ll U'_{min})_L$
		$(L \ll V_a \leq U''_{min})_H$
		$(L'_{max} \ll \#V_a \leq U''_{min})_T$
8	agreed($V^i_a\mid_{i=1,\ldots,n}$) to responder i agreed(V_a^1) to initiator	

Figure 6.2 1:n multicasting negotiation.

the three basic negotiation roles, i.e. *initiator, arbiter* and *responder* which are adopted by the parties involved. In a *1:N*-party negotiation scenario the initiator and arbiter roles are each adopted by one party only. However, the responder role can be adopted up to N times by different players. It is important to realise that the initiator and responder roles do not determine the sender or the receiver of the data streams for which the players want to negotiate resources or QoS characteristics. The initiator role, for example can be adopted by either the sender or by the receiver. This is not true for the arbiter role. The arbiter role must be adopted by a player which is next to the initiator in the chain of streaming parties, and which is in-between the initiator and the set of responders. Thus, the arbiter role can be played by the sender in co-operation with its initiator role but also by the streaming channel or network that is between the initiator and the responders. The latter case is assumed to be the normal case.

The initiator role is characterised by taking the initiative for the negotiation. The initiator of course knows the quality and resource that can minimally be provided for the service. Hence it is able to provide initial values of quality parameters or initial requests of resources needed. It is possible to negotiate either a single target, or the lower or upper limits of a range. In case the initiator wants to negotiate the lower limit, the upper limit or both at the same time, it selects an appropriate range of quality values with the bounds *(#U, #L)*. This range is then sent to the arbiter player at the channel. If it cannot guarantee the requested lower quality or does not have sufficient resources, the player rejects the initiator's request and negotiation is finished. When it accepts, it is allowed to adjust the boundaries according to its own needs. The channel that is assumed to play the arbiter role must at least provide a quality that fulfils the conditions determined by the lower bound of the initiator. However, it might not be able to fulfil the conditions determined by the upper bound. So the channel may reduce the requested range by lowering its upper bound only, i.e. by choosing $(L < \#U' \leq U)$. It must be noted that this selection can be done on an individual basis for each participating multicasting party. Hence, there can be up to N selections for the new quality values $\#U'_i$, $i = 1,...,N$ that are now transmitted to the N waiting responder players. On receiving, each responder in turn checks the modified requested range according to its individual capabilities. If the responder behaves out of the requested range, it has to reject the request. Otherwise it will accept; but it is allowed to modify both bounds. Therefore, each individual responder $(1 < i \leq N)$ can suggest a change for the lower bound by choosing $(L \leq \#L_i' \leq U)$, and for the upper bound by choosing $(L \leq \#U_i'' \leq U)$. These selections will individually be returned and collected by the arbiter player. The arbiter player then looks at the N responder returns and chooses the maximum of the lower bounds and the minimum value of the upper bounds. The maximum of the lower bound must obviously be less than any upper bound chosen by the responder players. Finally, the arbiter returns the chosen lower and upper bounds to the initiator as initially requested and the negotiation is successfully finished.

6.4.4 Monitoring

QoS monitoring is an important activity that is required by many other QoS functions, such as QoS policing and QoS re-negotiation. It presumes that a QoS measuring function is available. Basically, the task of monitoring is to detect and notify any QoS violations. A QoS violation has occurred when the measured value of a QoS parameter no longer meets the value that was originally agreed. In this case the QoS management system must be informed.

6.4.5 Tuning

For QoS management to be effective there must be remedy mechanisms. If a user exceeds the initially agreed amount of system resources, e.g. a user sends 3 Mbps although only 2 Mbps were initially agreed, appropriate action must be taken. Possible remedy actions include adaptation of the initially agreed QoS context, or the tuning of the performance of the used transportation paths. Remedy actions are necessary in order to protect other users who keep within their agreed QoS context. The actions taken can vary depending on the available resources. For example, the user's violation can simply be ignored, the user could be charged a fine, or the traffic could be re-shaped corresponding to the agreed QoS.

Otherwise, the QoS parameters that have been agreed upon during the negotiation phase might need to be adjusted due to changes in the environment. It might not be possible to further maintain the agreed QoS and so a graceful QoS degradation has become necessary. Lowering the provided QoS in case of unexpected resource shortage is more desirable than the complete abortion of the service.

Tuning is a mechanism that keeps a system variable $y(t)$ between an upper and a

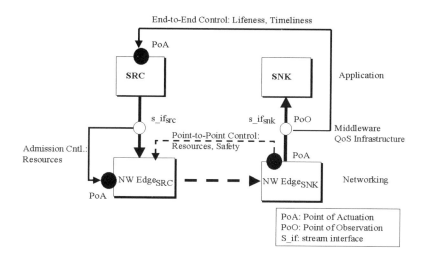

Figure 6.3 QoS management architecture.

lower threshold, e.g. (*UTH, LTH*). Each threshold is controlled by a separate discriminator. A signal will be generated, e.g. to steer the source of $y(t)$, if either the upper or lower threshold value is violated.

6.4.6 Termination

After the termination of a service, the reserved resources need to be freed again. This means that all system components that were involved in the service provision, have to be notified and asked to free the resources and to update their amount of available resources. This has to be done in a reliable way otherwise resources will be wasted.

6.5 Quality of Service Management Architecture

In this section we develop criteria by which we can identify locations to place active QoS management elements and mechanisms such that they will support QoS system-wide. Basically, we assume that a QoS-aware system architecture is constructed in such a way that a certain set of applications can be run and the performance of the application's service quality can be managed by built-in QoS management functions. We have chosen a three-jar architecture that separates QoS management functions from service providing and service applying functions. Hence, there is the application jar, the networking jar and as a third jar (the middleware) there is the infrastructure of testing, monitoring, tuning, negotiating, terminating etc. in order to do QoS management (see Figure 6.3).

The set of anticipated applications provided with guaranteed service quality that shall be supported by a system architecture that supports QoS, is defined as the class of interactive multimedia (IMM) services. In Section 6.2, the characteristics of IMM have been introduced by a 4-dimensional property space, comprising continuity, capacity, timeliness, and integrity. Continuity requires the support of streams at the application–network interface. High capacities require high bandwidths from the network and high storing capacities from end systems. Timeliness implies short turn-around delays of actions triggered. To provide integrity and safe transmission facilities synchronisation mechanisms must be built-in features of the QoS architecture.

The mechanisms and interfaces of the 4-dimensional property space of the IMM service class will dynamically be applied by instances of an application. The mechanisms and interfaces provided by the system architecture must hence dynamically be managed by an additional built-in control policy. The controlling policy employs different mechanisms to deal with safety using point-to-point flow control mechanisms, or, to deal with QoS adaptation using end-to-end tuning mechanisms, or, to deal with resource management using admission control mechanisms. For example, the Internet provides admission control functions in combination with remedy operations like packet dropping or transmission request queuing in case of overloaded resources.

The architectural principle of flow-control and tuning is *feedback* and the architectural principle of admission control is *feed-forwarding*. Both links connect a *Point of Observation* (PoO) with a *Point of Actuation* (PoA) as outlined in Figure 6.3, but with the difference that in the feedback case the PoA steers a source of the controlled flow and in the feedforward case the PoA steers remedy activities at a network's edge. The difference comes from the observation that admission control does not prevent applications from the misuse of resources. Hence, a forward controlling policy must include remedy operations which are applied after the misuse has been observed. In contrast, backward controlling policies operate on specific targets of one or more critical variables observed, such that misuse cannot occur at all. Since these control policies serve different purposes, a QoS-aware architecture has to support both kinds of control. The control mechanisms are applied at different levels of abstraction, because of their different purposes and of their "direction of effect". Direction of effect means a cause–effect relationship. The cause for controlling occurs first at the "point of observation" and finally triggers an action at the "point of actuation". This means that we can identify "horizontal" and "vertical" control mechanisms. As depicted in Figure 6.3, the admission control mechanism is vertical and the flow control and tuning mechanisms are both horizontal. Admission control is said to have a vertical effect because it is normally located at the edges of networks and is thus not an operational element of a horizontal flow-control mechanism of a protocol. More details can be found in [29].

Any QoS architecture that will be discussed in the following sections provides an individual sub-structure that is transparent to the proposed QoS management architecture as shown in Figure 6.3. Hence, the structure of an architecture is not a matter of evaluation but of their built-in policies and capabilities for managing and controlling QoS. The capabilities and policies provided by the architectures must fit into the above-mentioned 4-dimensional property space of IMMs. This means that continuity requires a tight connectivity among the interfaces of various components. Tight connectivity requires that interfaces are able to handle multimedia flows without disruptions. The speed of interconnected interfaces may however synchronously vary over time. The working conditions at the interfaces must be negotiable, i.e. resources will be reserved prior to the start of the service and freed at its termination. The second dimension, capacity, requires access control mechanisms such as admission control or point-to-point flow control mechanisms in order to avoid resource congestion. Mechanisms that are suited to handle the timeliness are mechanisms that permanently keep control of the interaction between end-to-end clients. For instance, if a degradation of speed is observed, the feedback mechanism may assign more bandwidth to the component that is lacking resources. The requirements of the fourth dimension of integrity can be fulfilled by mechanisms that provide safety and lifeness qualities. Safety can be achieved by simple retransmission mechanisms but lifeness needs advanced feedback control mechanisms.

T. Walter *et al.* [31] evaluates system architectures from the QoS testing point of view. Since testing is restricted to probing, observing and monitoring activities the structure of the suggested "QoS test architecture" is very simple. Monitors, i.e. testers, are attached to the distributed components of the system observed. The behaviour of QoS variables can only be evaluated correctly if the behaviour of the embedding network is predictable during testing. By this philosophy, QoS in a critical state can only be evaluated if the embedding network is forced to perform a predefined behaviour, i.e. a specified test case that instructs the network as well. Certain similarities between a QoS test architecture and a QoS management architecture can be manifested. The tester is a built-in component in the recursive structure of a valid QoS management architecture as suggested in this chapter. The monitor or the tester respectively provides a link between the point of observation at the component to the generating "source" of the behaviour that is expected at the PoO. Thus the testing structure is very similar to the structure of the QoS management architecture with its feed-back and feed-forward links with the only difference that the monitor cannot be removed from the system because this would delete the adaptivity property.

Hence, the architecture of a system must be designed such that it is "testable", which means being observable. Furthermore, QoS-aware systems must also be controllable from outside via the points of actuation. In other words, observability and controllability can be expressed in terms of continuous functions. These functions represent flows in which behaviours change over time. In QoS-aware systems the internal state is defined by a continuous state function $x(t)$, the egress behaviour, e.g. the egress flow at the edge of a network or a component's interface, is defined by the continuous service function $y(t)$. The tuning capabilities are defined by the steering function $u(t)$ (see Figure 6.4).

A system or a component S is observable if the service $y(t)$ comprises all internal system states that are represented by $x(t)$, which means S is testable (observable) by inspecting $y(t)$. S is said to be completely observable, if and only if the state $x(t)$ can uniquely be determined from $y(t)$ in a finite period of time.

A system or a component S is controllable by monitor M, if any internal state of $x(t)$ can be triggered by a given steering function $u(t)$, which means $x(t)$ is adjustable by modifying $u(t)$. S is said to be completely controllable, if $u(t)$ can translate any

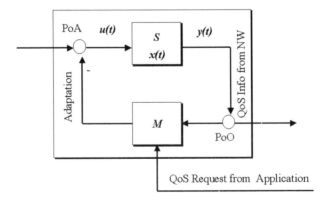

Figure 6.4 Continuous QoS model.

state $x(t_0)$ into any other state $x(t_1)$.

Due to design constraints, some of the continuous variables of the system's or component's state $x(t)$ cannot be determined from observing $y(t)$. In that case a so-called observer must be constructed that estimates the state value of a continuous variable from observing $y(t)$. The condition that such an observer can be designed is called the observability of the system[32].

C. Aurrecoechea *et al.* [1] investigates QoS architectures with the aim of summarising and comparing capabilities and mechanisms of QoS provision, QoS control and QoS management of various approaches in a tabular form. This table provides an interesting overview of the extent to which QoS mechanisms have already been implemented. With respect to the functions listed the most complete architectures are QoS-A, the Heidelberg architecture and the Tenet architecture. On the other hand, the authors of [1] have concluded that

> ...it is still too early to decide which approach is more suitable for future QoS architectures given the need to support both, high-end (e.g. tele-surgery and time-critical applications) and low-end (e.g. video conferencing and audio tools) multimedia applications.

The reference architecture suggested in this chapter does not provide a final answer to the question for a suitable QoS-architecture that has initially been raised. However, the answer offered here goes beyond the pure enumeration of QoS mechanisms and parameters. In order to achieve end-to-end control, mechanisms are required that span all components between source and sink of an interaction. This is preferably the case for feedback control mechanisms, because they operate by relating effects directly back to their causes. Normally, causes are observed at the sink, which are several components away from the source. Sources get informed by derived control information from observations. Contrarily, feed-forward mechanisms observe violations from normal behaviour and inform the next node about the violation. There, remedy processes are activated in order to correct observed malfunctions.

Control structures can be adopted by the application and the networking layer in order to provide stream and resource control capabilities over point-to-point and end-to-end distances. Feedback control mechanisms have a so-called tuning effect on the observed streaming behaviour. This effect enables designers to construct architectures with built-in mechanisms that provide some kind of guaranteed quality of service to users.

6.6 Quality of Service Architectural Approaches

During the last few years a considerable amount of research has been done in the area of quality of service for distributed multimedia services. This research has been conducted by academia as well as by industry. Most of the research has been within the scope of an individual architectural layer, such as the transport or network layer, the operating system, etc. By far less research has been done in the area of comprehensive end-to-end QoS features supporting multimedia applications. The following paragraphs give brief introductions into some of the research projects that address QoS architectures.

6.6.1 Communication Object Request Broker Architecture (CORBA)

The early work of the Object Management Group (OMG) was published in the so-called QoS Green Paper [17]. The basic idea of OMG was to extend the ISO ODP-RM [23] in order to make QoS characteristics and functions suitable for object-based distributed systems.

Both organisations, OMG and ISO, agreed to work on QoS in close collaboration, in order to adapt standards and specifications to new or changed product requirements as quickly as possible. Recent achievements on the issue of QoS can thus most rapidly be adopted by new products. Items of work of the OMG which are related to QoS are considered in answers to OMG's RfP on the Messaging Service [13]. An actual specification has recently been developed within the OMG that covers the three topics of asynchronous method invocations, of transporting requests asynchronously to replies, and of Quality of Service. The specification defines a possible integration of QoS characteristics and functions into CORBA that consists of a set of policies to represent QoS characteristics. Unfortunately, it differs from the one that is used by ISO for defining QoS in the ODP-RM [23].

The OMG model distinguishes three levels of specifying and handling of QoS characteristics. The lowest level corresponds to the *ORB level* at which QoS characteristics for the ORB can be defined by using a default specification option. The next higher level is the *thread level*. Threads describe certain client–server

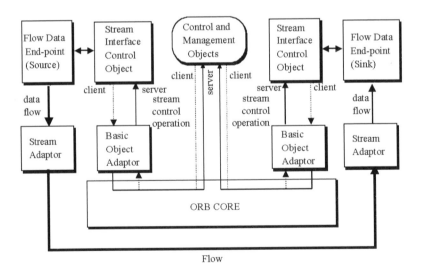

Figure 6.5 CORB architecture.

relationships. At this level, it is allowed to override QoS characteristics from the ORB level. The highest level is the *object level*, at which QoS characteristics are processed in the order of priorities. QoS characteristics specified at the thread or at the ORB level are allowed to be overridden at this level.

When a server gets deployed, a set of policies concerning the handling of QoS characteristics is deployed as well. At the same time, when a server becomes accessible after having exported its reference, policy functions are added. In turn, by importing the reference, the client provides to the ORB a validation capability. Therefore, the ORB Core can check the QoS characteristics of the client with respect to the criteria exported by the server.

Basically, OMG's approach of specifying QoS using abstract policies is still very generic. However, it is possible to specify certain QoS characteristics in conjunction with the following CORBA messaging features:

–   Rebind Support
–   Synchronisation Scope
–   Request and Reply Priority
–   Request and Reply Timeout
–   Routing
–   Queue Ordering

Figure 6.5 shows the principles of control of the CORB architecture. Client and server control functions are separately handled from data flow control functions. At each data flow end-point there exists a server object that controls the flow of data. The server objects at the data flow end-points interact with a central controlling object. This structure of control is similar to the control structure of TINA (see Section 6.6.2). Both architectures handle data and control paths separately.

6.6.2 Telecommunications Information Networking Architecture (TINA)

The Telecommunication Information Networking Architecture (TINA) of the European TINA Consortium is described in detail in [11] and [28]. Architecturally, TINA is separated into the Native Computing and Communication Environment (NCCE), the Distributed Processing Environment (DPE) the Application Layer (AL). The NCCE contains the operating systems and the communication protocol stacks. It is composed of a set of heterogeneous interconnected computing nodes. The DPE hides the heterogeneity and distributive nature of the NCCE. It thus minimises the knowledge required by the Application Layer about NCCE technology. The Application Layer contains management capabilities for the resource sub-layer and the service sub-layer. The service sub-layer comprises the specific part of the telecommunication service, e.g. a video-on-demand service, and additionally some generic procedures for the association of users to a service invocation. More importantly, the same sub-layer also contains the service session manager which deals with negotiation and control of service resources. In

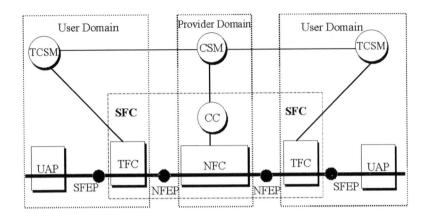

Legend: TCSM: Terminal Communication Session Manager,
        CSM: Communication Session Manager,
        CC: Connection Coordinator, UAP: User Application,
        N/S/T FC: Network/Steam/Terminal Flow Connection,
        N/S FEP: Network/Stream Flow End Point

Figure 6.6 TIN-Architecture.

co-operation with the service session manager, the network resource manager provides connection configuration capabilities.

The components that provide services for setting-up and for managing connections are captured by the so-called TINA Network Resource Architecture (TNRA), which is outlined in Figure 6.6. TNRA is the structure of the resource sub-layer described above. At the top level of the TNRA there is the Connection Session Manager (CSM). The CSM provides service-independent interfaces about the control of end-to-end Stream Flow Connections (SFC). A SFC is separated from its user application components (UAP) by its Stream Flow End-Points (SFEP). CSM shares control of a SFC with its local Terminal Communication Session Manager (TCSM) from the associated user domains. The part of the SFC which is controlled by the local TCSMs is called the Terminal Flow Connection (TFC) and bridges the gap between the SFEP at the user application and the Network Flow End-Point (NFEP) at the communication network. Both SFEP and NFEP are either application-independent or network-independent end-points respectively, i.e. they provide transparency of the service or technology. The inter-connections between NF end-points are provided by Network Flow Connections (NFC). NFCs are controlled network internally by Connection Coordinators (CC). SFC and TFC are logical representations of a connection, whereas the NFC is their physical counterpart.

The TIN-Architecture provides the necessary flexibility to get information from resources and from service components used by an application. The management components are optimally distributed in order to control local resources and to co-operate with remote management components, i.e. to feed-back or to feed-forward steering information, such that end-to-end control of QoS can be achieved.

6.6.3 Lancaster Architecture (QoS-A)

The Quality of Service Architecture (QoS-A) [3] has been developed at Lancaster University, UK and research is now continuing in collaboration with Columbia University, USA. The architecture consists of a number of layers and planes (see Figure 6.7). The highest layer consists of a distributed application platform augmented with services to provide multimedia communications and QoS specification. The task of the orchestration layer is to control jitter and regulate the rate for continuous media streams. This layer is supported by the transport layer which contains various configurable QoS services and mechanisms. The network layer is very closely linked with the transport layer and supported by the lowest two layers, the data-link layer and the physical layer.

QoS management is done in three vertical planes. The protocol plane separates control and data because of their different QoS requirements. The QoS maintenance plane contains several layer-specific QoS managers, each one being responsible for the monitoring and maintenance of their associated protocol entities. The flow-management plane is responsible for flow establishment, which includes admission control, QoS-based routing and resource reservation, QoS mapping (i.e., the translation of QoS parameters between layers), and QoS scaling (which constitutes QoS filtering and adaptation).

QoS-A is a very comprehensive framework that addresses many aspects of QoS provision, control and management. It can provide deterministic, statistical and best-effort service guarantees. In general, it can be said that its main focus is on the end

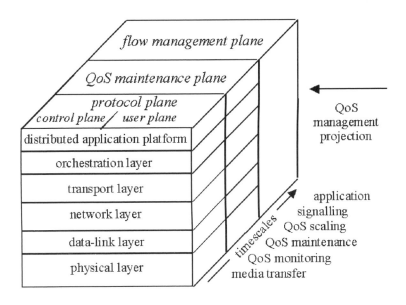

Figure 6.7 Lancaster Architecture

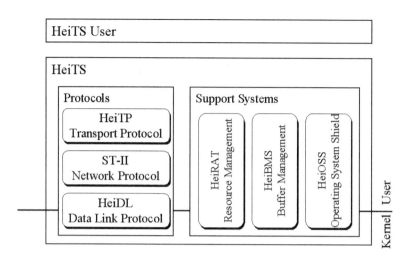

Figure 6.8 Heidelberg architecture.

systems rather than on the network. Flow synchronisation, flow scheduling, flow control and resource allocation in the network require further attention.

6.6.4 Heidelberg Architecture

The HeiProjects at IBM's European Networking Center in Heidelberg, Germany, have achieved a comprehensive framework for providing QoS guarantees in the end-systems and the network. The projects include the development of HeiTS (Heidelberg Transport System) for the transport of continuous media streams across the network [22] and HeiRAT (Heidelberg Resource Administration Technique) that provides a well-defined QoS for this transport [21].

HeiTS is designed for the communication of continuous media data. Its purpose is to exchange digital audio and video with QoS guarantees. This can be done in a one-to-one or multicast fashion. It uses HeiTP (Heidelberg Transport Protocol) as transport protocol, ST-II as network protocol and HeiDL as data-link layer protocol [8]. Although HeiTS uses the old-fashioned ST-II protocol for resource reservation, it can be adapted for RSVP [3].

HeiTS has several support mechanisms. As can be seen in Figure 6.8, it provides support for buffer management with the HeiBMS (Heidelberg Buffer Management System) and for platform portability with the HeiOSS (Heidelberg Operating System Shield). However, HeiRAT is the most important subsystem. It manages all resources that are critical for the processing and transmission of continuous media data: CPU time, bandwidth and memory. The QoS values are given in terms of maximum end-to-end delay, minimum throughput required and reliability class. The latter defines how the loss of data is treated. Furthermore, an application can specify an interval from desired to worst-acceptable QoS values. In order to offer guaranteed or statistical QoS, QoS routing is employed to find the best path through the network.

A big advantage of the HeiProjects is their scalability [5]. In the case of MPEG, the continuous media stream can be divided into sub-streams. The stream that contains the important I-frames is transmitted over a guaranteed connection. The P- and B-frames are less important and can be transmitted over a best-effort connection. However, this division into sub-streams requires good synchronisation, which is still a weak point in this architecture.

6.6.5 Tenet Architecture

The Tenet architecture [2] has been developed at the University of California at Berkeley and consists of a family of protocols that run over networks which can provide guaranteed-performance services, such as FDDI or ATM. The user specifies the desired QoS in terms of delay, jitter and loss rate together with traffic characterisation parameters.

The protocol suite defines five protocols (see Figure 6.9). At the network level the Real-Time Internet Protocol (RTIP) delivers packets to meet the channels' real-time requirements. It is connection-oriented and performs rate control, jitter control and scheduling based on the QoS parameters of each connection. It provides an unreliable, simplex, guaranteed-performance, in-order packet delivery service.

Two protocols are defined for the transport layer, the Real-Time Message Transport Protocol (RMTP) and the Continuous Media Transport Protocol (CMTP). RMTP is concerned with message-based real-time transport between end-points. It is unreliable and depends on RCAP to manage connections so that there is no congestion and on RTIP to provide rate-based flow control. One of the main services

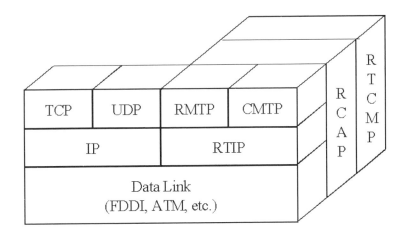

Figure 6.9 Tenet architecture.

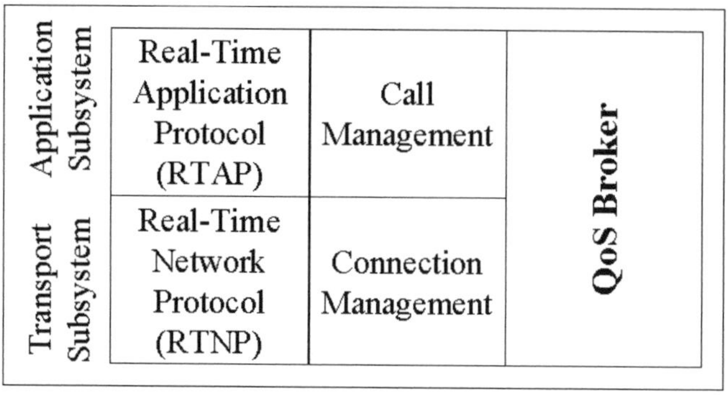

		Real-Time Application Protocol (RTAP)	Call Management	QoS Broker
Application Subsystem				
Transport Subsystem		Real-Time Network Protocol (RTNP)	Connection Management	

Figure 6.10 Omega architecture.

provided by RMTP is fragmentation and reassembly. CMTP is concerned with the transport of continuous media and offers a stream-based interface for isochronous applications.

The remaining protocols are control protocols. The Real-Time Channel Administration Protocol (RCAP) provides the signalling and control services in the Tenet suite. Its main functions are the set-up and tear-down of real-time channels in a heterogeneous internetwork and to provide status inquiries about already established channels. Finally, the Real-Time Control Message Protocol (RTCMP) is there to detect and manage error conditions. In the event of a network failure it computes a new route and allocates resources before redirecting a data stream.

Compared with the aforementioned QoS architectures, Tenet is much more focussed on the network rather than the end systems. In order to provide comprehensive end-to-end QoS, a more detailed consideration of the end systems would be necessary.

6.6.6 Omega Architecture

Omega [15] was developed at the University of Pennsylvania. It is built on a network that provides bounds on delay and errors and that can meet bandwidth demands. The architecture concentrates on the provision of QoS in the end-points.

The system can be partitioned into two parts, the communication model and the resource model. The communication model (see Figure 6.10) contains the application subsystem layer that provides functions such as call management, as well as rate control, fragmentation, I/O functions, etc. which are the core of the Real-Time Application Protocol (RTAP). The transport subsystem layer provides connection management, FEC, timing failure detection, etc, which form the core of the Real-Time Network Protocol (RTNP). The service guarantees provided to the applications are negotiated by the so-called QoS Broker [16] during call establishment. The broker is responsible for the management of local and global end-point resources.

The resource model addresses the management of multimedia devices, CPU scheduling, memory allocation, and network resources. The resources in each of these domains (application, operating system, network) are described with appropriate QoS parameters. The application specifies its resource requirements with high-level (application) QoS parameters (such as frame rate and resolution). The operating system provides system resources (such as CPU slots, buffers and processing). The network finally provides network resources (such as bandwidth and packet size).

The essence of Omega is resource reservation and management of end-to-end resources. The architecture includes the application layer and allows the re-negotiation of the initially negotiated QoS parameters. However, it does not address QoS filtering or flow synchronisation.

6.7 Advances in Quality of Service Architectures

Without the possibility of retrieving appropriate information from system components QoS management cannot be performed. The previously invented QoS architecture, as sketched in Figure 6.3, shows access points and signalling paths which are necessary for providing reflective or adaptive QoS management respectively in the application layer and on the networking layer. Obviously, the mechanisms in the transport layer are resource-oriented, and the mechanisms in the application layer are service-oriented. Resource-oriented mechanisms are, for example, the point-to-point flow control or the admission control mechanism. These mechanisms can be found in the Lancaster architecture, the Heidelberg architecture and the Tenet architecture. CORBA, which can also be classified as being resource-oriented, has a very low level of visibility of its resources and is thus not open enough for introducing resource control mechanisms suitable for QoS-awareness. In contrast TINA, which is object-oriented, provides a very fine-grained structure on the application level. It further structures the interaction activities between application entities into phases of access, transportation and termination. It is thus possible for the application layer to assign QoS tasks to some of the TINA management objects and to identify access points at object interfaces and signalling paths between managing objects.

One of the most important features of QoS-aware architectures is the openness of their structures. Openness provides the necessary visibility of internal behaviour. Visibility is required for the various activities to enable QoS control, like controlling, filtering, shaping, monitoring etc. More precisely, openness is subdivided into observability and controllability as presented in Section 6.5. Whereas observability defines the constraints between the internal state variables and the outputs, controllability defines the relationship between the input and the internal state of a component or a system. To take these constraints into account a system designer must know which of the state variables are stringent to QoS.

Control requires decision procedures. Decision procedures interpret observations and generate actuation signals for the adaptation of resources or sources. Thus, decision procedures are policy-driven and may change according to traffic or service characteristics. Therefore, the following design constraints can be derived:

1. To identify openness constraints for a known QoS policy in terms of observability and controllability.
2. To identify continuous variables that are stringent to the QoS policy to be achieved. Define their relationships to input and output of the system.
3. To separate, architecturally, control functions from service functions. Define a clear interface between the control plane and the service or network plane.

The structure of the advanced QoS-aware middleware fulfils the three constraints introduced above, by which QoS control is achieved. This kind of middleware plays the role of a mediator between the application layer and the networking layer. The sensors are attached to the interfaces of components coping with transportation resources. These components are found at the edges of the network, i.e. routers, shapers etc. Actuators are either plugged to application interfaces or to resource management interfaces of the networking jar. Placing actuators depends on the adaptation policy applied. For example, the adaptation policy adapts the behaviour of an application to the observed traffic situation. Alternatively, the resources can be rearranged such that the same quality of service is maintained even after the observation of scarce resources. The third class of agents of the QoS-aware middleware are the discriminator agents. Discriminators may reside not only as part of the middleware but also in the various domains of the application and of the network edges. Thus, discrimination looks like a distributed process that provides the decision-making task of the adopted QoS policy. During execution, the decision-making process refers to the negotiated values, thresholds, limits etc, that are captured by the QoS contract. The QoS-aware middleware is thus capable of providing the adaptation infrastructure to the QoS management, that includes signalling between sensor, actuators and discriminators, the access to QoS contracts from any location, and the roaming of decision-making agents, i.e. the discriminators. This approach achieves a clear distinction between QoS control, i.e. management function and service function.

6.8 Conclusions

This chapter has introduced quality of service mechanisms and architectures for interactive multimedia services. It first listed some of the issues in QoS management functions and then surveyed the most common architectures that claim to be QoS-aware. Research in recent years has shown that it is not enough to provide guarantees with respect to network resources. The sole reservation of bandwidth in the network cannot ensure high quality of IMM services. Although these guarantees are essential, they need to be combined with service guarantees with respect to end-systems. The scheduling of multimedia streams at the end-systems is an important factor. Furthermore, QoS guarantees need to be provided on an application-to-application basis. Resource management at the end-systems as well as in the network needs to be related to QoS parameters given by applications or users.

Multimedia communication is very dynamic in nature. Unfortunately, most reservation schemes and QoS architectures are still quite static. What is required are more adaptable structures, similar to the suggested QoS reference architecture, that can respond to QoS violations and network or device failures. However, the diversity of networks and applications makes it very difficult to implement such a comprehensive and reflective system structure as is required for the deployment of high-quality interactive multimedia services on a large scale.

Glossary of Architectural Concepts

BER   Bit Error Rate
CC   Connection Coordinator
CHQ   Controlled Highest Quality (Negotiation term)
CMTP   Continuous Media Transfer Protocol
CORBA   Common Object Request Broker Architecture
CSM   Connection Session Manager
DPE   Distributed Processing Environment
HQA   Highest Quality Attainable (Negotiation term)
IMM   Interactive Multimedia
LQA   Lowest Quality Acceptable
Mbps   Mega Bits per Second
MPEG   Moving Pictures (Definition) Expert Group
NCCE   Native Computing and Communication Environment
NFC   Network Flow Connection
NFEP   Network Flow End-Point
ODP   (ISO) Open Distributed Processing
OSI   (ISO) Open Systems Interconnection (Reference Model)
PoA   Point of Actuation
PoO   Point of Observation
QoS   (ISO) Quality of Service
RCAP   RT Channel Administration Protocol
RMTP   RT Message Transfer Protocol
RSVP   Resource Reservation Protocol
RT   Real Time
RTAP   RT Application Protocol
RTCMP   RT Control Message Protocol
RTIP   RT Internet Protocol
RTNP   RT Network Protocol
RTTP   RT Transport Protocol
SFC   Stream Flow Connection
SFEP   Stream Flow End-Point
S_IF   Stream Interface

TCSM   Terminal Communication Session Manager
TFC   Terminal Flow Connection
UAP   User Application Component

Glossary of Standardisation Institutions

ETSI   European Telecommunication Standards Institute
IETF   Internet Engineering Task Force
ISO   International Standardisation Organisation
ITU-T   International Telecommunication Union – Telecommunication Standardisation Sector
OMG   Object Management Group
TINA-C Telecommunications Information Networking Architecture Consortium

References

[1]   Aurrecoechea, C., Campbell, A.T. and L. Hauw, (1998) "A Survey of QoS Architectures", ACM/Springer Verlag Multimedia Systems Journal, Special Issue on QoS Architecture, Vol. 6 No. 3, pp. 138–151, May 1998. [A former version can be found in: "A Review of QoS Architectures", Proceedings of the 4th International IFIP Workshop on Quality of Service IWQoS96, Paris, March 6–8, 1996.]

[2]   Banerjae A., Ferrari D., Mah B.A., Moran M., Verma D.C. and Zhang H. (1996) "The Tenet Real-Time Protocol Suite: Design, Implementation and Experiences", IEEE/ACM Transactions on Networking, 4 (1), pp. 1–10.

[3]   Campbell A., Coulson G. and Hutchison D. (1994) "A Quality of Service Architecture", ACM Computer Communication Review, 24 (2), pp. 6–27.

[4]   OMG (1998) "CORBA Messaging, Joint Revised Submission", OMG TC Document, OMG, May 18, 1998, ftp://ftp.omg.org/pub/docs/orbos/98-05-05.pdf

[5]   Delgrossi L., Halstrick C., Hehmann D., Herrtwich R.G., Krone O., Sandvoss J. and Vogt C. (1993) "Media Scaling for Audiovisual Communication with the Heidelberg Transport System", Proceedings of the ACM Conference on Multimedia (Multimedia'93), Anaheim, CA.

[6]   Eberlein A. (2001) "Interactive Multimedia: A Review", International Journal of High Performance Computer Graphics, Multimedia and Visualization 1 (1), pp. 9-29.

[7]   Guo X. and Pattinson C. (1997) "Quality of Service Requirements for Multimedia Communications", Proceedings of the Time and the Web Symposium, UK.

[8]   Huard J.-F. and Lazar A.A. (1997) "On QoS Mapping in Multimedia Networks", Proceedings of the Twenty-First Annual International Computer Software & Applications Conference, Washington, DC.

[9]   R. Bradsen ISI, L Zhang UCLA (1997) "Resource Reservation Protocol (RSVP)", Network Working Group, www.ietf.org, RFC 2209.

[10]   Y. Bernet et al. (1998) "A Framework for Differentiated Services", Internet Draft draft-ietf-diffserv-framework-01.txt

[11]   E.Koerner (1998), "Methods and Elements for the Construction of Collaborated Services in TINA", These de doctorat, University de Liege, ISSN 0075-93333.

[12]   Little T.D.C. and Venkatesh D. (1994) "Prospects for Interactive Video-on-Demand", IEEE Multimedia, 1 (3), pp. 14–24.

[13]   OMG(1996) "Messaging Service RfP", OMG, November 1996, ftp://ftp.omg.org/pub/docs/orbos/1996/96-03-16.pdf

[14] Nahrstedt K. and Steinmetz R. (1995) "Resource Management in Networked Multimedia Systems, Computer", 28 (5), pp. 52–63.

[15] Nahrstedt K. and Smith J.M. (1996) "Design, Implementation and Experiences of the OMEGA End-Point Architecture", IEEE Journal on Selected Areas in Communications, 14 (7), pp. 1263–1279.

[16] Nahrstedt K. and Smith J.M. (1995) "The QoS Broker", IEEE Multimedia, 2 (1), pp. 53–67.

[17] OMG (1997) "Quality of Service (QoS)" OMG Green Paper, Working Draft, Version 0.4a, OMG, June 1997, ftp://ftp.omg.org/pub/docs/ormsc/97-06-04.pdf

[18] Svend Frølund and Jari Koistinen (1998) "Quality of Service Aware Distributed Object Systems", Hewlett-Packard, April, 1998.

[19] Tanenbaum A.S. (1996) "Computer Networks", Prentice Hall.

[20] Vogel A., Kerhervé B., von Bochmann G. and Gecsei J. (1995) "Distributed Multimedia and QoS: A Survey, IEEE Multimedia", 2 (2), pp. 10–19.

[21] Vogt C., Wolf L.C., Herrtwich R.G. and Wittig H. (1998) "HeiRAT – Quality of Service Management for Distributed Multimedia Systems", to appear in ACM Multimedia Systems Journal - Special Issue on QoS Systems.

[22] Wolf L.C. and Herrtwich R.G. (1994) "The System Architecture of the Heidelberg Transport System", ACM Operating Systems Review, 28 (2), pp. 51–64.

[23] ISO (1995) IS10746-2 "IT ODP-RM Open Distributed Processing Part 2: Descriptive Model".

[24] ETSI (1995) ETSI and the Information Society – "State of Art 1995".

[25] ISO (1997) ISO/IEC ITU-T Recommendation IS 13236 / X.641, "Information Technology – Quality of Service – Framework", December 1997.

[26] ISO (1998) ISO/IEC ITU-T Recommendation TR 13243 / X.642, "Information Technology – Quality of Service – Guide to methods and mechanisms", September 1998.

[27] ISO (1999) CD15935 (1999) "IT ODP-RM – Quality of Service", ISO/IEC JTC1/SC7 N1996.

[28] TINA-C (1995) "Computational Modelling Concepts", Archive Label TB_A2.HC.012.1.2.94, February 1995.

[29] J.B. deMeer (1999) "On the construction of Reflexive System Architectures", Middleware Workshop RM2000, N.Y.C.

[30] I.Foster, A.Roy, V.Sander (2000) A Quality of Service Architecture that combines Resource Reservation and Application Adaptation. IWQoS2000 Proceedings pp. 181–188.

[31] T.Walter, I.Schieferdecker, J.Grabowski (1998) Test Architectures for Distributed Systems – State of the Art and Beyond. IWTCS 1998 Proceedings pp. 149–174.

[32] B.C.Kuo 1995 Automatic Control Systems, Prentice Hall.

Chapter 7

Changes and Challenges: Mass Customised Media and the Internet

Klaus Goldhammer

7.1 Introduction

Personalisation of net services will probably be the main factor for future success of Internet media. The user obtains the content they want, and is not overwhelmed with unnecessary material. The Internet is the first electronic medium with which this interactive personalisation has been possible. This trend will also be developed by online radio and television, as they move away from general and special interest programming, towards narrowcasting and supply on demand. At the same time, the user is turning into Toffler's pro-sumer, creating the product they themselves desire. Involving users in production of content and the creation of communities increases attractiveness and thus profitability (e.g. AOL and AOL's scouts). Besides supporting user input with web pages, chatrooms and online games also increase involvement. Personalisation is also aided by two technical means: agents and collaborative filters. Agents, e.g. as used by search engines, search the Internet and compile information on the subject required by the user. These are now also being used for e-commerce. Collaborative filters batch users into "affinity groups", people with similar interests, by use or purchasing patterns, etc. This is a powerful marketing and programme planning tool. Both methods also help increase user loyalty. All these approaches to personalisation are currently being used by several webcasters, to develop their webcasting services. Accordingly, the other major trend on the Internet is away from globalisation towards niche marketing: content is focussed more and more by interest or locality, dividing the former masses using a single medium into many different users with their "own" medium. These very small target groups (fewer than 10,000 people) can be provided with their own webcasted programme. Pornography currently heads this market. Former mass media thus become the first meso-media on the Internet and finally the fully personalised "Me-channel".

7.2 The State of Things on the Internet – And Where it is Going

Northern Europeans continue to lead the Internet boom, whilst Southern Europeans lag behind. Whilst even in Germany one still cannot speak of a "People's Net", it is catching up with the Scandinavian countries. According to an Empirica study from October 1999, every 24 hours about 15,000 Germans take the plunge onto the Net.

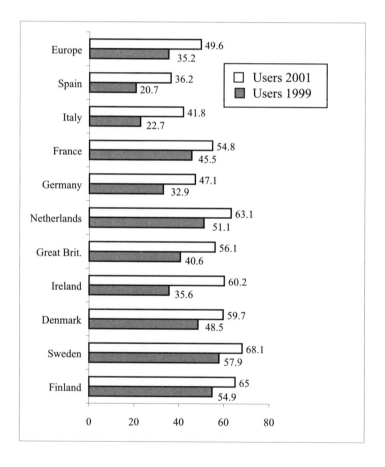

Figure 7.1 Internet users (per cent).

By 2001 the current European Internet population of 22 million users is expected to rise to 32 million. By 2003, four million Germans are expected to be using the data-highway either privately or for business (see Figure 7.1[1]).

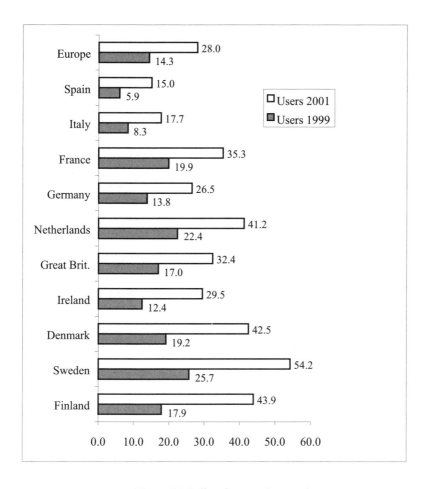

Figure 7.2 Online shoppers (per cent).

Germany will number 18 million online shoppers in 2001. By 2003 every other German is expected to swap the shopping basket for the mouse (see Figure 7.2[2]).

The development in German companies is also rapid, with approx. 46 per cent of them currently represented on the Internet. By 2001 this is expected to reach 70 per cent (Figure 7.3[3]).

---

[1] Source: Capital No. 10; October 1999

[2] Source: Capital No. 10; October 1999

[3] Source: Capital No. 10; October 1999

The average Internet user is well educated and of an average to higher educational level. The educational boundaries will become hazier in the future with increasing penetration, as shown in Figure 7.4[4].

7.3 Personalisation of Content: Media as Daily Me or I-Channel

Probably the most important factor for success of online offers in the future is the possibility of personalising available content. Personalisation of content primarily helps the user to obtain the offers he or she personally desires, and secondly protects users from being overloaded with information. The Internet is the first electronic medium to make personalised offers at all possible either technically or economically.

The fact that there is a need for individualised content is shown by the numerous offers from Yahoo, Netscape, etc. For example, after an appropriate registration

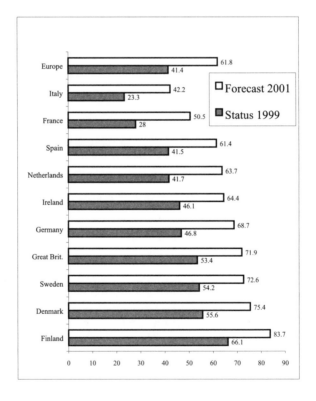

Figure 7.3 Company presences on the Internet.

---

[4] Source: Capital No. 10; October 1999

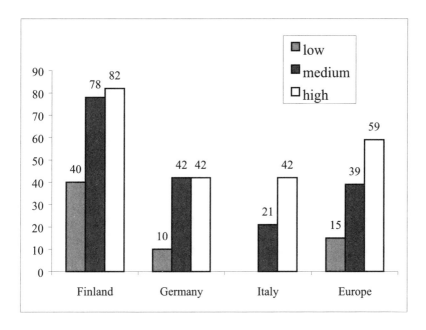

Figure 7.4 Internet use according to educational level (per cent).

procedure at *MyYahoo* where the user defines their interests, they can, on the second visit to the page, enjoy content collected just for them from the available database.

This gives rise to the niche medium for one person, the "I-channel". According to Eli Noam this sort of personal or personalised program offer is the third stage of development of television [12,13].

Thus online media are continuing to develop the classic radio-broadcaster concept of formatting in general or special interest programming [4]. The individual

Figure 7.5 Personalisation pyramid of online content.

user comes into the focus of the provider as a target group which receives its daily and personal (online) radio offer, the personalised program. The personalisation pyramid of contents in Figure 7.5[5] explains this.

The idea of the "Daily Me", the personalised program, is becoming increasingly important for radio and television broadcasters – and in the end this can only be realised via the Internet. Currently it is mainly online radio broadcasters such as Spinner, Imagine or Rolling Stone who are venturing into this new territory. But music broadcasters such as MTV and VIVA are already considering similar approaches to individualisation as the leaders of the development in TV.

Besides the general concept of individualisation of content for the user, individualised compilation of content by the user must however also be studied.

7.4 Personalisation of Content Production: Pro-sumer

The idea of transferring production to consumers, was already developed by the futurologist Alvin Toffler in his book *Future Shock* in 1970: he predicted that *consumers* and *producers* would develop into *pro-sumers*.

The consumers themselves become the producers of what they use. Even now it is often the case that those who (have to) use a product know the most about it: the customers. Tying in their expertise is a significant success strategy on the Internet, particularly in the production of content.

"Content is King" is the motto of the media industries and there is certainly more than a grain of truth in this: without attractive content, even the most technically perfect medium is not attractive enough to prevail in the market. Creating sufficiently high-value content therefore is always the Achilles' heel of every new medium.

The Internet has been able to avoid this problem with remarkable ease, due to its anarchic structure: as many individuals have the possibility of placing content which appears relevant to them on the Net for a relatively small expense, it was possible to avoid the start-up problem for the new medium:

> In the first 1,000 days of the web's life, several hundred thousand webmasters created over 450,000 web sites, thousands of virtual communities, and 150 million pages of intellectual property, primarily for free. [5, p.56]

Open access to the platform was a fundamental requirement for its success. Instead of having to commission a few professional and very expensive editors with the task of creating very little content (possibly also the wrong content), the potential recipients took charge of production themselves and in their spare time created the content which interested them. The almost revolutionary significance of this wholesale privatisation of content creation can still be easily seen in the Internet. The Internet was able by this means to generate net effects itself which could not have been planned by any company.

---

[5] Source: Rundfunk Online 1998/1999

7.4.1 Examples of Personalised Content Production: Communities

A good example of a successful attempt at personalised content production is online communities, e.g. Geocities (www.geocities.com). Here, the provider's aim was to entice as many users/pro-sumers to establish their own websites on Geocities, by providing hard-disk space free of charge. There are only two conditions attached to the offer: firstly, the user must accept a notice on their own website stating that they are hosted by Geocities, and secondly they have to accept advertising banners, which Geocities themselves market.

The system has been successful: Geocities' portfolio of content, which in 1998 was compiled by about 1.9 million users, is growing and growing. At the same time, the number of visitors is climbing almost automatically and thus the attractiveness of buying advertising banners grows. Already by 1997 the company had a turnover of about 4.6 million dollars. Today, Geocities (with 13.7 million visitors in July 1998) is one of the Top 10 most-visited websites in the world – and all this without the operator having had to compile any content [16]. Kevin Kelly describes this effect very aptly:

> The more dimensions accessible to member input and creation, the more increasing returns can animate the network, the more the system will feed on itself and prosper. [6, p.186]

Similarly, all the experts questioned by us are trying to develop their own communities. In the end, the Internet will need the radio in order to generate attention for itself and the radio will need the Internet to find communities [5]. Also, the more influence the customers win over the (media) product, the greater is the possibility that they are satisfied with the end product and the stronger loyalty becomes (see [9, pp.189–190]).

Another good example of the concept of personalisation of content production is also provided by the online service AOL: most of the content AOL offers its customers today comes from itself, whether postings or chatrooms. It took AOL years to find out that it was far better value for the service, and made a far more attractive range of offers, if it integrated its own customers into the process of content compilation, instead of just buying in offers from professional journalists and expensive external media providers.

The point when AOL realised that its own customers were behaving like employees and were themselves compiling AOL's services almost free of charge, is the point when the online service began to earn money [5].

7.5 The Role of Online Radio: Aggregator and Infrastructure Provider

Until now, electronic media have primarily followed the principle of generating content themselves and/or collecting available content (*aggregating*), *bundling* or *repackaging* it in new ways and then broadcasting it. In this approach to media production, users are simply passive consumers.

But the online media have not only had to switch the accent, they have even had to create *a new role for the provider* themselves: as infrastructure provider for the pro-sumer previously mentioned. The classic production process described above is provided for this level and finally the users are themselves given the possibility of developing, collecting and bundling content, as well as distributing it. Online radio providers thus increasingly become genuine aggregators and infrastructure providers.

7.5.1 Examples: Chats and Online Games

Chatrooms are a perfect example of personalisation of content production and the need for infrastructure providers. In the end, the provider only has to make a platform or infrastructure available, the content is created by the users.

With Internet games like *Ultima Online*, the participant receives nothing more than access to a virtual world. Again, there is nothing more than an infrastructure and the players are then obliged to equip this world and develop it creatively.

This gives rise to the questions, how can these offers for users to participate productively be realised, what significance do the developments mentioned have for media providers themselves, and how can these trends be realised in practice?

7.6 Technical Means of Personalisation: Agents and Collaborative Filters

Besides the already discussed approaches of providing webspace, as with Geocities, or of offering other suitable surroundings (chatrooms, virtual gaming worlds) which visitors can use for their own contributions, two technical solutions should also be mentioned which likewise (will) have a great share in the continuing personalisation of content on the Internet. These are, firstly, *agents* [11] and, secondly, the "*collaborative filter*".

7.6.1 The User Aspect: Intelligent Agents

In relation to the Internet, intelligent agents are software programs which support the user to search for and prepare information. The agent program helps the user to filter and prepare the relevant content. "The aim is the personalisation of data quantities" [8].

Almost every search engine works with similar software agents, which search through the Internet systematically and archive the relevant pages. The search engine's software agent, called a robot, then calls up page after page, makes the relevant links and thus compiles a register which can be searched by key words.

Agents have also been developed for shopping which search out the best-value online provider for a product. For example, the business consultancy Andersen Consulting has developed an agent called "Bargain Finder" which can be used

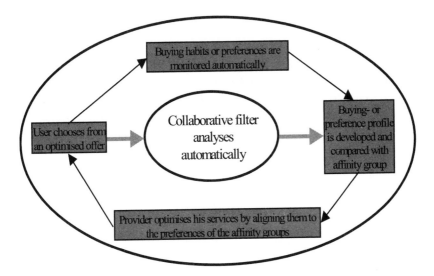

Figure 7.6 Function principle of collaborative filters.

exclusively to compare prices of CDs [17]. Various types of agents can be found for different areas of application.

There are intelligent agents in numerous areas of application. Besides e-commerce agent systems, other examples of media-related agents include news, financial information and entertainment-related agent systems.

Unfortunately although called intelligent agents, none is actually gifted with intelligence; but as an aid to personal selection in mountains of data and hence personalisation of content they are always useful.

7.6.2 The Provider Aspect: Collaborative Filters

A highly-promising tool for improving personalisation of online content is the concept of the *collaborative filter*: in principle, this is a database which compares the preferences of individual users with one another and similar groups' use or purchasing patterns (see Figure 7.6[6]). Thus as the number of members increases, the results improve. By this means, collaborative filters enable the formation of "affinity groups", i.e. users with an average quantity of preferences. With the help of data from affinity groups, the content of offers can be optimised for the individuals.

One of the first of these web-based recommendation systems was the software *Firefly* [18,19]. The software was developed by MIT Medialab and sold to Microsoft at the start of 1998. Another similar software originated from the company NetPerceptions and is called GroupLens. Both function in a similar way.

For example, a user registers with *My Launch* [20], a music website which uses the Firefly software, and names the ten CDs they most enjoy listening to. In order to

---

[6] Source: ECC 1999, 196

define their own preferences however, as many other CDs can be rated as the individual wishes.

Firefly takes this information and compares it with the information from about 500,000 other My Launch members who have already given their preferences. It seeks out the user information whose preferences best match with those of the new member. This creates a *virtual interest* or *affinity community*. The user then receives pointers to CDs which were not named by them, but which were enjoyed by other users with similar interests. The other users can receive (anonymised) pointers to the CDs that the new My Launch member has named, and which were not given by themselves (see [15, pp.232–247; 5, pp.119–121; 2, pp.195–197]).

At the heart of this is the assumption that a user is more likely to enjoy the CDs he does not know from his affinity group, than discs which, for example, are praised in a print magazine by a music critic he does not know. The attraction of systems like Firefly is not just the recommendations they can make, but also the development of preference or affinity groups. Firefly develops an individual affinity group for each user.

Apart from the music area, Firefly is used for similar services with a total of three million members for books, films and websites. "MyYahoo" also uses Firefly as its software tool, to serve users' demand for personalised offers better [8]. Collaborative filters are also of course very interesting for advertisers, because they make it possible to target offers more precisely.

Even bookshops like Amazon.com or Barnes & Noble/Bertelsmann use collaborative filter systems to make their customers personalised offers. For this, the purchasing pattern is directly compared, instead of the user having to input preferences themselves. Recommendations are made to the customer on the basis of what they have bought in the past and what others with similar purchasing patterns have ordered. These recommendations are regarded as Amazon's most powerful marketing technique [5].

Amazon cannot therefore simply be regarded as an online bookshop, but also as a company which sells connections. Everyone logging on to Amazon obtains access to a connection generator which gets to know the customer better and better, almost like a real salesman in an actual shop. It is safe to assume that this process of the collaborative filter will continue to expand. Not only in the media sector, for which some exemplary applications will be given, but for example also in the financial or health sectors [2, pp.195–197].

At the same time, these systems intensify *user loyalty*, the customer lock in: extra effort must be made by any participant who has given all their preferences into this kind of system to connect themselves to another collaborative filter system. So the connections between service and participant are generally longer-term.[7]

---

[7] Peppers/Rogers offer an example of intensified online connections which are not based on collaborative filters: "When the florist sends a note reminding you of your mother's birthday, and offers to deliver flowers again this year to the same address and charged against the same credit card you used with the florist last year, what are the chances that you will pick up the

If the radio providers succeed in learning the preferences of their recipients equally well and make suitable offers, which user would then want to switch to another online radio or television broadcaster?

In the end, therefore, collaborative filters succeed in simulating the old corner shop owner, by using software: the old shop owner got to know the customers over years, and knew what each one liked because they always bought there. On the basis of what other customers said about new products, he could tell who else would like the new product and recommend it to them. In the best cases he could present it to someone without asking - and be right.

For radio and television broadcasters, this software represents a revolution in programme scheduling. Collaborative filters offer webcasters the possibility of releasing their programme offers from yesterday's market research and the concept of formatting, which inevitably led to a programme of the "lowest common denominator", as they were searching for the statistical mean. But if the programme could be personalised with filter software instead, webcasters are taking a great leap in the individualised design of the programmes they offer on the Internet.

7.6.3 Collaborative Filters for Online Radio Broadcasters: Spinner.com and Imagine

In all, there are three major online radio broadcasters internationally, who use collaborative filters to personalise their offers. These are led by the former TheDJ.com now known as *Spinner* [21] then *Imagine Radio* [22], which went online in March 1998, and *Rolling Stone Radio* [23]. Another example is the German Website, Yosei [24] which went online in December 1999.

Spinner is definitely one of the most interesting models of online radio. The webcaster is trying to exploit almost all the programming possibilities of the Internet. The programme can be individualised with collaborative filters, chatrooms support interchange between the users and hence the formation of a community. The site is refinanced by advertising and a partner program with Amazon.com. In November 1998 about 750,000 different users visited Spinner. The site offers more than 130,000 songs as real audio files. The former "Nerd concept" has developed into a respectable company with about 30 employees. Many companies have tried without success to become involved with the company - the television company MTV was the last of these at the end of 1998. AOL bought Spinner and the company Nullsoft at the start of July 1999 for a total 400 million dollars in shares.

Spinner offers a total of 120 different channels by musical styles. The range stretches from "Female Voices of the 80s" through "Ska" or "Acid Jazz" to classical music. The user selects seven of these, which appear in an interface similar to a radio. Spinner then plays one channel, and the user can rate each individual track on a scale from 1 to 10. If the rating is positive, Spinner plays the track more frequently, if it is negative, the track isn't played any more. In time, Spinner can

---

phone and try to find a cheaper florist?" [15] – Presumably the chances for other florists are really small in this case.

develop a personal preference profile for the user and – thanks to collaborative filtering – design the programme offer optimally for the individual user with new tracks.

Imagine radio also offers the possibility of compiling the programme oneself. The parent company Imagine Media is one of the venture capital providers for Spinner [25]. As a programme Imagine provides four thematic talk channels and 16 different music channels, from Country to HipHop, and news from Associated Press. Other music channels concentrate on Hard Rock, Jazz, and Alternative Music. Added to this is one channel each just focusing on the music of the Rolling Stones or the Grateful Dead.

Imagine radio had about 100,000 registered users in November 1998. A "tuner" is simulated on the desktop, which is technically based on the RealPlayer. Here too, as with Spinner, background use during online time is possible. Transmission of video pictures is also being considered, in order for example to show participants in talk shows.

In contrast to Spinner, however, Imagine expects the user to develop their own profile after registration, by rating individual tracks from different categories of music. Also in contrast to Spinner, this profile is then stored on the user's hard disk. Then it goes on into the "programme". Commercial breaks and banners as well as sponsoring and a partner program, are intended to support Imagine radio financially. Banners and audio advertising should run simultaneously [10].

Imagine's target group are readers of the Imagine media magazine, Internet users in the workplace and younger Internet users such as students. Nonetheless, the programmes are produced with their world-wide reach in mind [7].

7.7 Regionalisation and Focusing: Meso-Media

This section deals with a further trend in content on the Internet and its effects. Besides the attraction of global distribution and the range of the Internet, it is also possible to discern an equally clear opposing development: focusing of content by content or by locality. Here, a general trend towards specialisation comes to bear, in order to master the mass of information, both on the part of the provider as well as on the part of the user. Netscape founder Marc Andreessen described the development towards focusing of content in an interview in Der Spiegel:

> The formation of groups independent of location is however just one side of the general trend towards focusing. On the other side, users' demands for regional content and services which are directly obtainable by them are growing, precisely because they are not only looking for global information."

In this context, the online service America Online (AOL) announced in July 1998 that it wanted to strengthen its regional offer, in order to increase the number of subscribers and advertising customers. Since version 4.0 of AOL's access software, which appeared in Autumn 1998, customers are greeted with their own region's start page. AOL thus not only attacked the advertising market of local papers, but also drew itself closer to the needs of its users. To do this, about 60 volunteers, called "AOL scouts" compile regional pages for 57 German cities in return for a free AOL subscription.

The reaction of advertising agents like AdDoubleclick to this development, has been the offer of operating regionalised advertising since mid-1998, in order to give advertising customers the option of advertising for a business which is actually in the close vicinity of the customer. To do this, the user's IP address is analysed and, if a company advertising with them has a branch in the neighbourhood, a dedicated banner referring to the local business is operated instead of the general banner.

7.7.1 Focusing by Locality and Content: Narrowcasting

Until now, regional subjects and media needs have primarily been dealt with by local papers and advertising sheets. Electronic media are affecting economic barriers with contents for the smallest target groups.

However, the Internet can also reproduce the user's interests in focusing by content and locality by electronic means. In a four-field matrix, this development towards *narrowcasting*, which was previously carried out by different classic media, can easily be reproduced (see Figure 7.7[8]).

Internet offers first entered the Net as wide-ranging offers both in content and locality. They were comparable with national TV broadcasters. However, the trend is for the Internet to copy the regional and local structures more and more and therefore offer online media-orientated content, as is done today by local advertising sheets. The multiplicity and spatial structure of the real world finally also have to be copied on the Internet, because they match the users' interests and experiences

		Local focusing	
		narrow	broad
Content focusing	narrow	Personal Radio / TV (www.spinner.com) *Advertising pages*	Online sport services (www.sport1.de) *TV channel broadcaster*
	broad	Digital city *Local newspaper* *Local TV*	Search engines / portals/ communities (www.netcenter.com) *National TV broadcaster* *Satellite broadcaster*

Figure 7.7 Local vs. content focusing of media offers on the Internet.

---

[8] Source: Rundfunk Online 1999 after ECC 1999: 204

better. This means not just more content in the local language, but also more information from a city, a district, a street. In this, information on regional weather (see the approach on MyYahoo) is equally significant as the question of what a chop costs at the two butcher's shops in town [2].

7.7.2 The Discovery of Small and Medium Groups: Meso-Media

There are mass media, such as television, radio and print, which reach millions of people at one time with a single message. And there are micro-media like the telephone, letters, fax and e-mail which all enable one-to-one communication between individual persons. But the average levels, smaller groups and circles of fewer than 10,000 people rarely appeared in the classic electronic media world, as these media could largely only be realised economically with financial losses.

Until now there was hardly any media technology besides print which made it possible to supply small groups of perhaps 5,000 people with media-oriented content. Electronic media could not until now offer an economic basis [5]. Just a few cable television channels such as C-SPAN in the USA sometimes registered under 100,000 viewers per day. Local German TV channels are mostly barely relevant economically.

Providers become a crystallisation point for small and medium groups on the Internet, because they offer an overview, access and orientation, in an apparently immense Net world. They represent the levels which have previously been missing in the electronic communications world: the *meso-levels*. As a Very-Special-Interest Program they represent a segment whose existence was only made economically possible by the Internet. Meso-media on the Internet, which are called online special interests in Figure 7.8,[9] can place themselves precisely on the interface between mass and individual communication, both in the speed of their distribution and in their range.

Online radio or webcasting should besides competing for existing advertising budgets be able to achieve new yield potential which enables the content producers to make completely new offers. One highly-promising approach is the *"differentiated online subscription"*. This can be used by a content provider to organise a small group of subscribers who are prepared to pay perhaps DEM 50 per year for special content or offers. If the provider can gain just 10,000 subscribers world-wide, then as producer he generates an annual turnover of half a million Deutschmark: enough to produce one broadcast a week, which can be distributed at low expense via the Internet and/or can be called up by the subscribers *on demand*.

Meso-media will therefore probably appear in great numbers and unimagined variety as Very-Special-Interest Programs on the Internet, as the infrastructure of the Web offers not just a good-value platform for production and distribution, but will also provide a long-term functioning basis for the previously expensive billing of these closed user groups.

---

[9] Source: Rundfunk Online 1998/1999 after: Lars B. Karle, Thyssen Telecom 1998

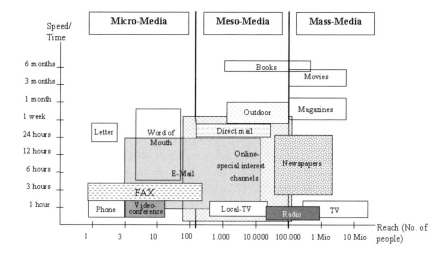

Figure 7.8 Speed and range of media.

7.8 Summary

Internet radio and television therefore offer the possibility for the first time to provide small to very small target groups of fewer than 10,000 recipients with their own electronic program offer (at present pornography offers are leading this on the Web). By this means, the Internet opens up the way to these small groups via several aspects [5]:

– There are no limited frequency wavelengths on the Internet. The falling cost of distributing information on the Internet makes it possible to establish small interest groups – beyond the limits of country or frequency – and to link members with one another. This makes it possible for the first time to create a specialised website for every hobby, every enthusiasm, every interest ("the macramé-channel") and further to develop a community with this interest.

– The possibility of symmetrical exchange of messages (text, audio, video, 3D-rooms, etc.) improves the chances of placing these virtual communities on long-term, stable foundations.

– Electronic cash also enables the development of commercial structures on these networks. Every niche group can easily sell its special knowledge to outside interests and thus further stabilise their existence. At the same time, these small groups represent an optimal target group for providers with that specialism to make sales.

– By networking the participants and exchanging information with one another, these groups can develop extensive knowledge almost free of cost.

In spite of this, mass media like radio and television will not die out, because they make it possible for large masses to orient themselves precisely, which would inevitably lead to chaos if there were a splintered multiplicity of small niche groups.

References

[1]   European Communication Council (Eds.) (1997) "Exploring the Limits. Europes Changing Communication Environment", Springer, Berlin.

[2]   European Communication Council (Eds.) (1999) "Die Internet-Oekonomie. Strategien für die digitale Wirtschaft", Springer, Berlin.

[3]   Goldhammer, Klaus; Zerdick, Axel "Rundfunk Online. Entwicklung und Perspektiven des Internets für Hörfunk- und Fernsehanbieter", Vistas, Berlin.

[4]   Goldhammer, Klaus (1995) "Formatradio in Deutschland. Konzepte, Techniken und Hintergruende der Programmgestaltung von Hoerfunkstationen", Spiess, Berlin.

[5]   Kelly, Kevin (1998) "New Rules for the new economy. 10 radical strategies for a connected world", Penguin Books, New York.

[6]   Kelly, Kevin (1997) "New Rules for the new economy. Twelve dependable principles for thriving in a turbulent world", Wired Magazine, No. 11/97, 140—197

[7]   Lipton, Beth "Imagine tries Net Radio", Under: http://www.news.com/News/Item/0,4,19811,00.html; dated 9.3.1998.

[8]   Lux, Harald (1998) "Intelligente software hilft suchen. Entwickler arbeiten an Programmen, die das Internet transparenter machen", Horizont, No. 5/98, 51.

[9]   Miles, Peggy (1998) "Internet World Guide to Webcasting. The Complete Guide to Broadcasting over the Web", Mecklermedia, New York.

[10] Mitchell, Dan (1998) "Imagining Things? A computer magazine publisher hopes to capture the ears of Internet users", Under: http://www.redherring.com/insider/1998/0310/imagine.html; dated 3.10.1998.

[11] Negroponte, Nicholas (1995) "Being digital", Vintage Books, New York.

[12] Noam, Eli M. (1995) "Die Entwicklungsstufen des Fernsehens", in Bertelsmann Stiftung (pub.), 15–28.

[13] Noam, Eli M. (1996) "Cyber-TV. Thesen zur dritten Fernsehrevolution", Guetersloh.

[14] Noam, Eli M. (1997) "Systemic Bottlenecks in the Information Society" in: European Communication Council (Eds.), 35–44.

[15] Peppers, Don / Rogers, Martha (1997) "Enterprise One to One. Tools for Competing in the Interactive Age", Currency/Doubleday, New York.

Web Site References

[16] www.wired.com/news/news/business/story/14266.html

[17] bf.cstar.ac.com/bf/

[18] www.ffly.com

[19] www.firefly.net

[20] www.mylaunch.com

[21] www.spinner.com

[22] www.imagine radio.com

[23] www.rsradio.com/home/home page.html

[24] www.yosei.de

[25] www.hotwired.com/collections/venture_capital/ 6.01_silicon_valley10.html

Chapter 8

Regulatory Trends in Webcasting in the United States, the European Union, and Japan: Focusing on Universal Service

Jae-Young Kim

8.1 Introduction

There is no specific policy targeting on webcasting, sometimes known as Internet broadcasting, in the world. In fact, policy-makers are increasingly facing challenges of how to deal with new communication services that use the Internet to deliver contents to users in ways that take on many of the characteristics of traditional communications services. Webcasting is a leading example of the emerging group of new services. It is not an easy task for policy-makers to promptly respond to fast-growing Internet-based services like webcasting.

At the same time, there are few barriers to entering into the webcasting sector because of the low cost of providing webcast services. This indicates that government regulations such as issuing or renewing licenses that are necessary for the traditional broadcasting industry are not needed in the field of Internet broadcasting. This explains another reason for compelling policy-makers to be laggards in developing webcasting policies.

Therefore, this study explores the regulatory trends of webcasting in a roundabout way that deals with convergence between telecommunications and broadcasting. Convergence is one of the most popular terms applied to the communication industry in a number of different ways. One type of convergence is evident in the technologies used by infrastructure providers. Other forms occur between different communication platforms and the services offered over them. Convergence is raising challenges for the existing regulatory frameworks and requires adjustment in terms of emerging services. Internet broadcasting was born as a typical result of convergence between different telecommunications and broadcasting infrastructures and services and, currently, is the most representative example of this phenomenon.

Accordingly, regulatory trends of webcasting can be understood by examining the regulatory measures designed to address or to remedy technological convergence. Convergence constitutes a broader and larger problem in the analysis of webcasting policies.

This study selects the relevant experiences of the United States (US), the European Union (EU), and Japan as the main areas of research concern, not only because they have advanced telecommunications systems, but because they have each taken a different path in developing their telecommunications sectors. The US has the most sophisticated telecommunications system, and its regulatory framework rests on private ownership and market incentives. By establishing the first and most conspicuous telecommunications deregulation, the US could serve as a model for other less-developed countries, though its experience has by no means been uniformly positive.

On the other hand, the development of telecommunications policy in the EU has been marked by a relatively sceptical attitude toward "the workability of the market-economy system and . . . the possibility of catering to public benefits via the market mechanism" [22, p.55]. Perhaps because the weight of European history has favoured retaining the public monopoly model, the EU lags a little behind in telecommunications reform. Its member countries are, however, undergoing telecommunications liberalisation efforts and recognising the importance of competition in this area. Therefore, the EU can be considered a principal test case for the liberalisation of telecommunications services.

Japan liberalised its telecommunications after the US but leads Asia in deregulatory efforts. Since 1985 when the telecommunications industry was substantially reformed, Japan has shifted from government monopoly to market competition. However, this trend proceeds in Japan in a manner different from that in the US and the EU because of various cultural, legal, and social differences between East and West. Japan has much in common with other far eastern Asian countries in political, economic, social, and cultural respects including a traditionally slower pace of administrative reform. The Confucian commitment also maintains the cohesion of the social system. With due consideration of this distinctiveness, Japanese telecommunications policy is expected to be a useful laboratory for the policy-makers who are considering a non-Western type of telecommunications development.

8.2 Universal Service and Webcasting

This study focuses on universal service among various Internet policies because it is a public policy objective that lays the essential groundwork for the growth of Internet broadcasting. A universal service policy ensuring that all members of society have not only the greatest but also equal access to channels of information needs to be guaranteed if webcasting is to evolve.

No precise definition of universal service has ever been agreed upon among policy-makers and researchers. Any definition poses as many controversies as it settles issues. Resolving this ambiguity is not an easy task; nor is it the purpose of this study. Rather, this study adopts a broad view of universal service that probably fits to see how government furnishes environment advantage to the development of webcasting.

Among others, Miller [31] described universal service as having five components: (1) access, (2) usability, (3) training, (4) purpose, and (5) affordability (pp. 181–182). *Access* provides a connection for everyone who wants to plug in no matter where they live or work. *Usability* creates an interactive device and interface, with sufficient power and flexibility to be usable by people desiring to either produce or consume information for a wide variety of purposes. *Training* provides adequate support in a way that is sensitive to people's backgrounds and is integrated into the institutional context of their everyday lives. *Purpose* makes sure that the system can be used to accomplish personally and socially meaningful tasks for most of our population, an infrastructure for personal satisfaction and citizenship as well as economic gain. *Affordability* makes sure that the system is generally affordable and cost effective relative to other alternatives.

Concerning Internet broadcasting, the five elements of universal service can be converted into the following:

1. diffusion of computer terminals,
2. convenience of Internet use environment,
3. education of digital or information literacy, and
4. cost of Internet access.

The fact that universal service obligations exist as a primary policy objective in every developed country implies that similar benefits from widespread interconnectivity are perceived around the world. What are the factors leading to such similarity? Perhaps the best way to answer the question is to see how some of society's essential functions relocate within the new infrastructure.

Sawhney [47] stressed the importance of universal service at three distinctive levels (pp. 378–383). The first level is individual. The argument at this level starts with the assumption that access to the many modern communication services of the Internet is a basic human right – not unlike the right to speak. Every person has a right to these services by the mere virtue of being a citizen. The moral basis of this argument is that Internet services have now become so indispensable that an individual without access to them is not equipped for everyday life.

The second level is the social system. The basic argument is that the provision of services on a universal basis makes it possible for the social system as a whole to function more efficiently. The third level is general humanity. The discourse at this level is based on the natural connection between the craving for ubiquity and the desire for communion. The Internet is not simply a conduit for transporting information. The connections it creates have more to do with human interaction than do traditional, one-way electronic communications like television and radio.

For these reasons, universal service on the Internet is recognised by nearly all societies as being of immense social value. Moreover, because the Internet delivers value only to people using it regularly, a universal service policy regarding the medium is becoming more worthy of attention.

8.3 Technological Convergence and Free Market Ethos: The American Case

From its inception, US telecommunications has evolved differently from that of most other countries. Whereas European governments operated telecommunications directly, mainly in association with the post office, the US government allowed private companies to operate as regulated monopolies. Since the beginning, the US has relied on competitive forces to spur technological innovation and to enhance telecommunications services. However, during the last two decades, the US telecommunications industry has evolved from one dominated by a handful of closely regulated firms[1] to one in which a wide variety of providers using a multitude of new technologies compete to meet the increasingly sophisticated communications needs of businesses and consumers.

In the process, the divestiture of American Telephone and Telegraph (AT&T) especially undermined many of the traditional principles of the US telecommunications policy. It was closely linked to a broader trend in that the breakup was "used to expand the program of the deregulation of telecommunications" [23, p.244]. Indeed, the decade following divestiture saw competitive market forces dramatically reshape the telecommunications landscape.[2] Shaw [48] defined the period from the mid-1980s through 1995 as "an era in which, through initial experimentation with deregulation, the nation would experience unprecedented services" (p. 35).

---

[1] The most common justification for the reasoning is the problem of natural monopoly. It is defined as an industry in which the production technology is such that one producer can supply the entire market more cheaply than two or more producers. Examples are the public utilities such as telephony, water, gas, and electricity, where there is a requirement for a network of pipes or cables.

[2] Snow [49] offered, in considerable detail, an evaluation of the costs and benefits of the AT&T divestiture from the perspective of the 11 years since it entered into force.

The deregulatory trend reached a peak with the passage of the Telecommunications Act of 1996.[3] The overarching purpose of the Act was to deregulate all telecommunications industries and to permit the market to determine the telecommunications system. Until 1996, federal regulations kept telephone, cable television, and broadcast television industries separate from each other. The 1996 Act, however, changed the playing field considerably. It allowed cross-ownership across these media in an effort to encourage competition and technological innovation. Indeed, the local telephone markets, which had been serviced by the seven independent, but monopolistic RBOCs, were completely opened to the long-distance carriers and cable operators without any restriction.

With the lifting of the cross-ownership restriction, traditional cable companies also can start local phone businesses without any franchise. Both phone and cable companies may opt to create "open video systems" – pay television services – using any communications technology, by opening two-thirds of the channels on their systems to outsiders on an equal basis. In a word, the 1996 Act marks the biggest overhaul of US telecommunications policy since the Communications Act of 1934. The boundaries recognised and codified between broadcasting and telephony in the 1934 Act were broken down.[4]

By tearing down entry barriers, existing regulations no longer stand in the path of technological convergence. This approach seems to be adequate for the development of webcasting because the trend reflects technological convergence. Indeed, it is the convergence of technology that leads to even further deregulatory measures in US telecommunications. The tenet that a competitive marketplace is preferable for achieving the purpose has been mostly unquestioned because it is well suited to the political, economic, social, and legal atmosphere in the nation. The development of the Internet is highly illustrative of this belief.

The Internet, whose suzerain state is the US, was born during the 1960s out of an effort by the US Department of Defense (DOD) Advanced Research Projects Agency (ARPA) to create a non-centralised computer network. The rationale behind the development of the ARPAnet was the DOD's concern for maintaining the

---

[3] Public Law No. 104-104, 110 Stat. 56 (codified in scattered sections of 47 U.S.C.). The Act is simple in its basic principles. It covers three domains of communications: local and long-distance telecommunications services, broadcasting, and cable and video services. A special title of the Act, referred to as the "Communications Decency Act of 1996," addresses violence and obscenity on networks. The entire content of the 1996 Act is available at http://www.fcc.gov/Reports/tcom1996.txt. It is also included in an appendix of a book written by Shaw [48], along with a condensed version of the primary features of the Communications Act of 1934. An annotated bibliography about the 1996 Act is available in *Federal Communications Law Journal*, vol. 49 no. 3 (1997), pp. 771–783.

[4] Even though telecommunications in the US are subject to the primary jurisdiction of the federal government, potential conflicts with state regulators remain. On the state level, telecommunications enterprises are typically regulated through state public service commissions. Their activities resemble FCC regulation, but a wide variety exists between each of the 50 states. The 1996 Act does not make significant alterations to the existing state-level regulatory structure.

military's ability to communicate in the face of the destruction of one or more key links in the chain of command that might happen during a nuclear engagement.

The initial form of the Internet was not originally intended to provide any access to the general public. It was reserved strictly for military use. The turning point was the advent of USENET news, which resulted from the effort of computer scientists, responsible for the construction of the ARPAnet but excluded from connecting to the defense establishment. They built their own network to provide themselves with communication channels similar to ARPA's computer network in 1976 and interconnected the two networks in 1979. The advent of USENET marked the beginning of a rapid growth in the life of publicly accessible computer networks as well as the end of the military's control of the computer network [20, pp.129–132].

The ARPAnet split into military and civilian components in 1983, with the civilian component giving rise to what is now known as the Internet. In 1985, the National Science Foundation (NSF) began a program to establish Internet access across the US by creating a research "backbone"[5] called the NSFnet. For more than a decade, the networks of the Internet were all non-commercial and, if not directly subsidised, were indirectly subsidised by virtue of their free use of the cross-country NSFnet backbone. The services to operate the Internet were supplied under contract to the NSF by a service company, Advanced Network & Services (ANS), which was established by MCI, IBM, and Merit Networks. They sold ANS to America Online at a time when the contract with the NSFnet was terminated in 1995. The sale marks the transition of the backbone infrastructure of the Internet from federal funding to full private commercial operation [2, 26].

Today, the Internet is almost completely operated by private enterprises. They operate regional network access points, which in turn sell Internet access to local service providers, private enterprises, universities, and government agencies [2, p.62]. Both public organisations like government agencies, research institutes, and universities which rely on government funds, and private groups such as corporations and individuals not associated with government funds pay substantial monthly fees for access to the private companies which serve the Internet [5]. In this vein, the infrastructure on which communication via the Internet relies is almost entirely managed by commercial vendors, although "the assumption that the Internet is government-subsidized lingers" [26, p.6].

In addition, commercial use of the Internet greatly overshadows its academic and research uses. The commercial domain, ".com", replaced the educational one, ".edu", as the single largest domain in 1994. As Golding [21] noted, "the most significant change in the character of the WWW [World Wide Web] has been the irresistible rise of commercial sites" (p. 73). Indeed, the Internet itself has become "a commercial more medium", which is used to communicate marketplace information [44, p.239].

Indicative of this shift is the change of the mandate of the US government in the development of the Internet. Instead of intervening in Internet development directly, the government now takes a hands-off policy, relying on competitive market forces

---

[5] A backbone is a continental network carrier providing connectivity to regional networks.

to accelerate the deployment of advanced services through the nation. In particular, the Federal Communications Commission (FCC) has only taken numerous affirmative steps to ensure that the marketplace, not regulation, allows innovation and experimentation to flourish. The tendency of this kind is called "unregulation" beyond "deregulation".

The most representative example is *The FCC and the Unregulation of the Internet* which was released by the FCC Office of Plans and Policy on 19 July, 1999 [42]. The report analysed the FCC's 30-year history of not regulating the data services market and how that tradition of unregulation was a significant factor in the successful growth of the Internet. It stated that market forces had driven the Internet's growth, and the FCC had played a crucial role in creating a deregulatory environment in which the Internet could flourish. To take advantage of the lessons learned in three decades of unregulation of data networks, the report concluded that the FCC should not impose legacy regulations on new communication technologies. In particular, the report recommended that the FCC deregulate the old instead of regulate the new, when Internet-based services replace traditional communications services. Accordingly, Internet broadcasting is likely to evolve in the US without any restrictions.

The webcasting sector has rapidly grown in the US, but it is next to impossible to count how many Internet broadcasting stations provide services. In fact, the number of webcasters varies according to different ways of conceptualisation of the term, "webcasting".

Webcasting services are immature relative to traditional media services in terms of quality and accessibility. In particular, streaming video is still in an early development state owing to bandwidth. For this reason, the use of video is less than that of audio. By October 1998, five percent of American radio stations had been webcasting. At that time, broadcast.com carried some 345 commercial radio stations and sports broadcasts for 350 college and professional teams [45].

A study, conducted by Arbitron New Media and Edison Media Research, shows interesting results concerning Americans' Internet webcast usage [52]. The portion of Americans who have listened to radio stations over the Internet has soared from 18% to 30% between 1998 and 1999. A greater number of men have listened online compared with women, and most Internet tuning occurs at home. Most webcast users find Internet audio a very positive experience. Music, news coverage, and talk shows draw the largest Internet listening audiences. However, online radio listenership is not habitual yet.

Even though the US webcasting is to evolve without any government guidance, the governmental role will not invariably be pushed to the margins. This is because the development of webcasting can be affected by some form of "positive" public policies. It is universal service that the regulation itself can be credited as furthering, rather than limiting, the widespread use of Internet broadcasting.

In the US, a universal service principle grew out of 19th century populist concerns about equal access to basic services such as rail transport for agricultural foods. The concept developed as one of the basic themes of telephony policy. Theodore Vail, the architect of the AT&T system, expanded the concept of universal service in the early 1900s by defining it as a telephone in every home connected to every other telephone in the country [51]. He had attempted to deliver telephone services everywhere at an affordable cost as a corporate strategy of extending monopoly status for the powerful Bell company in return for embracing state regulation.

The concept of universal service was loosely articulated in Section 151 of the Communications Act of 1934. Since then, this notion has evolved with ongoing changes in technology and the marketplace.[6] The most recent codification of universal service was the Telecommunications Act of 1996 in which the FCC identified universal service as one of three main goals. As a result, universal service mainly applied to the monopoly telephone systems has become a public policy which is applicable to multimedia service.

The 1996 Act did not, however, specifically provide the definition of universal service. Instead, it required the FCC to create the Federal-State Joint Board on Universal Service for making recommendations to the FCC on a formal definition.[7] In 1997, the Joint Board proposed new rules to implement the provisions of universal service of the 1996 Act guaranteeing affordable telecommunications services, and the FCC adopted them on 7 May 1997. The new rules are grounded in seven general principles: (1) quality and rates; (2) access to advanced services; (3) access in rural and high-cost areas; (4) equitable and non-discriminatory contributions by service providers; (5) specific and predictable support mechanisms; (6) access to advanced services for schools, health care facilities, and libraries; and (7) competitive neutrality.[8]

Overall, the American attempt to fulfill the commitment to universal service is represented by the basic theme of the 1996 Act itself: the creation of competition across the full telecommunications field, even in areas that had previously been monopoly controlled. Even though universal service is a policy goal which government itself has to actively try to obtain, its approach is propelled by the governmental belief that a new marketplace will create not only the advantages of competition, but the unforeseeable benefits that result from new synergetic relationships between previously separated businesses and technologies [30, p.287].

Actually, the goal of universal service was articulated and implemented by the National Information Infrastructure (NII) initiative launched by the US government with the publication of *The National Information Infrastructure: Agenda for Action* on 15 September 1993. Since then, the NII has become a centrepiece of the current

---

[6] For more detailed explanations of conceptual changes of universal service, see [28, p.282].

[7] The Joint Board is made up of federal and state-appointed representatives and a state-appointed utility consumer advocate. The FCC will convene the Board to review the definition of universal service on or before 1 January 2001.

[8] While the first six were originally outlined in the 1996 Act, the last one was newly advanced by the Joint Board. Competitive neutrality suggests "universal service support mechanisms and rules [that] neither unfairly advantage or disadvantage one provider over another, and neither unfairly favor or disfavor one technology over another". For detailed explanations of each principle, see at http://www.fcc.gov/ccb/universal_service/fcc97157/97157.html or http://www.benton.org/Updates/summary.html.

Clinton Administration's information policy. In the general context of the NII, universal service has been referred to as a process of eliminating barriers so that everyone has the opportunity to use the telecommunications systems for effective participation in all aspects of society.

A central premise behind the NII universal service policy is also the encouragement of private investment, which ultimately promotes competition [43, p.95]. In this context, the NSFnet (which began as a DOD communication tool in the 1970s and functioned as backbone infrastructure) was shut down in 1994 when its governmental subsidy was removed. The government has gradually transferred the US portion of the global computer network to private companies since then.

The major reasoning behind the government's grander plan to deregulate cyberspace was well expressed in the *Agenda for Action* [24]. Identifying nine specific principles to guide governmental action, it presented the need for promoting private sector investment to extend universal service to guarantee that information resources were available to all at affordable prices. Working under the premise that deregulation would bring increased services, lower costs, and technological development, the government has attempted to realise the policy goal of universal service as well as build the NII within a market context.

Such a goal is consistent with the theme of deregulation that has guided US telecommunications policy on which the present Internet policy for universal service is also predicated. Telecommunications policy concerning universal service is closely related to the growth of webcasting because the widespread use of webcasting relies upon ubiquitous computer environment and computer literacy which are major elements of universal service. In this respect, the US has the basic conditions for the progress of webcasting.

8.4 Overcoming a Regional Unbalance: The European Case

The European approach to media policy significantly differs from the American one for a variety of historical reasons. Telecommunications policy is not an exception at all. When the telegraph and the telephone were first introduced throughout Europe in the latter part of the 19th century, there was a strong belief that telecommunications was a natural monopoly and that economies of scale were such that competition did not make sense. Therefore, telecommunications in most European countries was dominated by government-owned monopolies. Administration of telegraph and telephone networks was generally merged with the existing postal authority, which had had a monopoly over mail for generations. The new administration became known as the PTTs, for Post, Telegraph, and Telephone.[9]

Since the 1980s, many deregulatory reforms have been implemented in the hope of stimulating innovation and efficiency in this sector. Presently, the PTTs of Europe

---

[9] Noam [40] provided an excellent historical analysis of the development of telecommunications in Europe.

are experiencing unprecedented change. A major influence has been the divestiture of AT&T in the US, which has called into question the prevalent public concept of natural monopoly. Additionally, the privatisation and liberalisation of telecommunications in the United Kingdom beginning in 1984 provided a clear alternative to the monopoly model.

More broadly speaking, European countries' approaches to telecommunications restructuring have been boosted by the European integration process, aimed at creating a single common market.[10] Since the EU became fully aware of the enormous strategic importance of telecommunications in a global economy and recognised that the inefficiencies and high prices plaguing European telecommunications are detrimental to industrial development, it has developed itself into a major force in the reform of European telecommunications. Every telecommunications policy in Europe has to be balanced with new European policies.

The major policy-making institutions at the EU level include the Council of Ministers, the European Commission, and the European Parliament. In particular, the Commission was empowered by Article 90 of the 1957 Treaty of Rome to issue "directives"[11] that introduce or safeguard competition in sectors controlled by public enterprises that have been granted exclusive rights by national governments. Indeed, the Council plays a major role in guiding the various treaties signed by member states of the EU, in initiating policies, and in proposing legislation to the European Council. It also has the authority to control and regulate anti-competitive practices.

Since the mid-1980s when the European Commission listed the telecommunications sector as an industrial policy priority, telecommunications reforms in Europe have been strongly guided by a general blueprint in the form of directives, decisions, resolutions, recommendations, and community legislation. The most important Commission policy document regarding telecommunications is the *Green Paper* [6]. The principles laid out in it can be summarised as liberalisation and harmonisation. By illuminating the major characteristics of the future market structure in European telecommunications, the paper identified areas in which member states would have to take action to achieve the common goals, and it proposed how liberalisation and privatisation of member state telecommunications monopolies could take place. Specifically, four major goals were established in the *Green Paper*:

1. opening of terminal equipment markets to competition,
2. progressive introduction of competition in services,

---

[10] Under the framework of the Maastricht Treaty, which came into effect in 1993, the member states of the European Community are in the process of creating a broader EU where goods, services, capital, and people can move freely across national borders and many social and economic policies are to be harmonised. The content of the Treaty is available at http://europa.eu.int/en/record/mt/top.html.

[11] Directives as indirect forms of legislation are addressed to all EU countries. Directives lay down policy objectives to be realised by member states through national legislation. Since 1988, the European Commission has issued more than 90 directives.

3. separation of regulatory and operational activities, and
4. movement toward more cost-based tariffs.

The most significant step came with two directives approved on 28 June 1990. One is the Services Directive, a cornerstone for liberalising the European telecommunications market [7].[12] The other is the Open Network Provision (ONP) Directive, which established the framework for access to and use of telecommunications networks and services [14].[13]

The EU has approved various directives since 1990 that apply the principles to specific types of network infrastructures such as public-switched telephone networks, public-switched packet data networks, mobile services, intelligent networks, ISDN, and broadband communications networks. For example, the Commission enacted directives on competition in the markets for satellite services and equipment [9] and for mobile and personal communications [11]. Also, the Council extended the ONP principles to leased lines in 1992 [15] and to voice telephony services in 1995 [16] which was replaced by a new voice telephony directive in 1997 [17] .

Caby and Steinfield [4] concluded that these liberalisation trends by the EU can be summarised as efforts for

(a) creating an open and comprehensive market for telecommunications equipment, (b) progressively opening national markets to competitive supply of value-added services, and (c) curtailing the power of existing telecommunications administrations to use their regulatory authority to constrain competition in services or equipment. (p. 42)

Currently, the *White Paper on Growth, Competitiveness, and Employment* [8], with the full political support of the European Council, has placed the EU's telecommunications policy at the heart of the EU's general policy. As a follow-up to the *White Paper*, the Bangemann Group's [1] report on *Europe and the Global Information Society* has confirmed the EU's telecommunications regulatory agenda. The report pleads for a break with the past, ending state-owned monopolies and making rapid progress towards a fully liberalised environment. The strategic approach of this report was delineated in *Europe's Way to the Information Society*

---

[12] The Services Directive initiated an opening up to competition of the telecommunications services by providing for the removal of special or exclusive rights granted by member states for value-added services and data services. However, key basic services such as public voice telephony were temporarily permitted to remain under monopoly control. It also established deadlines for full liberalisation and required the separation of operational and regulatory functions.

[13] The ONP Directive sought to ensure open access to and harmonisation of conditions of access to publicly available telecommunications networks and services for both users and new service providers. Harmonisation covers three domains: (1) technical interfaces and/or service features, (2) supply and usage conditions, and (3) tariff principles. These conditions of ONP must not restrict access to networks and services, except for narrowly defined public interest reasons.

[10] and is still an underlying theme of the updated Action Plan adopted by the Commission in November 1996 and regularly updated.

As Waverman and Sirel [53] indicated, however, "while the European Commission recognized the importance of competition in telecommunications, implementing this understanding with long-established state-owned monopolies has not been an easy task" (p. 114). In spite of the EU's harmonising efforts, each European country has maintained its own unique approach to the provision of telecommunications. Indeed, according to a report in the *Economist*, even if all 12 of the EU countries became a single telecommunications market on 1 January 1998, the actual liberalisation would not proceed without a hitch [25, p.59].

For instance, new consortia such as Mannesmann Arcor and o.tel.o. in Germany, Cegetel in France, and Albacom in Italy have been formed to offer competitive telephone services. However, the consortia have been forbidden in most EU member states from offering public voice telephony—the biggest and most lucrative part of the service, even though this market is opened in Europe.

The discord between the EU and its member states also occurs in obtaining universal service goals which are essential for the development of Internet broadcasting. The maintenance of provision and financing of universal service in a deregulated environment as well as the concept of the service itself are based on the principles of universality, equality, continuity, and affordability. They appear in a number of EU legislative texts, in particular in the Voice Telephony [16,17] and the Interconnection Directives [18].[14] Universal service is specifically defined in the Interconnection Directive as "a defined minimum set of services of specified quality which is available to all users independent of their geographical location and, in the light of specific national conditions, at an affordable price". Currently, universal service obligations comprise connection to the public telephone network – at a fixed location – for telephone, fax, and data communications, as well as the provision of operator assistance, emergency and directory inquiry services (including the provision of subscriber directories), public pay-phones, and, where appropriate, special facilities for customers with disabilities or special needs. By including network access, this definition ensures that users access any service provided over today's telecommunication networks, most notably online services including the Internet.

Affordability is so crucial to the extension of telecommunications services to every citizen that it has emerged as a key element in any concept of universal service, but is not yet an explicit requirement of the Voice Telephony Directive. Affordability remains a matter to be determined at a national level because it is closely linked to specific national circumstances and national policy objectives.

---

[14] Whereas the Interconnection Directive defines the scope of universal service for funding purposes, the Voice Telephony Directive provides a detailed picture of the level of service users should receive. One of the most important elements introduced by the Voice Telephony Directive is the requirement for member states to ensure that universal service is provided at an affordable price.

The shift from a monopoly environment to competition suggests that rules are needed to determine the extent to which any financial burden associated with providing universal service is shared among market players. Nevertheless, no requirement is imposed on member states to set up schemes for sharing the financial burden of universal service. Each nation is just required to respect Community law and common rules for calculating and financing universal service without discriminating between competitors when it decides to establish some schemes. Likewise, the EU framework does not require member states to take specific measures on crucial points of universal service policy. It just provides the general principles necessary to unite member states under a single market.

Each EU member state used the EU suggestions to formulate its own schemes for universal service so that they do not conflict with European efforts to achieve regional co-operation. For example, the German universal service program is strongly based on the belief that "market forces will supply everybody with telecommunications services at an affordable price and that government intervention will only be necessary if it turns out that this is not the case in certain areas" [29, p.408]. Although effective competition is conceived to benefit both residential and business Internet users in terms of choice, quality, and prices, specific measures have not been well refined for the smooth operation of the market mechanism. This indicates that universal service supposed to contribute to the growth of Internet broadcasting would not be realised with little trouble.

Additionally, Germany has undertaken two legislative initiatives to create specific rules for the Internet and to codify existing laws to ensure their applicability to the Internet. They are the Interstate Media Services Treaty (*Mediendienste-Staatsvertrag*, MdStV) and the Information and Communication Services Act (*Informations- und Kommunikationsdienste-Gesetz,* IuKDG).

These two multimedia laws went into effect on 1 August 1997, after the states developed the MdStV and the federal government the IuKDG.[15] With the introduction of the laws, media services have been differentiated from tele-services. The MdStV is only concerned with media services which are offered to an unspecified, general public such as tele-shopping, videotext, and media on demand. The IuKDG regulates information and communication services which are designed for individual use and which are based on transmission by means of telecommunication. They include online services, tele-banking, and tele-medicine.

This approach is adequate in terms of technological convergence. Nevertheless, by attempting to apply existing, strict restrictions on Internet speech, for example, German policies make the EU's general aim to cohere different national approaches in the age of convergence difficult to realise. This incongruity could become a barrier to webcast use in the EU as well as in Germany.

---

[15] The enactment of both laws is characterised as a compromise or a tentative agreement between the states and the federal government which had fought a bitter feud over who would regulate new online and multimedia services. While the states argued that the Internet and other online services should fall under their authority to regulate the media and broadcasting, the federal government assumed the Internet to be under its authority to regulate interpersonal communication and commerce [3].

By the same token, the challenges the EU is facing were well illustrated in the *First Monitoring Report on Universal Service in Telecommunications in the European Union*[16] [13]. According to the report, the current state of universal service in the European telecommunications sector can be characterised by the different levels of development. Only 13.9 percent of Portuguese households had one or more PCs compared with 53.5 percent and 47.8 percent in the Netherlands and Sweden, respectively. There were only 1.8 Internet hosts and 35.8 webpages per 1,000 population in Portugal compared with 65.4 hosts and 283.1 pages in Finland.[17] Also, only four member states had provided estimates of the net cost of universal service, but nine out of 15 member states did not find that specific funding for universal service was required at the moment of opening their markets to full competition. These different levels of development substantially undermine the goal of realising universal service, because the existence of a certain minimum set of infrastructure is essential for the widespread use of webcasting. The unequal levels in the member states will hamper the take-off of Europe-wide webcasting services.

Nevertheless, webcasting in Europe has rapidly grown relative to other new media. According to the European Broadcasting Union's extensive report on the state of streaming players via the Internet in Europe, the number of pure audio webcasters was about 8,000 and the number of audio and video webcasters was around 750 [19].

One of the major reasons that the European webcasting market has not developed as fast as in the US is the high price of leased lines or dedicated circuits. Furthermore, most European countries have no flat-rate structure for local service, so all calls to service providers are charged per minute. Both Internet provider and user telephone rates are very high, which makes it costly both for business and private customers to link to the Internet and for service providers to develop their networks and provide cost-effective services.

To reduce and remove these barriers and stimulate development, the EU has encouraged its member states to adopt the prospect of telecommunications competition and to enhance Internet access and use in educational institutions. In 1997, general indications were that, depending upon the type of school and member state concerned, between 15% and 60% of schools were connected to the Internet and that the numbers were growing fast. Currently, a wide range of initiatives are underway in the context of the action plan, "Learning in the Information Society". This policy drive can be evaluated as positive to Internet broadcasting growth and vitality.

---

[16] This report followed from the first systematic survey of telecommunications service indicators in the EU which was published in March 1996 [12] and responded to the call of the European Parliament for the Commission to report on a regular basis on universal service in the EU. It also examined for the first time the private and public use of the Internet drawing on information provided by National Regulatory Agencies.

[17] The *First Monitoring Report* noted that, in the absence of systematic and comparable information on Internet users, the main pointer to the level and rate of development of Internet services can be such indicators as personal computer penetration, the growth of Internet hosts, and the number of webpages.

8.5 Government Guidance for an Information Society: The Japanese Case

Webcasting in Japan is a subject that stands in the path of technological convergence between telecommunications and broadcasting. Most debates concerning the issue have been evolved around the term, "info-communications".

The Japanese Ministry of Posts and Telecommunications (MPT) is forging ahead with "secondary info-communications reform" as a means of reforming socioeconomic structures for the 21st century [37]. Since the first info-communications reform started in 1985 with the liberalisation of the telecommunications sector and privatisation of Nippon Telegraph and Telephone Public Corporation (NTT), there have been a significant number of new entrants and a drastic reduction in the number of non-competitive areas of the telecommunications market [41].

This process has promoted benefits and greater convenience for Internet users in Japan. According to the *White Paper* [33], there is increasing use of the Internet in Japan. By January 1998, the number of access points for Internet dial-up IP connections had reached about 4,600 nationwide (p. 40). In 1997, 6.4 percent of households held subscriptions to Internet access services, which was up 3.1 percentage points from a year earlier (p. 4). In addition, as of January 1998, Japan had the second largest number of hosts in the world with about 1.17 million or 3.9 percent of the total (p. 40).

However, Japan had become a lumbering giant with slow economic growth by the mid-1990s. The telecommunications sector now faces an entirely new situation driven by the globalisation of the industry, the diversification and sophistication of consumer needs, and the introduction of multimedia services supported by technical innovation. These are growing increasingly important and are major tasks for the future of Japan. These factors, together with the success of the first reform, provided an impetus for the initiation of the secondary reform.

To imbue the telecommunications sector with a new dynamism, the Japanese government implemented a "three-in-one" policy: promotion of deregulation, promotion of network connection, and reorganisation of NTT [39,41]. The three policy programs depend on the market mechanism for obtaining the goal of the secondary reform. But the government does recognise that there are problems that cannot be resolved by this approach alone. It is particularly concerned that inequality will arise between regions and between individuals in their ability to participate in the new information system if everything is left to market forces. Therefore, the Japanese government has taken the lead in establishing the second deregulatory policy in the telecommunications sector. The *Vision 21 for Info-Communications* specifically stipulated that the government play the roles of presenter of a clear vision, developer of information infrastructure, promoter of dynamic competition, and ensurer of social fairness [39].

The most recent policy document stressing the significance of the secondary info-communications reform is *Principles of Major Info-communications Policies for Fiscal 2000* [34]. It proposed three major aims of government measures to rebuild the Japanese economy:

1. building a foundation for growth in the 21st century,
2. creating new industries and jobs, and
3. enabling all citizens to participate in the information-based society.

The document did not present any specific vision for the development of Internet broadcasting. But concrete policy targets under the first principle are set to develop advanced Internet technologies, to improve network infrastructure, and to advance a low-cost and secure Internet environment which are essential components for the development of webcasting. The document also placed promotion of opportunities for disabled people, improvement of information literacy, and introduction of information technology to local communities as main policy targets to achieve the third principle. This policy trend is expected to build a foundation for the widespread use of Internet broadcasting.

A document more related to webcasting is *Diversified Info-communications Developments on the Road to Creation of the Cyber Society* [36]. It described how radical changes had emerged as a result of the tremendous growth in the use of the Internet and then mentioned the convergence of telecommunications and broadcasting as one of the major issues to deal with. According to the document, convergence occurs in four areas: services, lines, businesses, and terminals. Internet broadcasting is a typical example of the convergence of services which covers the area between telecommunications and broadcasting.

Although the four forms of convergence are mutually connected, they are different from each other in nature. Because they cannot be covered by the same measures, it is imperative to make it clear what aspects of convergence are to be the subjects of the discussions on convergence. With regard to the types of distributing information other than existing broadcasting, for instance, discussions should take place on whether the existing disciplines for broadcasting like the obligation to establish a consultative organisation on broadcast programmes could be applied to Internet broadcasting. It has also become necessary to discuss whether special measures applied to telecommunications, such as the legislation of exception on secrecy of communications, are needed in Internet broadcasting. However, the document did not provide any answer to these matters. They remain topics of continuing debate.

In addition, the document pointed out key elements for the improvement of circumstances on the road to the cyber society as long-term goals. They include improving Internet users' ability, protecting the rights and benefits of users, and assisting elderly people and handicapped persons. What is worthy of mention here is the Japanese governmental efforts to enhance information literacy which is closely related to the goal of universal service.

Universal service became a national issue in October 1994 when the Japanese Study Group for Research into Universal Services and Rates in the Multimedia Age was formed. The group carried out a comprehensive study from various perspectives concerning desirable universal services and tariff systems to facilitate new business deployment and access by all people to advanced information services in the coming multimedia age. It issued an interim report in 1995 and a final report on 31 May 1996.

The interim report mainly discussed the telephone rate structure. Because the metered local system was not suitable for computer communications, a local flat-rate service was proposed. NTT, considering the rapid rise of peak usage and the capacity problem, introduced in 1995 a local flat-rate only during the off-peak period (11:00 p.m. to 8:00 a.m.).

The final report has two sections titled "Rates in the Multimedia Age" and "Universal Services in the Multimedia Age" [32]. The first section noted that "demand-stimulating rates"[18] were necessary and suitable for the coming multimedia age. The adoption of rate systems that are independent of the data volume and more suited to calls of extended duration such as a flat-rate system was also recommended.

The second section explained that multimedia services would be indispensable in people's daily lives in the near future. At the same time, it proposed that the scope of universal service – which was then limited to plain old telephone service – be expanded because there was a fear that social inequities might increase due to differences in accessibility.

Therefore, the section classified universal services into two types: multimedia access service and multimedia service. While multimedia access service covers broadband network service and network facility services, multimedia service includes several kinds of application services such as tele-education and tele-medicine. In this regard, the telephone carrier (including NTT and private carriers) is supposed to provide access service, and non-telephone companies are to offer multimedia services. For example, tele-medicine can be provided by hospitals and tele-education by schools. Internet access service falls between them.

This indicates that defining multimedia universal service is easy, but it is difficult to define who would be service providers and who would be participants of the universal service fund. According to Sugaya [50], the easiest way to solve such complicated problems is to exclude multimedia service from advanced universal service. But this is so unattractive that the rather broad concept, as defined by the Universal Service Group, is currently supported by the majority (p. 184).

As a whole, the Japanese approach is predicated on establishing a competitive marketplace, but it permits a significant degree of governmental involvement in realising universal service obligations. The services are proposed as forms of regional information plans by various government ministries. For instance, the Ministry of International Trade and Industry projects "new media communities", while the MPT sponsors "teletopias", and the Ministry of Agriculture has its own "greentopia" [54, p.87]. The role of the ministries is to propose the general design of

---

[18] In this concept, rates would be set low from the initial stage of network implementation to promote the diffusion of multimedia services, thereby expanding the market and consequently lowering the charges paid by users.

a particular information plan to local governments. If local governments authorise any model, the central government will give tax reductions and low-interest loans to the local government to construct the projected telecommunications infrastructure in a particular region [50, p.180].

The provision of universal services in Japan depends upon dynamic competition in the regional markets, which is similar to the cases of the US and the EU. However, the Japanese approach differs from the others in that it allows both central and local governments to be involved more actively in introducing an advanced multimedia system in each region in addition to establishing a neutral, independent support system. This propensity does not conflict with a larger political and social climate in which excessive competition unbounded by governmental guidance is not believed to be beneficial to the public. Actually, the government itself has had an important role in pursuing the secondary reform as well as in creating a postwar economic miracle in Japan.

Recently, the Japanese government has become particularly concerned that information disparity has emerged between different geographical areas because the market gives priority to metropolitan areas in establishing the new infrastructure. The information gap also occurs between the information-literate and information-illiterate like the elderly, the handicapped, and the low-income class. This gap, in turn, increases economic disparity. A MPT study found white-collar workers in Japan who were able to use PCs earned 19 percent more than those who could not [27].

To fill these gaps by making it easier to access the Internet and by improving PC and network literacy, the Japanese government actively intervenes in realising universal service, assumed to be a new basic human right in the info-communications society [38]. These efforts are supposed to create an environment conducive to the growth of Internet broadcasting.

Contrary to the positive factors for webcasting, a survey conducted by the MPT in March 1999 showed that the medium would not be popular among Japanese Internet users in the near future. According to a *Fiscal 1998 Communications Usage Trend Survey* [35], online services usage increased from the previous year only 4.5 percentage points to 10.2%. The number of households that would like to use an online service within one year or one of these days was 52.0%, which was a 5.5 percentage points increase from a year earlier. In a similar way, Internet usage rate increased just 4.6 percentage points to 11.0%. Household heads who would like to use the Internet were 53.0%, which was up 4.5 percentage points since the previous year. In terms of the rapid expansion of Internet users in most advanced countries, the rates are very low.

Additionally, households' purposes for online services and Internet usage were "acquisition of business information, business documentation" (59.1%), followed by "contact with particular people/communication" (57.1%) and "acquisition of personal information for travel or hobby" (52.9%). Among services anticipated in the near future due to advances in Internet technologies, Japanese respondents most wanted to try "screen medical consultation with a physician" (46.6%), followed by "government administration services such as reserving public facilities" (26.8%).

The fact that most of the services mentioned here are not related to services typically provided by webcasters darkens the outlook for the future of Internet broadcasting.

One of the reasons for the negative prospect comes from the fact that Japan is a non-individualist, group-centered society which is the most timeworn of all truisms about the country [46, p.219]. In Japan, the locus of identity is identified in very cohesive groups rather than isolated individuals and diverse views largely emanate from the former. Furthermore, the freedom of expression of groups is better protected than that of individuals. This "groupism" culture values individual reticence and, in many contexts, views aggressive assertion of personal opinion as reprehensible. This point can be extended to other far eastern Asian countries that are in the midst of structuring their Internet environments in one way or another.

8.6 Summary

The US has led the worldwide deregulatory movements in telecommunications. It has had little difficulty in adopting deregulatory measures in this sector. Its prevailing social and political culture has an explicit deregulatory intent. Governmental restrictions are kept to a minimum to enhance a competitive atmosphere. For this reason, the US lays underlying groundwork to deal with legal problems arising out of the rapid technological convergence of new information services and to bring the American legal system into line with the requirements of the changing environment. In particular, the US adheres to a hands-off policy in the Internet, believing a competitive marketplace is preferable for accelerating the deployment of advanced services throughout the nation. This policy propensity is likely to continue in the field of webcasting. Universal service is a major means of spreading the benefits of market developments to all Internet users. Its policy objective is in the context of the vision for the NII whose success is predicated on the effective operation of market mechanisms. This set of factors – free market ethos and consistency of telecommunications policy – has provided fertile soil for webcasting growth and vitality.

This is not the case in the EU, where a belief in the public telecommunications system imputed a different meaning to regulation. There, telecommunications deregulation is better understood in terms of regional pressures than in terms of a faith in market mechanisms. The EU's initiatives for the economic integration of Europe are the key regional factors for member states adopting deregulatory policies in telecommunications. The EU has generated various policy documents and directives since 1990 that apply free marketplace reasoning to technological convergence between telecommunications and broadcasting. The universal service policy of each member state especially reflects the EU's belief that a competitive market can achieve its goals. However, unequal levels of development concerning the Internet environment as well as little experience of utilising a competitive marketplace obstruct the widespread deployment and use of Internet broadcasting.

The Japanese case provides a rather different story. Its approach is predicated on establishing a competitive marketplace in general, but it permits a significant degree of government involvement in both entering into an information society and realising universal service obligations. Recognising telecommunications as an expanding economic sector with potential for growth, the government has made efforts to enhance the industry competitiveness by permitting and facilitating intensified competition among telecommunications companies. Despite the relevancy of the deregulatory policy in telecommunications in terms of technological convergence, the policy transition has had to contend with the existing cultures and traditions of the relevant nation. Such nation-specific considerations as groupism culture often take precedence over the universal driving force for telecommunications deregulation in Japan. This makes it difficult to witness the take-off of webcasting services in the country.

References

[1]   Bangemann Group (1994) "Europe and the global information society", available at http://www2.echo.lu/eudocs/en/bangemann.html, accessed on 15 October 1999.

[2]   Baran N (1996) "Privatization of telecommunications", Monthly Review: An Independent Socialist Magazine, 48, 3, 59–69.

[3]   Braun P & Schaal A (1997) "Federalism, the nation state and the global network: the case of German communications policy", paper presented at the Harvard information infrastructure project conference, available at http://ksgwww.harvard.edu/iip/iicompol Papers/Braun-Schaal.html, accessed on 12 May 2000.

[4]   Caby L & Steinfield C (1994) "Trends in the liberalization of European telecommunications: community harmonization and national divergence" in Steinfield C, Bauer J & Caby L (Eds.) "Telecommunications in Transition: Policies, Services and Technologies in the European Community", 36–48, Sage, Thousand Oaks.

[5]   Calabrese A & Borchert M (1996) "Prospects for electronic democracy in the United States: rethinking communication and social policy", Media, Culture & Society, 18, 2, 249–268.

[6]   Commission of the European Communities (1987) "Towards a dynamic European economy – green paper on the development of the common market for telecommunications services and equipment", COM (87) 290.

[7]   Commission of the European Communities (1990) "Commission directive of 28 June 1990 on competition in the markets for telecommunications services", 90/388/EEC; OJ L 192/10, available at http://www.ispo.cec.be/infosoc/legreg/docs/90388eec.html, accessed on 12 May 2000.

[8]   Commission of the European Communities (1993) "White paper on growth, competitiveness, and employment", COM (93) 700, available at http://europa.eu.int/en /record/white/c93700/contents.html, accessed on 12 May 2000.

[9]   Commission of the European Communities (1994) "Commission directive of 13 October 1994 amending directive 88/301/EEC and directive 90/388/EEC in particular with regard to satellite communications", 94/46/EC; OJ L 268/15, available at http://www.ispo.cec.be/infosoc/legreg/docs/9446ec.html, accessed on 12 May 2000.

[10]   Commission of the European Communities (1994) "Europe's way to the information society: an action plan", COM (94) 347, available at http://www2.echo.lu/eudocs/en /com-asc.html, accessed on 12 October 1999.

[11] Commission of the European Communities (1996) "Commission directive of 16 January 1996 amending directive 90/388/EEC with regard to mobile and personal communications", 96/2/EC; OJ L 20/59, available at http://www.ispo.cec.be/infosoc /legreg /docs/962ec.html, accessed on 12 May 2000.

[12] Commission of the European Communities (1996) "Communication to the European parliament, the council, the economic and social committee and the committee of the regions: universal service for telecommunications in the perspective of a fully liberalised environment – an essential element of the information society", COM (96) 73 final, available at http://www.ispo.cec.be/infosoc/telecompolicy/en/d8.htm, accessed on 12 May 2000.

[13] Commission of the European Communities (1998) "Communication to the European parliament, the council, the economic and social committee and the committee of the regions: first monitoring report on universal service in telecommunications in the European Union", available at http://www.ispo.cec.be/infosoc/telecompolicy/en /ip98182.html, accessed on 12 May 2000.

[14] Council of the European Communities (1990) "Council directive of 28 June 1990 on the establishment of the internal market for telecommunications services through the implementation of open network provision", 90/387/EEC; OJ L 192/1, available at http://www.ispo.cec.be/infosoc/legreg/docs/90387eec.html, accessed on 12 May 2000.

[15] Council of the European Communities (1992) "Council directive of 5 June 1992 on the application of open network provision to leased lines", 92/44/EEC; OJ L 165/27, available at http://www.ispo.cec.be/infosoc/legreg/docs/9244eec.html, accessed on 12 May 2000.

[16] Council of the European Communities (1995) "Council directive of 13 December 1995 on the application of open network provision to voice telephony", 95/62/EC; OJ L 321/6, available at http://www.ispo.cec.be/infosoc/legreg/docs/9562ec.html, accessed on 12 May 2000.

[17] Council of the European Communities (1997a) "Common position adopted by the council on 9 June 1997 with a view to adopting council directive 97//EC of the European parliament and of the council on the application of open network provision to voice telephony and on universal service for telecommunications in a competitive environment", available at http://www.ispo.cec.be/infosoc/legreg/docs/onpvoice.html, accessed on 12 May 2000.

[18] Council of the European Communities (1997) "Directive 97/33/EC of the European parliament and of the council of 30 June 1997 on interconnection in telecommunications with regard to ensuring universal service and interoperability through application of the principles of open network provision", OJ L 199/32, available at http://www.ispo.cec.be/infosoc/telecompolicy/en/d1-en.htm, accessed on 12 May 2000.

[19] European Broadcasting Union Webcasting Group (1999) The New Range of Opportunities for Traditional Broadcasters, available at http://www.rnw.nl/corporate /ebu.html, accessed on 12 May 2000.

[20] Giese M (1996) "From ARPA to the Internet: a cultural clash and its implications in framing the debate on the information superhighway" in Strate L, Jacobson R & Gibson S (Eds.) "Communication and Cyberspace: Social Interaction in an Electronic Environment", 123–141, Hampton Press, Cresskill.

[21] Golding P (1996) "World wide wedge: division and contradiction in the global information infrastructure", Monthly Review: An Independent Socialist Magazine, 48, 3, 70–85.

[22] Hoffmann-Riem W (1984) "Policy research on telecommunications in West Germany" in Mosco V (Ed.) "Policy Research in Telecommunications: Proceedings from the Eleventh Annual Telecommunications Policy Research Conference", 55–70, Ablex, Norwood.

[23] Horwitz R (1989) The Irony of Regulatory Reform: The Deregulation of American Telecommunications, Oxford University Press, New York.

[24] Information Infrastructure Task Force (1993) The National Information Infrastructure: Agenda for Action, U.S. Department of Commerce, Washington, DC, available at http://sunsite.unc.edu/nii/NII-Agenda-for-Action.html, accessed on 12 May 2000.

[25] "In the shark pond" (3 January 1998) The Economist, 345, 8049, 59–60.

[26] Kahin B (1995) "The Internet and the national information infrastructure" in Kahin B & Keller J (Eds.) "Public Access to the Internet", 3–23, MIT Press, Cambridge.

[27] "Keyboard allergy dangerous to financial health" (1999) Japan Internet Report, 34, available at http://www.tkai.com/jir/jir1_99.html, accessed on 15 October 1999.

[28] Kim J (1998) "Universal service and Internet commercialization: chasing two rabbits at the same time", Telecommunications Policy, 22, 4/5, 281–288.

[29] Kubicek H (1997) "Multimedia: Germany's third attempt to move to an information society" in Kahin B & Wilson E (Eds.) "National Information Infrastructure Initiatives: Vision and Policy Design", 387–423, MIT Press, Cambridge.

[30] Meyerson M (1997) "Ideas of the marketplace: a guide to the 1996 telecommunications act", Federal Communications Law Journal, 49, 2, 251–288.

[31] Miller S (1996) Civilizing Cyberspace: Policy, Power, and the Information Superhighway, ACM Press, New York.

[32] Ministry of Posts and Telecommunications (1996) "Report submitted by study group for research into universal services and rates in the multimedia age", available at http://www.mpt.go.jp/pressrelease/english/telecomm/news7-7-2.html, accessed on 12 May 2000.

[33] Ministry of Posts and Telecommunications (1998) White Paper: Communications in Japan, 1998, available at http://www.mpt.go.jp/policyreports/english/papers/White Paper 1998.pdf, accessed on 27 November 1999.

[34] Ministry of Posts and Telecommunications (1999) "Principles of major info-communications policies for fiscal 2000: reviving the Japanese economy through info-communications", available at http://www.mpt.go.jp/whatsnew/Major_Policy.html, accessed on 12 May 2000.

[35] Ministry of Posts and Telecommunications (1999) "Fiscal 1998 communications usage trend survey", available at http://www.mpt.go.jp/data/communications/trend_survey 1998_1-1b.html, accessed on 12 May 2000.

[36] Ministry of Posts and Telecommunications Communications Policy Bureau (1998) "Diversified info-communications developments on the road to creation of the cyber society", available at http://www.mpt.go.jp/policyreports/english/group/communica-tions/convergence.html, accessed on 12 May 2000.

[37] Ministry of Posts and Telecommunications Telecommunications Council (1994) "Reforms toward the intellectually creative society of the 21st century: program for the establishment of high-performance info-communications infrastructure", available at http://www.mpt.go.jp/policyreports/english/telecouncil/Report1993No5/contents.html, accessed on 12 May 2000.

[38] Ministry of Posts and Telecommunications Telecommunications Council (1995) "For achieving globalization of an 'intellectually creative society': interim report", available

at: http://www.mpt.go.jp/policyreports/english/telecouncil/Interim_Report/index.html, accessed on 12 May 2000.

[39] Ministry of Posts and Telecommunications Telecommunications Council (1997) "Vision 21 for info-communications: policies to be promoted as we approach the 21st century and the specific socioeconomic conditions that will emerge", available at http://www.mpt.go.jp/policyreports/english/telecouncil/v21-9706/v21-9706-e.html, accessed on 12 May 2000.

[40] Noam E (1992) Telecommunications in Europe, Oxford University Press, New York.

[41] Organization for Economic Cooperation and Development (1999) Communications Outlook 1999, available at http://www.oecd.org/dsti/sti/it/index.htm, accessed on 12 May 2000.

[42] Oxman J (1999) "The FCC and the unregulation of the Internet", available at http:www.fc.gov/Bureaus/OPP/News_Releases/1999/nrop9004.html, accessed on 12 May 2000.

[43] Perritt Jr H (1995) "Access to the national information infrastructure", Wake Forrest Law Review, 30, 1, 51–103.

[44] Pridgen D (1997) "How will consumers be protected on the information superhighway?" Land & Water Law Review, 32, 1, 237–255.

[45] "Remarks by William E. Kennard to NAB radio convention" (16 October 1998), available at http://www.fcc.gov/Speeches/Kennard/spwek832.txt, accessed on 12 May 2000.

[46] Rosen D (1997) "Surfing the sento", Berkeley Technology Law Journal, 12, 1, 213–230.

[47] Sawhney H (1994) "Universal service: prosaic motives and great ideals", Journal of Broadcasting & Electronic Media, 38, 4, 375–395.

[48] Shaw J (1998) Telecommunications Deregulation, Artech House, Boston.

[49] Snow M (1995) "The AT&T divestiture: a 10-year retrospective" in Lamberton D (Ed.) "Beyond Competition: The Future of Telecommunications", 207–226, Elsevier, Amsterdam.

[50] Sugaya M (1997) "Advanced universal service in Japan", Telecommunications Policy, 21, 2, 177–184.

[51] Temin P (1987) The Fall of the Bell System: A Study in Prices and Politics, Cambridge University Press, New York.

[52] Verdino G & Rosin L (1999) "Arbitron/Edison media research Internet study III: webcasters vs. broadcasters – which business model will win?", available at http://www.arbitron.com/studies/internetIII.pdf, accessed on 12 May 2000.

[53] Waverman L & Sirel E (1997) "European telecommunications markets on the verge of full liberalization", Journal of Economic Perspectives, 11, 4, 113–126.

[54] West J, Dedrick J & Kraemer K (1997) "Back to the future: Japan's NII plans" in Kahin B & Wilson E (Eds.) "National Information Infrastructure Initiatives: Vision and Policy Design", 61–111, MIT Press, Cambridge.

Chapter 9

A Source-adaptive Multi-layered Multicast Algorithm for Internet Video Distribution

Célio Albuquerque, Brett J. Vickers and Tatsuya Suda

9.1 Introduction

The simultaneous multicast of video to many receivers is complicated by variation in the amount of bandwidth available throughout the network. The use of layered video is commonly recommended to address this problem. A multi-layered video encoder encodes raw video data into one or more streams, or layers, of differing priority. The layer with the highest priority, called the *base layer*, contains the most important portions of the video stream, while additional layers, called *enhancement layers*, are encoded with progressively lower priorities and contain data that further refines the quality of the base layer stream. For each unique bandwidth constraint, the encoder generates an enhancement layer of video, thereby ensuring that all receivers obtain a quality of video commensurate with their available bandwidth.

However, multi-layered encoding of video is not sufficient to provide ideal video quality and bandwidth utilisation. Due to competing network traffic, bandwidth constraints change continually and rapidly. To improve the bandwidth utilisation of the network and optimise the quality of video obtained by each of the receivers, the sender must persistently respond to these changing network conditions. It should dynamically adjust the number of video layers it generates as well as the rate at which each layer is transmitted. For the sender to do this, it must have congestion feedback from the receivers and the network.

We define a Source-Adaptive Multi-layered Multicast (SAMM) algorithm as any multicast algorithm that uses congestion feedback to adapt the transmission rates of multiple layers of data. Our previous work [1, 2 , 3, 30, 31] has focused on network-based SAMM algorithms, in which it was assumed that network switches were capable of executing complex flow and congestion control algorithms. However, in most existing networks and internetworks, where datagram routing and forwarding are often the only universally shared operations, the existence of such congestion control functions cannot be assumed.

We focus on an end-to-end SAMM algorithm that can be implemented in next generation Internets. Prerequisites for its implementation include router-based priority packet discarding and flow isolation via either class-based queueing or fair queueing. In the algorithm, video receivers generate congestion feedback to the sender by monitoring the arrival rate of video traffic, and feedback packets are merged by an overlaid virtual network of feedback merging servers. Network switches or routers are not required to implement flow or congestion control algorithms.

The remainder of this work is organised as follows. Trade-offs between sender-driven and receiver-driven approaches to layered multicast are considered in Section 9.2. The details of the end-to-end SAMM algorithm are described in Section 9.3. An encoder rate control algorithm for adaptive, multi-layered video encoding is presented in Section 9.4. The performance of the algorithm in terms of scalability, responsiveness, and fairness is compared with that of a non-adaptive algorithm in Section 9.5. Concluding remarks are provided in Section 9.6.

9.2 Sender-Driven vs. Receiver- Driven Adaptation

Adaptation to network congestion may be sender-driven or receiver-driven. In a sender-driven algorithm, the source adapts its transmission rate in response to congestion feedback from the network or the receivers. In a receiver-driven algorithm, the source transmits several sessions of data, and the receivers adapt to congestion by changing the selection of sessions to which they listen.

9.2.1 Background

Sender-driven congestion control for adaptively encoded video was first examined in the context of point-to-point communications. A number of works in this area have proposed algorithms in which information about the current congestion state of the network is passed via network feedback packets to the video source, and the source adjusts its encoding rate in response [17, 18, 19, 23, 27]. These works illustrate the effectiveness of transmitting video using sender-driven adaptation to congestion but do so only for the unicast case.

One of the first examinations of sender-driven congestion control for multicast video was performed by Bolot, Turletti and Wakeman [10]. In their algorithm, the source adaptively modifies the video encoding rate in response to feedback from the receivers. This is done to reduce network congestion when necessary and increase video quality when possible. To prevent feedback implosion, each receiver probabilistically responds with congestion feedback at a frequency which is a function of the total number of receivers. While this algorithm considers the problem of multicast, it uses only a single layer of video, and thus a few severely bandwidth-constrained paths can negatively impact the rate of video transmitted across paths that have more plentiful bandwidth.

The Destination Set Grouping (DSG) algorithm by Cheung, Ammar and Li [11] was one of the first to deal with the problem of heterogeneous bandwidth constraints in multicast video distribution, and it shares features of both receiver-driven and sender-driven approaches. The algorithm attempts to satisfy heterogenous bandwidth constraints by offering a small number of independently encoded video streams, each encoded from the same raw video material but at different rates. The streams are targeted to different groups of receivers, and their rates are adjusted according to probabilistic congestion feedback from each group. However, one important drawback of this algorithm is that the transmission of independently encoded video streams results in an inefficient use of bandwidth.

McCanne, Jacobson and Vetterli proposed the first truly receiver-driven adaptation algorithm for the multicast of layered video [21]. In the algorithm, known as Receiver-driven Layered Multicast (RLM), the video source generates a fixed number of layers, each at a fixed rate, and the receivers "subscribe" to as many layers as they have the bandwidth to receive. Congestion is monitored at the receivers by observing packet losses. This approach has the advantage that it uses video layering to address heterogeneous bandwidth constraints. However, it limits the receivers to choosing among the layers the source is willing to provide, and in many cases the provided selection may not be adequate to optimise network utilisation and video quality. Furthermore, RLM is relatively slow to adapt to changes in the network's available bandwidth. If the background traffic is particularly bursty, the receivers may not be able to adapt appropriately, resulting in degraded utilisation and video quality. Extensions and variants of RLM (namely, Layered Video Multicast with Retransmission (LVMR) [20], and TCP-like Congestion Control for Layered Data [29]) have recently been proposed to ameliorate some of these weaknesses.

Another potential solution to the multicast of video to receivers with heterogeneous bandwidth constraints—although it is not sender-driven or receiver-driven—is transcoding [5, 6, 7]. In this approach, a single layer of video is encoded at a high rate by the source, and intermediate network nodes transcode (i.e., decode and re-encode) the video down to a lower rate whenever their links become bottlenecked. While this approach solves the available bandwidth variation problem, it requires complex and computationally expensive video transcoders to be present throughout the network.

9.2.2 Trade-Offs

There are several trade-offs between receiver-driven and sender-driven approaches, particularly for the case of layered video multicast. The first trade-off is the granularity of adaptation. In a receiver-driven algorithm, the source typically generates a fixed number of layers at a coarse set of fixed rates. Hence, if the path to one of the receivers has an amount of available bandwidth that does not exactly match the transmission rate of a combined set of offered video layers, the network will be underutilised and the quality of that receiver's video will be suboptimal. Sender-driven algorithms do not suffer from this problem, because they are able to fine-tune layer transmission rates in response to network bandwidth availability. They can therefore achieve better network utilisation and video quality.

Another trade-off arises in the ability of sender-driven and receiver-driven algorithms to respond to rapidly fluctuating background traffic. Video sources using sender-driven algorithms receive a continuous stream of congestion feedback from the network, and thus they may adapt to changing bandwidth constraints either by adding a new layer of video or by adjusting the rate of an existing layer. Furthermore, this can be done rapidly, usually within a single round-trip time. Most receiver-driven algorithms, on the other hand, adapt to changing network congestion through a combination of "layer join experiments" and branch pruning, both of which occur at time intervals greater than the round-trip time.

The layer subscription and unsubscription strategies of receiver-driven algorithms also have negative consequences for overall video throughput and loss—consequences that sender-driven algorithms do not share. In most receiver-driven algorithms, receivers perform occasional join experiments, during which they request a new layer of data. If the join experiment creates congestion, packets may be lost and the experiment is considered by the receiver to be a failure. Since receiver-driven algorithms like RLM do not rely on priority discarding, packets from any video layer—even the base layer—may be lost during failed join experiments, causing brief but severe degradation in video quality for some receivers. Receiver-driven algorithms also rely on the receiver's ability to prune itself from the distribution tree of a given layer should there be insufficient bandwidth to support that layer. However, there is a significant "leave latency" associated with the pruning of a branch from a multicast tree. During this time, traffic congestion on the branch may be exacerbated, resulting in greater packet loss and delay for downstream receivers of other flows. In a network environment where bandwidth availability is continually and sometimes severely fluctuating, the effects of join experiments and long leave latencies can result in periods of significant packet loss and, for the case of video, significantly degraded video quality.

Receiver-driven algorithms have the advantage that they are naturally more friendly to competing network traffic than are sender-driven algorithms. Sender-driven algorithms typically send all video data on a single transport layer connection and use priority indications to specify the drop precedence of each layer. This inevitably results in some low-priority traffic being sent needlessly down some branches of the multicast tree, only to be discarded further downstream. If this extraneous traffic shares FIFO queues with competing traffic that is adaptive (e.g., TCP flows), then the adaptive flows may experience an unfair degree of discarding or delay within the network. Receiver-driven algorithms do not share this deficiency with sender-driven algorithms, because they send each layer of video in a different flow and allow for the pruning of flows that have no downstream receivers. One way to correct this deficiency of the sender-driven algorithms is to isolate video traffic from other traffic. This can be done by implementing class-based queueing [16] or weighted fair queueing [14, 25] within the routers or switches. There is, however, a non-negligible degree of complexity involved in the implementation of class-based and fair queueing at intermediate network nodes.

9.3 Architecture and Algorithm

In the SAMM paradigm, the sender adjusts its encoding parameters, including the number of video layers it generates and the encoding rate of each layer, in response to a continuous flow of congestion feedback from the network and/or the receivers. In this section, we consider a network architecture capable of supporting this paradigm and a SAMM algorithm in which congestion control is performed on an end-to-end basis with minimal network participation.

9.3.1 The SAMM Architecture

The network architecture necessary to implement a SAMM algorithm for video consists of four basic components: adaptive layered video sources, layered video receivers, multicast-capable routers, and nodes with feedback merging capability. A sample configuration of this architecture is shown in Figure 9.1.

9.3.1.1 Adaptive Layered Video Sources

In a SAMM algorithm, it is assumed that the video source is capable of generating layered video data. There are a number of ways for a source to generate layered video data. For instance, it may simply mark a subset of the video frames as base layer data and the remaining frames as enhancement layer data. Or, the source may coarsely quantise the video stream's frequency coefficients to produce the base layer

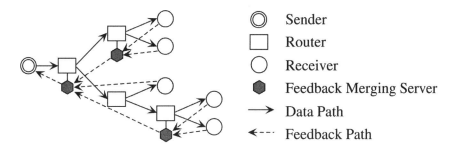

Figure 9.1 Network architecture for SAMM.

and add refinement coefficients to produce enhancement layers. For the purposes of this chapter, we will assume sources that adopt the latter approach, since a finer granularity of layer transmission rates can be achieved this way. However, it is important to note that the SAMM architecture does not mandate that any one type of layering is performed by the video source.

The video source must also participate in the SAMM algorithm being used. This means it must observe congestion feedback arriving from the network and adaptively modify (1) the number of video layers being generated, and (2) the encoding and transmission rates of each video layer.

9.3.1.2 Layered Video Receivers

Layered video receivers collect layered video data arriving from the source and reconstruct a decoded video image. All video receivers must use a layered video decoder that is compatible with the layered video encoder used by the source. Video receivers also co-operate with the SAMM algorithm by returning congestion feedback toward the source as specified by the algorithm.

9.3.1.3 Multicast-Capable Routers

Routers or switches within the network must, at a minimum, be capable of performing the following functions:

- *Multicast forwarding and routing.* Whenever a packet reaches a branch point in its multicast distribution tree, the router produces one copy of the packet for each branch. The router also builds its multicast routing tables according to a multicast routing protocol such as DVMRP [32], MOSPF [22], CBT [8], or PIM [13], although no specific multicast routing algorithm is mandated by SAMM algorithms.
- *Priority drop preference.* To support layered video transmission, the router must be able to distinguish packets with different priorities. During periods of congestion, routers drop low-priority packets in preference over high-priority packets.
- *Flow isolation.* To prevent low-priority packets from negatively impacting the performance of rate-adaptive flows that share the router's output links, the router isolates SAMM flows from other flows. Examples of mechanisms capable of doing this include class-based queueing [16] and weighted fair queueing [14,25], although SAMM is not married to any one particular flow isolation mechanism.
- *Congestion control.* For network-based SAMM algorithms, the router must perform the congestion control functions required by the algorithm. Examples of congestion control algorithms that are network-based and may potentially be used as part of a network-based SAMM algorithm include Random Early Detection (RED) [15], the Explicit Proportional Rate Control Algorithm (EPRCA) [4] and others.

9.3.1.4 Feedback Mergers

Feedback mergers should be deployed to prevent feedback implosion, an undesirable situation in which a large number of receivers consume significant return-path bandwidth by sending feedback packets to a single source. In order to alleviate this problem, feedback mergers consolidate information from arriving feedback packets and route the resulting feedback packets upstream towards the next feedback merger on the path to the source. The idea of designating nodes in the network to alleviate feedback implosion has appeared in a number of other contexts, most notably in the context of reliable multicast [24, 26, 28].

Feedback mergers ultimately form a virtual network overlaid on top of the underlying datagram network as shown in Figure 9.1. The feedback merging function may be implemented at the source, at routers which have been enhanced to perform the merging function, at dedicated nodes inside the network, and/or at one or more participating receivers. Furthermore, feedback mergers do not have to be present at every branch point in the multicast tree in order to operate properly. Obviously, a larger number of feedback mergers in the network guarantees a greater reduction in the amount of feedback returning from receivers to video sources. However, in realistic scenarios, feedback mergers are likely to be incrementally deployed as the load created by feedback packets becomes a greater issue.

The primary task of the feedback mergers is to consolidate the feedback packets returning from receivers. For each video multicast flow, feedback mergers store the most recent feedback packet arriving from the nearest downstream feedback merger or receiver. A flow's stored feedback packets are merged and routed to the next upstream feedback merger whenever (1) a feedback packet from the downstream feedback merger or receiver that triggered the last merge arrives, or (2) two feedback packets from the same downstream merger or receiver arrive after the previous merge. To prevent the merging of feedback from downstream receivers that have left the multicast distribution, stored feedback packets that have not been updated are removed from the merger after a sufficient time-out interval.

In addition to its simplicity, this merging policy has several attractive properties. First, it does not require feedback mergers to know in advance how many feedback packets are going to arrive from downstream. This is important, because many multicast models (e.g., IP multicast) do not have built-in provisions for determining the membership of a multicast group. Second, the policy allows merged feedback packets to be returned at the arrival rate of the fastest incoming stream of feedback packets. This is also important, since with heterogeneous bandwidth constraints, some receivers may generate feedback at faster rates than others. This is especially true for congestion control algorithms (like the one presented in this chapter) that return feedback at a rate proportional to the data arrival rate.

Note that we have not explained how the content of feedback packets is merged, since this is dependent on the congestion control algorithm being used. We leave this discussion to Section 9.3.2.

9.3.2 End-to-End SAMM Algorithm

In this section we introduce an end-to-end SAMM algorithm, where congestion control functions are performed solely at the source, the receivers, and the feedback mergers. Network routers and switches are not assumed to perform any complex or novel congestion control functions apart from those necessitated by the SAMM architecture. The video source simply adjusts the number of video layers it generates and the encoding rate of each layer in response to a continuous flow of congestion feedback from the receivers. The behaviour of the end-to-end SAMM algorithm's receiver is enhanced to compensate for the lack of congestion control functions within the network. The receiver estimates the available bandwidth on the path from the source by monitoring its received video rate and periodically returns feedback packets toward the source.

When a branch of the multicast tree experiences (or is relieved of) congestion, available bandwidth decreases (or increases) on the branch, and the arrival rate of video packets at downstream receivers changes accordingly. Due to this fact, an estimate of the bandwidth available on the path from the source can be obtained by monitoring the rate at which video packets arrive at the receiver. In the end-to-end SAMM algorithm, each receiver monitors the arrival rate of video packets by using Clark and Fang's time sliding window (TSW) moving average algorithm [12].

Typically, the receiver assumes the available bandwidth is equal to the received video rate. However, the actual available bandwidth may be higher than the video arrival rate when the network is under-utilised. In order to exploit the available bandwidth, the receiver may occasionally report a rate that is higher, by an increment, than the observed arrival rate of video packets. The receiver reports a higher rate whenever there is a change in the observed arrival rate and no packet losses have been recorded in a given interval of time. This allows the source to capture newly available bandwidth in an incremental, and therefore, stable manner.

Table 9.1 lists the fields contained within each of the feedback packets. When a forward feedback packet is generated, the source stores the maximum number of video layers it can support (L). The value of L depends on the the number of layers

Table 9.1 Contents of feedback packets used by the end-to-end SAMM algorithm.

Field	Description	Used in forward feedback packets	Used in backward feedback packets
L	Maximum number of video layers allowed	✓	✓
N_l	Current number of video layers		✓
r_I	A vector ($i = 1, ..., N_l$) listing the cumulative rates of each video layer		✓
c_i	A vector ($i = 1, ..., N_l$) listing the number of receivers requesting each layer in the rate vector r_I		✓

the video encoder is able to generate. For example, if the source uses a scalable encoder that can only generate four layers of video (one base layer plus three enhancement layers), then it sets L to 4. The value of L must also be less than or equal to the maximum number of priority levels the network can support.

After receiving a number of video packets, the receiver returns a feedback packet toward the source. The receiver generates a "backward feedback packet" and sets its contents to indicate the desired video rate. It does this by filling the first slot of the backward feedback packet's rate vector (r_1) with its estimated available bandwidth. It also sets the corresponding slot of the counter vector (c_1) to one in order to indicate that only one receiver has requested rate r_1 so far. The backward feedback packet is returned to the nearest upstream feedback merger. Feedback packets are collected and merged by feedback mergers or by the source.

When a feedback merger joins two or more backward feedback packets, it collects the components of the rate (r_i) and counter (c_i) vectors from each incoming feedback packet and stores them into a local array, sorted by rate. Each entry in the local rate array corresponds to a video rate requested by one or more downstream receivers, while the entries in the counter array indicate how many downstream receivers have requested each rate. Ultimately, the rate values will be used by the source to determine the rates at which to transmit each video layer. After filling the local rate array, the number of entries in the array is compared with the maximum number of video layers allowed for the connection (L). If the number of entries in the local rate array does not exceed L, then the merging is considered complete. However, if the number of entries exceeds L, then one (or more) of the rate entries must be discarded and its counter value added to the next lower entry. To determine which entry (or entries) to discard, the feedback merger attempts to estimate the impact of dropping each listed rate on the overall video quality. This is done through the use of a simple estimated video quality metric.

The estimated video quality metric attempts to measure the combined "goodput" of video traffic that will be received by all downstream receivers. The goodput for a single receiver is defined as the total throughput of all video layers received *without loss*. For instance, suppose a sender is transmitting three layers of video at 1 Mbps each. If a receiver entirely receives the most important first two layers but only receives half of the third layer due to congestion, then its total received throughput is 2.5 Mbps, but its *goodput* is equal to the combined rate of the first two layers, namely 2 Mbps. The goodput is a useful estimate of video quality because it measures the total combined rate of traffic from uncorrupted video layers arriving at a receiver.

As the feedback merger aggregates feedback packets, it attempts to determine the goodput that downstream receivers will observe. The combined goodput G is estimated from the values listed in the rate array and calculated as follows:

$$G = \sum_{i=1}^{N} r_i \times c_i \qquad (9.1)$$

where N is the number of entries in the local rate array, and r_i and c_i are the rate and counter values for entry i. To determine which entry to remove from the local rate array, the feedback merger calculates the combined goodput that will result from each potential entry removal. The entry removal that results in the highest combined goodput is then removed from the rate array. This process is repeated until the number of entries in the local rate array is equal to the maximum number of layers allowed. The rate and counter array entries are copied into the slots of the merged packet's rate and counter vectors, and the merged packet is transmitted to the next upstream feedback merger. This process is repeated at each upstream feedback merger until the final consolidated feedback packet arrives at the source. The feedback packet that arrives at the source will contain the number of video layers to generate as well as a list of cumulative rates at which to generate each layer.

The simplicity of the end-to-end SAMM algorithm is its most important feature. By transfering the congestion control functions to the end systems, the end-to-end SAMM algorithm becomes an attractive approach to support video multicast in Internet environments.

9.4 Video Encoder Rate Control

Encoder rate control is necessary to ensure that SAMM algorithms can dynamically adjust the encoding rates of several video layers. One possible encoder and rate control architecture is illustrated in Figure 9.2. The "encoder" block shown in the figure may be any type of layered video encoder (e.g., embedded zero-tree wavelet, MPEG-2, etc.), which accepts uncompressed video information. Uncompressed raw video naturally consists of a sequence of video frames, and we assume the encoder processes frames one block at a time (as in MPEG), where a block is defined as a rectangular component of the frame. The encoder receives a list of target bit rates for each video layer and attempts to produce layered video streams at rates that closely follow the target bit rates. However, since the compression ratio is dependent on video content, it is virtually impossible to produce compressed video at rates that precisely match the target bit rates. Therefore, the encoder returns a list of the rates that it actually generated for each layer of video. This data can then be used to

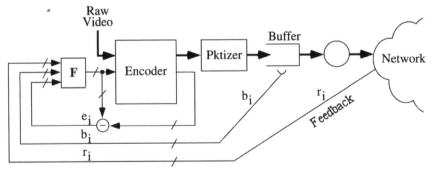

Figure 9.2 Video encoder and rate controller.

calculate an error term for use in the compression of the next block of video.

The rate control function F in Figure 9.2 determines the encoder's target bit rates for each layer. It has two purposes: first, to help the encoder produce several layers of video at rates requested by the network, and second, to prevent the video buffer from overflowing and underflowing. To achieve these goals, the rate controller determines the target bit rates F_i for layer i as follows:

$$F_i(r_i, b_i, e_i) = r_i - \left[\alpha e_i + \beta \left(\frac{b_i - T_d r_i}{\tau} \right) \right] \qquad (9.2)$$

where r_i is the rate requested for layer i in the most recently received feedback packet, e_i is layer i's encoder rate error from the previously encoded block, and b_i is the number of bits from layer i currently stored in the buffer. T_d is the target buffer delay, which determines the target buffer occupancy at the source. τ is the length of the video block interval. For example, if the raw video is captured at a rate of 10 frames per second and each frame is divided into 10 blocks, then τ is 0.01 seconds. The constants α and β are weighting coefficients. This rate control function adjusts the target bit rates according to the encoding error of the previous block and the current occupancy of the transmission buffer.

After being generated by the encoder, the layered bit streams are packetised and placed into the source buffer in Figure 9.2 for transmission into the network. Using a simple weighted round robin, the packetiser interleaves packets from each layer according to the layer's target bit rate in order to keep packets from clumping into layers. The packets are then fed into the network at the combined transmission rate of all the layers.

9.5 Performance

This section presents the results of several simulations designed to evaluate the performance of the end-to-end SAMM algorithm under various configurations. These configurations are designed to test the responsiveness, scalability with respect to delay, scalability with respect to the number of receivers, and fairness of the algorithm.

Unless otherwise specified, all simulations assume link capacities of 10 Mbps, propagation delays between end systems and routers of 5 µs, and propagation delays between routers of 100 µs. All packets are the size of ATM cells (53 bytes), and two class-based queues are used at each router hop to isolate background traffic from video traffic. To keep queueing delays minimal, only the amount of buffers necessary to tolerate 10 ms of feedback delay on a series of 10 Mbps links are used. For most simulation models, this works out to approximately 200 packets per router hop for each video flow. A receiver monitoring interval of 10 ms is assumed, and feedback packets are generated by receivers once for every 32 video packets received. Every router is assumed to be connected to a feedback merging server.

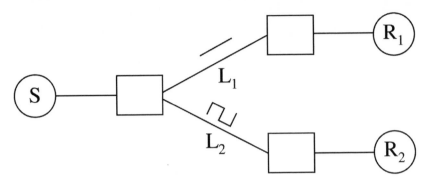

Figure 9.3 Simulation model for evaluating responsiveness.

9.5.1 Responsiveness

One of the most important requirements of a source rate adaptation algorithm is that it be able to respond rapidly to changes in network congestion. This simulation experiment illustrates the trade-offs between source-adaptive and non-source-adaptive algorithms. It also shows the impact of network propagation delay on the responsiveness of the end-to-end SAMM algorithm.

The model shown in Figure 9.3 is used to evaluate the responsiveness of the algorithm. It consists of one video sender and two receivers. Background traffic is applied on links L_1 and L_2, and two responsiveness experiments are conducted. The first experiment is designed to explore the transient response of the sender to changes in available bandwidth on one of the links. The second experiment explores the impact of the network propagation delay on the effectiveness of the algorithm.

In the first experiment, we apply CBR background traffic at a rate of 3 Mbps to link L_1 and sharply oscillating square-wave background traffic to link L_2. The square-wave traffic oscillates between constant rates of 4 and 7 Mbps over a period of 500 ms and is used to test the responsiveness of the sender to sudden and substantial changes in available bandwidth. As a basis for comparison, we also examine the performance of an algorithm in which the sender is non-adaptive and transmits three layers of video at cumulative rates of 1, 4.5 and 8 Mbps. This set of rates is admittedly arbitrary, but so is any choice of rates for a non-adaptive layered transmission mechanism.

Figure 9.4 shows the results of the simulation. As expected, the sender adapts the rate of one of its layers in response to the oscillating available bandwidth on link L_2. The remaining two layers are transmitted at cumulative rates of 1 and 7 Mbps, which correspond to the minimum transmission rate and the available bandwidth on link L_1, respectively. Note that the sender responds quickly to the square-wave traffic oscillations, usually within 10 milliseconds (the length of the receiver monitoring interval). The small spikes in the transmission rates are observed due to occasional over-estimations of the available bandwidth by receiver R_2. For the purpose of comparison, Figure 9.4(b) plots the cumulative transmission rates of each layer for the non-adaptive case.

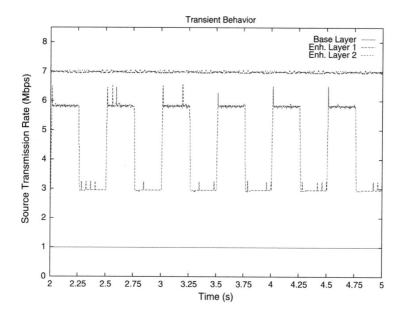

(a) Adaptive rates

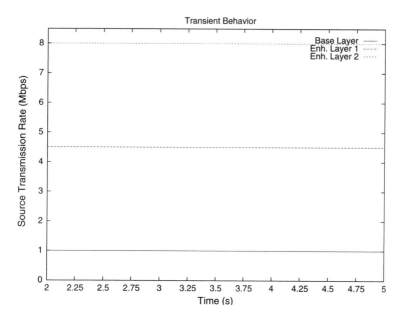

(b) Non adaptive rates

Figure 9.4 Responsiveness temporal behaviour.

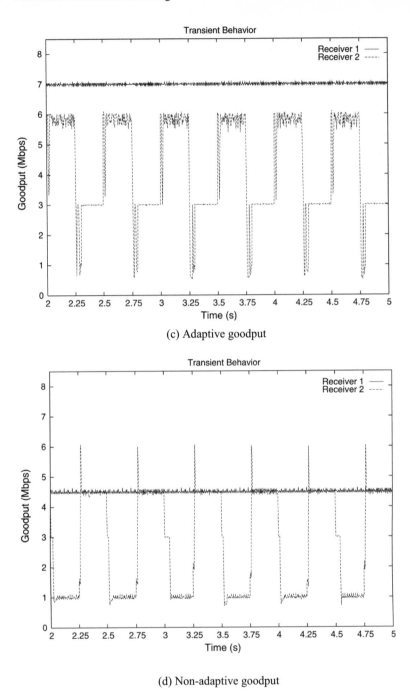

(c) Adaptive goodput

(d) Non-adaptive goodput

Figure 9.4 Responsiveness temporal behaviour.

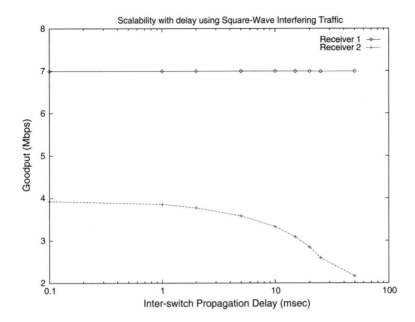

(a) Adaptive goodput

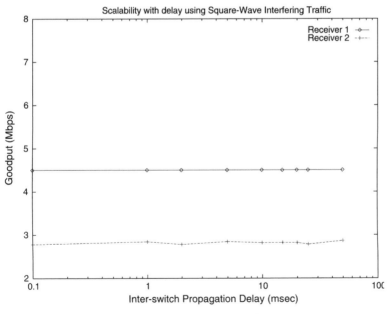

(b) Non-adaptive goodput

Figure 9.5 Responsiveness scalability with delay.

The receiver goodputs for the adaptive and non-adaptive mechanisms are shown in Figures 9.4(c) and 9.4(d). Recall that video goodput is defined as the total throughput of all video layers received *without loss* during a block transmission interval. Clearly the SAMM algorithm produces better goodput than the non-adaptive scheme due to its ability to adjust encoding behavior based on network congestion feedback. Although receiver R_2 experiences degradations of goodput during downward transitions due to buffer overflow, they are brief and the overall goodput levels are desirable. In contrast, the goodput of the non-adaptive mechanism suffers significantly from its inability to take the current state of the network into account.

In the second experiment, we explore the impact of propagation delay on the goodput. We apply CBR background traffic on link L_1 and square-wave background traffic with a period of 200 ms on link L_2. The background traffic transmission rates are the same as for the first experiment. Propagation delays between routers are varied from 0.1 to 50 msec, and each simulation is run for 60 seconds.

The average goodput delivered to each receiver is plotted in Figure 9.5. As propagation delay increases to the order of magnitude of the network transition interval, the average goodput delivered to receiver 2 by the SAMM algorithm drops almost linearly. This is due to the fact that as the propagation delay increases, the sender uses increasingly stale congestion feedback to adjust its layer transmission rates. Despite this drawback, the SAMM algorithm generally produces better goodput than the non-adaptive mechanism for both receivers and nearly all delays. The only exception is the goodput at receiver 2 for very high propagation delay (>20 ms).

9.5.2 Scalability

Scalability is perhaps the most important performance measure of any multicast mechanism. Multicast datagrams can reach dozens or even hundreds of receivers, each with varying bandwidth constraints. It is therefore important to understand how

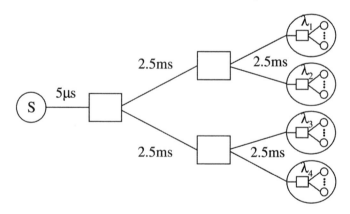

Figure 9.6 Simulation model for evaluating scalability.

a multicast mechanism performs as the number of receivers grows.

The network model used in the scalability experiments is shown in Figure 9.6 and consists of one video sender, four groups of receivers, and seven routers. Within each receiver group, the number of receivers is varied between 2 and 32. Independent background traffic streams are applied to each leaf link, and the traffic loads are divided into four heterogeneous groups (λ_1 = 2 Mbps, λ_2 = 4 Mbps, λ_3 = 6 Mbps, λ_4 = 8 Mbps). Background traffic is generated by a 10-state Markov-Modulated Poisson Process with state transition rates of 100 sec^{-1}. This traffic model captures the superposition of 10 on-off, interrupted Poisson processes and is generally much burstier than a simple Poisson process.

We first examine the performance of the SAMM algorithm as the number of receivers increases in Figure 9.7. The maximum number of video layers is varied from 2 to 8 in this figure. The goodput ratio is defined as the fraction of the available bandwidth used to transport uncorrupted video layers. To calculate the goodput ratio, the combined rate of video layers fully received by all receivers is divided by the total amount of bandwidth available to all receivers. These results reveal that the SAMM algorithm scales well with the number of receivers. They also illustrate the expected result that video goodput (and thereby video quality) can be improved by increasing the maximum number of layers generated by the sender.

In the second scalability experiment we encode and decode actual video sequences and transmit them through the simulated network shown in Figure 9.6. For this experiment we use an embedded zero-tree wavelet encoder to generate multiple layers of video from a raw video sequence. The raw video sequence we use

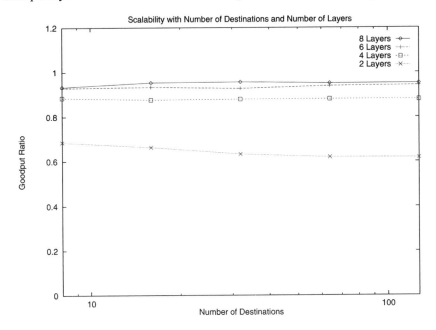

Figure 9.7 Average goodput ratio for all receivers vs. number of receivers.

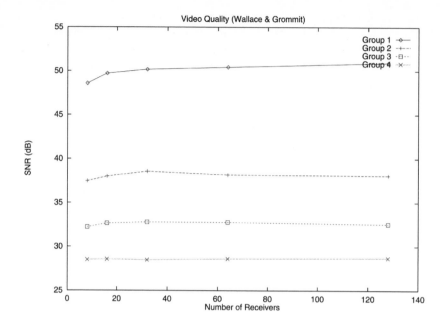

Figure 9.8 Average signal-to-noise ratio for all receivers vs. number of receivers.

is the Academy Award winning short animation *Wallace & Grommit*. The number of multicast receivers is varied between 8 and 128, up to 4 video layers are used, and the background traffic used in the first scalability experiment is reapplied to the leaf links.

Figure 9.8 plots the average peak signal-to-noise ratio of the decoded video sequence for a sampled receiver from each receiver group. (The peak signal-to-noise ratio is a measure of the video quality. The larger the value, the lesser the distortion. It is calculated by comparing the original and the received video image.) The video quality at each receiver remains relatively flat as the number of receivers increases, confirming that the SAMM algorithm is scalable. Furthermore, the quality of video obtained by a receiver is determined by the amount of bandwidth available to it, just as expected. Receivers from Group 1 experienced an average video quality of 50 dB while receivers from Group 4 experienced an average video quality of 28 dB.

In order to further understand and evaluate these objective video quality values, a set of subjective tests were conducted using the absolute category rating (ACR) method. In the ACR method the quality of the video is rated by viewers on a scale from 1 to 5 according to the ratings listed in Table 9.2. The maximum rate of 5 is given when the viewer considers the quality of the video excellent, or that the impairment to the video is imperceptible. Likewise, a minimum rate of 1 is given when the viewer considers the quality of the video bad or the impairment suffered by the video very annoying. In addition to the *Wallace & Grommit* video sequence used in Figure 9.8, an additional video sequence from the movie *Star Wars: Return of the Jedi* was used in this subjective video quality test.

Table 9.2 Absolute category rating for subjective quality of video.

Rating	Impairment	Quality
5	Imperceptible	Excellent
4	Perceptible	Good
3	Slightly annoying	Fair
2	Annoying	Poor
1	Very annoying	Bad

Table 9.3 Average subjective video quality from 20 viewers from each group.

Video sequence	Wallace & Grommit	Star Wars: Return of the Jedi
Group 1	4.05	4.50
Group 2	3.95	4.35
Group 3	3.25	3.40
Group 4	2.60	2.45

Table 9.3 lists the subjective assessment of the video quality for 20 viewers from each receiver group. The quality perceived by viewers varies slightly for each video sequence, however, on average, reconstructed videos at receivers from Group 1 show subjective video qualities between good and excellent, while the most congested receivers, receivers from Group 4, experienced video qualities between poor and fair. Despite the difference in signal-to-noise ratio (SNR) between the objective quality delivered to receivers from Groups 1 and 2, shown in Figure 9.8, the subjective quality perceived by receivers from Group 2 is only slightly lower than the quality perceived by receivers from Group 1. Nevertheless, consistent with the objective SNR results from Figure 9.8, as shown in Table 9.3, the subjective quality of video obtained by a receiver is determined by the amount of bandwidth available to it.

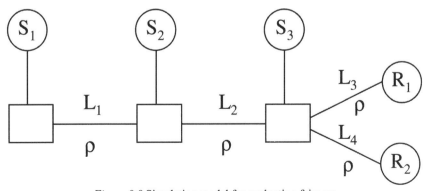

Figure 9.9 Simulation model for evaluating fairness

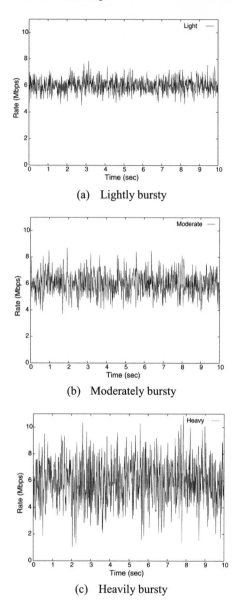

(a)   Lightly bursty

(b)   Moderately bursty

(c)   Heavily bursty

Figure 9.10 Sample traces of MMPP background traffic.

9.5.3 Fairness

An important factor in the evaluation of any traffic control mechanism is its fairness. If the mechanism fails to divide bandwidth equally between competing connections,

Table 9.4 Video transmission rates and fairness with FIFO queues and fair queueing.

Lightly Bursty Background

Scheduling	Rate (Mbps)			Fairness
	S_1	S_2	S_3	σ
FIFO	1.318	1.332	1.350	0.025
Fair Queueing	1.331	1.331	1.331	0.000

Moderately Bursty Background

Scheduling	Rate (Mbps)			Fairness
	S_1	S_2	S_3	σ
FIFO	1.312	1.316	1.349	0.035
Fair Queueing	1.333	1.333	1.333	0.000

Heavily Bursty Background

Scheduling	Rate (Mbps)			Fairness
	S_1	S_2	S_3	σ
FIFO	1.229	1.312	1.400	0.094
Fair Queueing	1.333	1.333	1.333	0.000

then some connections may unfairly receive better service than others. We use the simple "parking lot" model depicted in Figure 9.9 to examine the fairness of the SAMM algorithm. Propagation delays on links L_1, ..., L_4 are 10 msec, representing distances of 2000 km, and each of these links is loaded with 6 Mbps of background traffic generated by four independent N-state MMPP processes. To adjust the burstiness of the background traffic, three values for the number of MMPP states are used: $N=10$ (heavily bursty), $N=50$ (moderately bursty) and $N=2000$ (lightly bursty). Sample traces for each degree of burstiness are shown in Figure 9.10.

The allocation of bandwidth to competing video traffic streams is said to be optimal if it is *max-min fair*. A max-min fair allocation of bandwidth occurs when all active connections not bottlenecked at an upstream node are allocated an equal share of the available bandwidth at every downstream node [9]. In the model shown in Figure 9.9, a max-min fair allocation of bandwidth occurs if all three sources transmit at the same rate. To measure fairness, we calculate the standard deviation σ of the rates that each source transmits across the bottleneck links L_3 and L_4. An optimally fair allocation results in a standard deviation of zero.

Results for this set of simulations are shown in Table 9.4. There is a consistent degradation of fairness as the burstiness of the interfering traffic increases. This result was expected, since it is difficult for senders more distant from the shared bottleneck links (L_3 and L_4) to adapt their rates in response to rapid changes in the available bandwidth. Senders close to the shared bottleneck links unfairly grab a larger portion of the available bandwidth, especially when the background traffic is bursty. This kind of unfairness can be eliminated by using fair queueing within each of the router output ports. If traffic flows from senders S_1, S_2 and S_3 are buffered in isolated queues and served on a round-robin basis, then their allocations of bottleneck link bandwidth become virtually identical as shown in the table.

9.6 Conclusion

We have introduced the class of algorithms known as source adaptive multi-layered multicast (SAMM) algorithms and have studied their use for the multicast distribution of video. We have also proposed and investigated a simple end-to-end SAMM algorithm for possible use in the Internet. In SAMM algorithms, the source transmits several layers of video and adjusts their rates in response to congestion feedback from the receivers and/or the network.

We have also introduced a network architecture defining the source, receiver and network functions necessary to support SAMM algorithms. The architecture mandates that routers implement some form of priority packet discarding in order to support layered transmissions, as well as a class-based flow isolation mechanism at routers to prevent SAMM flows from negatively impacting the performance of other flows in the network. The architecture also includes feedback mergers, which prevent feedback implosion by consolidating the contents of feedback packets returning to the source.

Simulation results indicate that the proposed SAMM algorithm is capable of producing better video quality and network utilisation than algorithms which transmit video layers at fixed rates. Furthermore, the proposed end-to-end SAMM algorithm exhibits good performance in terms of goodput, video quality and scalability.

References

[1] Albuquerque C., Vickers B.J., and Suda T. (1998) Multicast Flow Control with Explicit Rate Feedback for Adaptive Real-Time Video Services. *Proc. of SPIE's 1998 Performance and Control of Network Systems II.*

[2] Albuquerque C., Vickers B.J., and Suda T. (1999) An End-to-End Source-Adaptive Multi-Layered Multicast (SAMM) Algorithm. In *Proc. of the Int'l. Workshop on Packet Video.*

[3] Albuquerque C., Vickers B.J., and Suda T. (2000) Credit-Based Source-Adaptive Multi-Layered Video Multicast. *Performance Evaluation Journal*, (40) 1–3, pages 135–159.

[4] ATM Forum Technical Committee, Traffic Management Working Group. (1996) ATM Forum Traffic Management Specification Version 4.0.

[5] Amir E., McCanne S., and Zhang H. (1995) An Application-level Video Gateway. In *Proc. of ACM Multimedia.*

[6] Amir E., McCanne S., and Katz R. (1998) An Active Service Framework and Its Application to Real-time Multimedia Transcoding. In *Proc. of ACM SIGCOMM*, pages 178–189.

[7] Assunção P. and Ghanbari M. (1996) Multi-Casting of MPEG-2 Video with Multiple Bandwidth Constraints. In *Proc. of the 7th Int'l. Workshop on Packet Video*, pages 235–238.

[8] Ballardie T., Francis P., and Crowcroft J. (1993) Core Based Trees (CBT): An Architecture for Scalable Inter-Domain Multicast Routing. In *Proc. of ACM SIGCOMM*.

[9] Bartsekas D. and Gallagher R. (1987) *Data Networks,* second edition. Prentice Hall.

[10] Bolot J., Turletti T., and Wakeman I. (1994) Scalable Feedback Control for Multicast Video Distribution in the Internet. In *Proc. of ACM SIGCOMM*, pages 58–67.

[11] Cheung S., Ammar M., and Li X. (1996) On the Use of Destination Set Grouping to Improve Fairness in Multicast Video Distribution. In *Proc. of IEEE Infocom*.

[12] Clark D. and Fang W. (1998) Explicit Allocation of Best Effort Packet Delivery Service. Technical report, MIT LCS.

[13] Deering S., Estrin D., Farinacci D., Jacobson V., Liu C., and Wei L. (1996) The PIM Architecture for Wide-Area Multicast Routing. *IEEE/ACM Transactions on Networking*, 4(2):153–162.

[14] Demers A., Keshav S., and Shenker S. (1989) Analysis and Simulation of a Fair Queueing Algorithm. *Proc. of ACM SIGCOMM*.

[15] Floyd S. and Jacobson V. (1993) Random Early Detections Gateways for Congestion Avoidance. *IEEE/ACM Transactions on Networking*, 1(4).

[16] Floyd S. and Jacobson V. (1995) Link Sharing and Resource Management Models for Packet Networks. *IEEE/ACM Transactions on Networking*, 3(4):365–386.

[17] Gilge M. and Gusella R. (1991) Motion Video Coding for Packet-Switching Networks—An Integrated Approach. *SPIE Conference on Visual Communications and Image Processing*.

[18] Kanakia H., Mishra P., and Reibman A. (1993) An Adaptive Congestion Control Scheme for Real-Time Packet Video Transport. *Proc. of ACM SIGCOMM*.

[19] Lakshman T.V., Mishra P.P., and Ramakrishnan K.K. (1997) Transporting Compressed Video over ATM Networks with Explicit Rate Feedback Control. In *Proc. of IEEE Infocom*.

[20] Li X., Paul S., and Ammar M. (1998) Layered Video Multicast with Retransmissions (LVMR): Evaluation of Hierarchical Rate Control. *Proc. of IEEE Infocom*.

[21] McCanne S., Jacobson V., and Vetterli M. (1996) Receiver-Driven Layered Multicast. In *Proc. of ACM SIGCOMM*, pages 117–130.

[22] Moy J. (1994) Multicast Extensions to OSPF. Request for Comments 1584, Internet Engineering Task Force.

[23] Omori Y., Suda T., Lin G., and Kosugi Y. (1994) Feedback-based Congestion Control for VBR Video in ATM Networks. *Proc. of the 6th Int'l. Workshop on Packet Video*.

[24] Papadopoulos C., Parulkar G., and Varghese G. (1998) An Error Control Scheme for Large-Scale Multicast Applications. *Proc. of IEEE Infocom*, pages 1188–1196.

[25] Parekh A. and Gallager R. (1993) A Generalized Processor Sharing Approach to Flow Control – the Single Node Case. *IEEE/ACM Transactions on Networking*, pages 344–357.

[26] Paul S., Sabnani K., Lin J., and Bhattacharyya S. (1997) Reliable Multicast Transport Protocol (RMTP). *IEEE Journal on Selected Areas in Communications*.

[27] Sharon C., Devetsikiotis M., Lambadaris L., and Kaye A. (1995) Rate Control of VBR H.261 Video on Frame Relay Networks. *Proc. of the International Conference on Communications (ICC)*, pages 1443–1447.

[28] Speakman T., Farinacci D., Lin S., and Tweedly S. (1998) PGM Reliable Multicast Specification. Internet draft (work in progress), Internet Engineering Task Force. ftp://ftp.ietf.org/internet-drafts/draft-speakman-pgm-spec-02.txt.

[29] Vicisano L. and Crowcroft J. (1998) TCP-like Congestion Control for Layered Multicast Data Transfer. *Proc. of IEEE Infocom.*

[30] Vickers B. J., Lee M. and Suda T. (1997) Feedback Control Mechanisms for Real-Time Multipoint Video Services. *IEEE Journal on Selected Areas in Communications*, 15(3).

[31] Vickers B.J., Albuquerque C., and Suda T. (1998) Adaptive Multicast of Multi-Layered Video: Rate-Based and Credit-Based Approaches. *Proc. of IEEE Infocom.*

[32] Waitzman D., Deering S., and Partridge C. (1988) *Distance Vector Multicast Routing Protocol.* Request for Comments 1075, Internet Engineering Task Force.

Chapter 10

An Adaptive Resource Broker for Multimedia Teleservices

Gábor Fehér and István Cselényi

10.1 Introduction

There is a steadily increasing number of multimedia teleservices, which require networks where quality of service (QoS) [1,2,3] is assured in order to achieve high quality services. Providing QoS is based on an agreement between the user and the provider where the QoS provider does not allow other connections to influence the service, then the quality of the user's service is assured. Unfortunately, for many reasons, until recently there were no protocols able to assure end-to-end QoS in large networks. Without agreed QoS these services run on best-effort networks, and they suffer quality falls when the network load is high. Therefore on the best-effort networks there was a need for adaptive applications and protocols that could adjust the transfer rate of a media connection to the bearer connection's quality [4,5].

Another alternative is an adaptive resource broker that is capable not only of adjusting the transfer speed of the connections, but of keeping its eye on the teleservice configurations and reconfiguring them according to the available resources. This approach can be more efficient since usually a teleservice consists of several coherent connections that depend on each other, therefore it cannot be handled as a bunch of independent connections.

Providing an acceptable level of QoS does not necessarily require adaptive applications and protocols or an adaptive controller but in many cases the latter can be very useful. In QoS-able networks when a teleservice configuration does not go through the resource reservation due to resource shortage then the user must modify the configuration itself and resubmit the initiation request. Putting this negotiation process inside the network would decrease the call setup time as it would require no user interaction and could achieve better teleservice configuration since the cause of the blocking would be known. In this way the adaptive service control can prevent teleservice blocking at teleservice setup time, when there would not be enough resources to realise all the desired high quality service realising a less resource demanding configuration, and it can extend the teleservice later, when other resources become available. There can also be physical or other reasons why even QoS-able networks are unable to provide the reserved resources (e.g. mobile networks) and in these situations reconfiguring the teleservice via an adaptive resource broker is also a great help.

There are existing standards related to teleservice session control, such as H.323 [6], an ITU standard for multimedia conferencing with control functions to operate conferences on Metropolitan Area Networks (MAN). Another proposal, being discussed in the IETF Multi-party Multimedia Session Control (MMUSIC) working group is called Session Initiation Protocol (SIP) [7], used to initiate different teleservices on the network. Both of these standards realise multimedia teleservice initiation and H.323 also maintains the teleservices and they are claimed to work on QoS-able networks. The problem is that they are restricted to handle teleservice sessions as a set of independent connections and this way they cannot solve the previously mentioned teleservice blocking problem and teleservice adjustment is less effective than in the case of an adaptive teleservice broker.

Adaptive teleservice management requires some intelligence in the network. The teleservice reconfiguration can be successful only if the network has knowledge about the teleservices and the user's preference. This intelligence can be introduced to the broker by describing the teleservices and expressing the user's preference in formal way, so the broker is able evaluate teleservice configurations in a user's view and can act as a human being with much more knowledge than the user would have.

The formal description of a teleservice is presented in Section 10.2. That section also covers the required knowledge base for the intelligence. Section 10.3 presents the teleservice reservation along with two teleservice reservation algorithms as examples. Section 10.4 gives a summary of the problems that have been solved using this approach.

10.2 Teleservice Description

When creating a new teleservice, the Service Provider has a conception how the teleservice will appear. They design the service for a particular user profile and determine what type of media sessions can exist among the participants. Additional to other management protocols, the broker is required to describe rules that can control the number of participants and their media sessions; and also the Service Provider can permit and force relations between any participant and media session. The *teleservice description* is the formal implementation of the previous, informal definitions. The description consists of the enumeration of involved party and media types that form the teleservice. These types are the behaviour models for participants: every user must act as described in their party type and they must handle media sessions as described in the media type. The description also contains the rules that express relationships among all of the participants and their media sessions. These rules will be detailed later.

The broker uses the teleservice description for three main purposes: teleservice validation, teleservice evaluation and teleservice assembly.

10.2.1 Teleservice Validation

To determine whether a certain teleservice configuration meets the teleservice description the broker uses a *teleservice validation* procedure. This description of a teleservice configuration can come from the user when he is initiating a service or else it might come from the broker itself when negotiating a blocked service or when the network conditions have changed and service reconfiguration is necessary. The teleservice configuration description populates the party and media types, coming from the teleservice description, with real participants, media sessions and the relations between them. Participants can take part in a media session in two ways: as receiver and/or as sender. The general rule is that all participants with a receiver attribute in a media session receive media information that originated from all the participants that have sender attributes in the same media session.

The teleservice description might contain rules also. Rules are to express arbitrary relationships among the participants and media sessions. For example, a rule can force the participants to listen on the audio media when they are in a videoconference; a rule in a network game can assure that players can have voice connections only inside a team but not outside.

Technically, each rule is a statement that uses the given configuration's participants and media streams as its input, and results in true or false depending on parameters and operators. These formal operators are derived from the world of set theory and mathematics, but any kind of operators can be implemented. Table 10.1 shows the most frequently used operators.

Table 10.1 The most frequently used operators in the teleservice description.

Operator	Meaning
$\sum type$	Number of elements with a given type
$\wedge$	Logical *and* operator
$\vee$	Logical *or* operator
$\in$	*Member of* operator

The validation procedure extracts the required parameters from the configuration description and substitutes them into the rule expressions of the teleservice description. If the results of all these expressions are true then the configuration is valid or in other words it is a configuration that matches the formal description of the teleservice. Figure 10.1 shows a teleservice description example for a videoconference service. The informal definition says that exactly one audio and a maximum of one video media session can exist in the service; the service is for one chairman and three other participants; everybody must transmit and receive the audio media and the chairman must be involved in the video media session.

Party Types: Chairman, Member

Media Types: Audio, Video

Rules:

Σ Audio $= 1 \wedge \Sigma$ Video ≤ 1

Σ Chairman $= 1 \wedge \Sigma$ Member < 4

Chairman(i) $\Rightarrow$ i $\in$ Audio$_S$ $\wedge$ i $\in$ Audio$_R$

Member(i) $\Rightarrow$ i $\in$ Audio$_S$ $\wedge$ i $\in$ Audio$_R$

Video(i) $\Rightarrow$ Chairman $\in$ i$_{SR}$

Figure 10.1 The description of a videoconference teleservice.

The validation procedure prevents users from creating meaningless teleservice configurations that would waste resources. This procedure also aids the teleservice resource reservation where reservation of invalid configurations would cause unnecessary resource waste for the Network Provider.

10.2.2 Teleservice Evaluation

Teleservice evaluation is designed to rank different configurations of a teleservice in different views. These views are the *configuration views* to promote ranking of alternative solutions during the teleservice reservation. These configuration views consist of the *user preference view* that expresses how much the user prefers one configuration to the others; there is a view for the network resource load called *network view* that covers the amount of network resources that are necessary to build up the configuration; further views are the *terminal view* that is the terminal resource load, which is similar to the network resource load but considers only resources in the terminals; the *cost view* that represents how expensive the assembled configuration is for the user; and finally, the *quality view* that refers to the media session qualities. To evaluate a configuration there are expressions for each view that take parameters from the components belonging to the configuration. Each party and media component has individual values for each view. These values are supplied by the Service Provider and are based on interviews that can explore the users' preference or calculations that determines the resource usage or marketing decisions that determine the costs. All of these values are stored in the teleservice description, but certain values like cost can only come from a given situation. Figure 10.2 shows an example for a videoconference teleservice, illustrating how these values and expressions can be stored in the teleservice description. The teleservice evaluation uses the same operators as the teleservice validation, but instead of giving a result of true or false, they express a value that has a meaning inside the view.

User's Preference values:
Chairman: 5, *Member*: 4
Audio: 6, *Video*: 4

User's Preference expression:
User's Preference: =
    Σ*Chairman* + Σ*Participant* + Σ*Audio* + Σ*Video*

Figure 10.2 Example of description of component values and evaluation expressions.

Figure 10.3 shows evaluations of two different videoconference configurations from the view of the user's preference. In the figure there are two configurations. The participants are denoted by small bullets, a black bullet represents the chairman and gray bullets represent the participants. The arrows mean media sessions. In the first configuration all the three participants share an audio session only, while in the second case there are only two participants: one chairman and one member, but they have not an only audio but a video session as well. We use the same teleservice description as shown in Figure 10.1 with the teleservice evaluation expressions in Figure 10.2 and as a result we get that the first configuration, where there are three participants, is the preferred one.

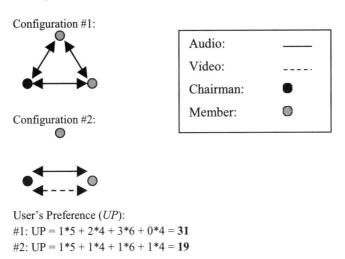

Configuration #1:

Configuration #2:

Audio:
Video:
Chairman:
Member:

User's Preference (*UP*):
#1: UP = 1*5 + 2*4 + 3*6 + 0*4 = **31**
#2: UP = 1*5 + 1*4 + 1*6 + 1*4 = **19**

Figure 10.3 Example of a videoconference configuration evaluation.

The configuration evaluation is the engine of the teleservice resource reservation as the algorithm creates a preference ranking among all of the possible configurations and adjusts the negotiation process to this ranking. Considering the user preference view, it is assured that the adjusted configurations will yield a successful configuration that has maximal user preference value and its resource need fits into the actual network conditions. Section 10.3 will present algorithms that are based on the network resource load view in addition to the user preference view. In certain cases the cost and quality views can be included during the teleservice resource reservation via the teleservice evaluation.

10.2.3 Teleservice Assembly

Teleservice assembly means the generation of a configuration based on the teleservice description. The assembly follows the service rules and its result is the complete set of all configurations that are valid within the teleservice. All configurations that do not belong to this set are invalid configurations. For configuration assembly, the rules can be considered as constraints and an adapted constraint logic programming application can speed up the generation procedure. The rules are described in such a way that only a minimal transformation is required to give them to a constraint solver application [8]. The result of the configuration assembly might lead to huge sets that could exceed the memory capacity of the broker, so there is a need for some methods to narrow down the result set. Therefore, the negotiation procedure chooses configurations that are close to each other, as will be described in Section 10.4, so this procedure has locality on the configurations. Using this locality it is enough to generate configurations that are close to one specified configuration that can be passed to the generator procedure as input. The assembly uses the previously introduced views when it gives meaning to the close configuration.

10.3 Teleservice Resource Reservation

Teleservice resource reservation provides the allocation of the necessary network and terminal resources for a certain teleservice configuration. The network reservation happens only on QoS-able networks as only this kind of network architecture assures that the necessary network resources carrying media session information are not affected by other traffic. Terminal resources can be assured in a similar way but there is no recent solution for this, as its importance is not so high and the problem can be treated locally.

In the QoS-able networks the reservation happens in the low-level layers, which means that the supplied information for reservation is suitable for individual connections only and multimedia teleservices that consist of coherent connections must not be handled this way. The resource reservation procedure for such teleservices requires a reservation scheme that can handle teleservices as a unity of coherent connections but represents them to the network layer as independent connections. To realise this, the resource reservation procedure uses a high-level description for the services that expresses the relations among the connections. This is the teleservice description, which has rules that define the base of the coherency. An additional difficulty is that in most cases there are no network components that can comprehend the state of all the resources in the whole network, so a teleservice established over a large network cannot count on help from such information bases. Furthermore, if a teleservice configuration requires a media session between two participants, the broker is able to ask the network for a QoS parameterised connection between the network end-points. However, when the network refuses the new connection then the broker might have no information as to why the reservation has failed. A better solution is to treat the QoS-able network as a black box. The resource reservation algorithm must handle it. It can request the network for resource reservation and can get reservation or blocking but no more information.

The resource reservation procedure converts the teleservice configuration into individual QoS connections and tries to make a reservation for them in the network. When the reservation of one connection fails then it initiates a negotiation procedure that resolves the resource conflicts and results in a valid configuration whose connections are reserved in the network and which is the most preferred configuration from the user preference view on the given network load. There are some basic requirements that this negotiation procedure should follow:

1. The configuration reservations must converge to a configuration that will be reserved finally and that should be the most preferred one for the user available on the current network load.
2. During the configuration reservation the procedure must make an effort to create as low an over-provisioning as it can. Over-provisioning means temporary allocation of resources, which will be released later. Here we mean resources that will not take part in the final configuration and they would block other user's teleservices unnecessarily.
3. As network load can change very frequently all reserved resources that will be part of the final configuration should be kept reserved.

Every negotiation is an iterative algorithm that probes a particular configuration and makes the next iteration based on the success or failure of the previous resource reservation step. Applied heuristics can improve the iteration.

10.3.1 The Life-Cycle of a Teleservice

A teleservice begins its life-cycle when an initiating user first creates a configuration from one of the Service Provider's teleservices. This configuration describes only a wish of the user giving the participants to be involved into the teleservice and the media sessions interconnecting the users. The user sends this configuration to the agent for initiation. The broker first makes a content negotiation by checking whether the terminals of the participants are capable of being involved in the teleservice. Meanwhile all terminals agree on a media format for each media session that will be commonly used. The broker extends the user's configuration description with the information of the agreed media formats and decomposes the configuration to connections. After the successful decomposition the broker makes resource reservation requests for all connections belonging to the teleservice and if all the reservations are successful then it launches the realised teleservice. However if there is a refused resource reservation request during the reservation process then the agent initiates a negotiation procedure and launches the teleservice configuration that resulted from the end of the negotiation. During the lifecycle of the teleservice session the broker maintains the service and when the amount of reserved resources changes or other resources become available then it adjusts the configuration to the new network conditions, which in case of a roaming mobile teleservice can happen frequently. At the end, when the teleservice is cancelled the broker releases all resources that were involved in the configuration.

The following two sections present two resource reservation algorithms that are available for the negotiation phase. The bottom-up algorithm is a pessimistic one and the top-down algorithm is an optimistic one.

10.3.2 The Bottom-Up Algorithm

The first algorithm is the bottom-up algorithm that builds up a teleservice configuration's connections from the null configuration to the maximum available configuration step-by-step. The procedure widens the configuration set by increasing the number and the size of the connections and tries to reserve the relevant connections in the network for each widening step. Each next step extends the previous configuration and these steps are repeated until the reserved configuration cannot be wider. Whenever the agent cannot reserve the new connections in the network, then the procedure examines an alternative widening of the last reserved configuration. Widening is based on the configurations' network resource load view and user preference view as detailed later. Figure 10.4 shows a block diagram of the algorithm that handles the negotiation and the description of it follows.

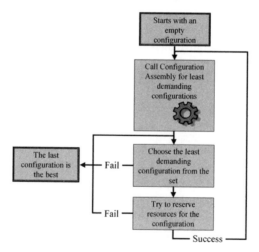

Figure 10.4 Block diagram of the bottom-up algorithm.

1. The algorithm is initiated with an empty configuration. There are neither participants nor media sessions defined in it. It is trivial that the network can always make reservations for this configuration, so at this point this is the last reserved configuration.

2. The algorithm calls the teleservice assembly with the last reserved configuration as input and makes some minor changes on this input configuration set. These minor changes can mean adding new participants or media sessions or replacing media session formats with new formats. The only requirement is that the newly created configurations should have a larger user's preference value than the previously reserved configuration and the teleservice assembly cannot release reserved resources. This set will be the set of possible next configurations.

3. If the set of possible next configurations is empty then the last reserved configuration is the most preferred for the participants that can fit into the network. The negotiation ends.

4. If the set of possible next configurations is not empty, the algorithm chooses one configuration from the set of possible next configurations where the network resource load value is the lowest. If there are more than one of these configurations then it chooses the one that has the highest user's preference value and if there is still more than one configuration then it chooses one of them randomly.

5. The algorithm tries to reserve resources for the new connections that were not involved in the last reserved configuration and modify the resource reservations for connections that were changed. If all creations and modifications are successful then the last reserved configuration will be the current configuration and the algorithm repeats from step 2. If there is a reservation failure then the current configuration will be dropped from the set of possible next connections and the algorithm repeats from step 3.

This is a pessimistic algorithm that can be used on heavily loaded networks as it has minimal over-provisioning. Unfortunately this algorithm has relatively high set-up time when the network load is light and the configuration is huge.

10.3.3 The Top-Down Algorithm

This algorithm is the opposite of the previously presented algorithm. The failure of the complete teleservice reservation initiates the negotiation and all successfully reserved resources are kept reserved. The idea is that a downgraded configuration can have smaller demand on resources where the previous reservation request failed so a downgraded reservation can be successful. Such downgrading continues until the negotiation reaches a configuration where all the resources can be reserved. During the procedure some of the reserved resources can be reduced or released. However, the algorithm decreases the reserved resource for a connection only when it is sure that no other configuration wants to use it. A block diagram of the algorithm can be seen in Figure 10.5, while the detailed description follows.

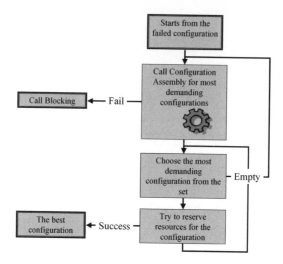

Figure 10.5 Block diagram of the top-down algorithm.

1. The algorithm is initiated with the user's complete configurations where all the resources that could be reserved are reserved. This configuration is called failed configuration, because this configuration had higher resource demand than the free network resources.

2. The algorithm calls the teleservice assembling procedure to produce downgraded configurations from the failed configuration. The generation takes minor changes similar to the bottom-up algorithm. The difference is that the expected set of configurations contains configurations where resource requirements are smaller along every connection than in the failed configuration. This set is called possible next configurations.

3. If the set of possible next configurations is empty, then this means that the failed configuration cannot be downgraded, so the negotiation resulted in failure and the teleservice will be blocked.

4. If the set of possible configurations is not empty, the algorithm chooses a configuration from the possible next configurations where the network resource load value is the highest. When there is more than one such configuration, then the user's preference value, and finally a random choice, makes the decision as it did in the bottom-up algorithm.

5. The algorithm tries to reserve network resources for the previously selected configuration. There are connections that already exist because of the failed configuration and there are new connections that could not be reserved when the failed connection's reservation happened. If all the new reservations are successful then the negotiation ends and this configuration is the result of the negotiation. When one of the reservations fails the algorithm keeps all resources reserved and the failed configuration will be changed to the previously tested configuration.

6. The algorithm reduces the amount of the reserved resources according to the next possible configurations. The reduced resources per connections cannot exceed the resource demands of those connections that are in the configurations that belong to the possible next configurations.
7. The algorithm repeats from step 2.

This is an optimistic algorithm, which supposes that the network resources are nearly enough to fulfil the user's configuration and a small amount of downgrading can achieve a fast negotiation. This algorithm works well with light loaded networks and has problems with heavily loaded networks where too much downgrading slows down the negotiation.

10.4 Simulation Study

In order to study the performance of the adaptive resource broker, we performed simulations. We investigated videoconference teleservices with three parties that are built up by the broker according to the two different algorithms. During the simulation we measured the *conference setup time* and the *conference blocking probability* as we increased the load in the network.

10.4.1 The Simulation Scenario

The network scenario can be seen in Figure 10.6. There are computer terminals behind the four routers and these routers are able to make resource reservations according the capacity of their links. The broker shown in the middle of the figure has connections to all of the routers and this way it is connected to all of the terminals, but does not perform resource reservation.

All terminals initiate a videoconference with two other participants selected randomly, but limited to computers that are connected to a router other than that connected to the initiator. The terminal makes its initiation according to an interrupted Poisson process: it is in silence for an exponential random long time with a mean of 30 minutes and then it makes a teleservice initiation. If the initiation is successful then the connection is kept for an exponential random interval with a

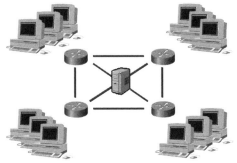

Figure 10.6 Network scenario for the simulation

mean value of 10 minutes and then released, while if the initiation fails it retries the initiation within 5 minutes.

According to the service rules, there are 9 different teleservice configurations. They are shown in Figure 10.7.

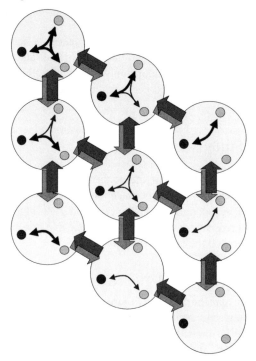

Figure 10.7 Videoconference teleservice configurations

Each circle is a configuration, where there are bullets representing the participants and arrows representing the connections. The darker bullet is the *chairman* and the lighter ones are the other *members*. Bold arrows represent an audio-video connection and light arrows an audio only connection. There are arrows between the configurations also. These arrows show the convergence of the algorithms: the darker arrow is for the bottom-up algorithm, while the light arrow is for the top-down algorithm.

10.4.2 Conference Set-Up Time

For *conference setup time* measurement we compared the two negotiation algorithms with each other and with an algorithm that has no negotiation built in. We considered that a single negotiation step takes 75 microseconds. During the simulations we increased the number of competing terminals behind the routers. As more and more terminals make reservation requests the network become saturated and according to this, the negotiation takes more and more time. Figure 10.8 shows the conference setup time as a function of the number of terminals.

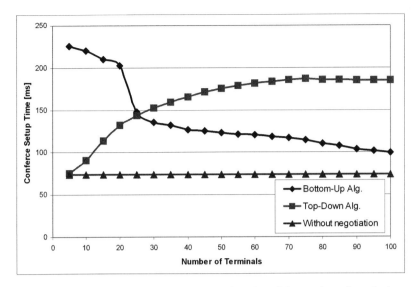

Figure 10.8 Conference setup time as a function of the number of terminals.

The results highlight the difference between the two negotiation algorithms. The top-down algorithm is very effective when there are lots of available free resources in the network, while the bottom-up algorithm is more effective when there is a resource shortage in the network.

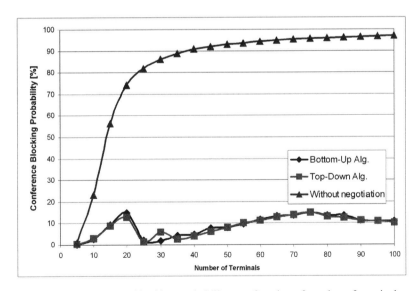

Figure 10.9 Conference blocking probability as a function of number of terminals.

10.4.3 Conference Blocking Probability

To find the *conference blocking probability* we measured the ratio between successfully launched and blocked conferences. Figure 10.9 shows the results. In the figure we can see that the broker has a great advantage using the negotiation algorithms. Without these algorithms the broker would not be able to build successful conferences if there are more then 20 terminals behind the routers. Using a negotiation algorithm the blocking probability is strongly reduced and we can see that both protocols produce almost the same conference blocking probability. This indicates that the conference blocking probability does not depend on the algorithm, but depends on the existence of the algorithm.

10.5 Conclusions and Future Work

The current teleservice management solutions cannot provide adaptive management for the whole teleservice and this way they are not able to prevent teleservice blocking. The solution is an adaptive resource broker that has an overall view of the teleservice and can cope with conference blocking problems and with the situations where the network resource conditions are changing.

This broker has high-level definitions for teleservices, called *teleservice descriptions* together with rules and expressions that the *teleservice evaluation* use to express the ranking between the possible teleservice configurations. The broker is implemented with various negotiation algorithms for the *teleservice resource reservation* that yield an optimal configuration that fits into the actual network conditions and this is the most preferred one among the possible configurations by the service initiator. This work presented two basic algorithms that have advantages and disadvantages in certain network situations, which shows that even the algorithms themselves can be adapted to the network conditions. Improvement of these algorithms or development of more complex ones might result in faster negotiation time.

This work was also extended with simulation measurements. The simulation measured the conference blocking probability, the conference setup time for both top-down and bottom-up algorithms and situations when there is no negotiation algorithm in the network. The simulation clearly showed that this intelligent negotiation could significantly decrease the conference blocking probability while the conference setup time remains reasonable.

This work can be continued by creating new algorithms or improving the teleservice description to concentrate more knowledge into the network. Future plans also contain the implementation of the broker into multimedia teleservice management systems like SIGNE/EMMA [9].

References

[1]   Blake, S., Black, D., Carlson, M., Davies, E., Wang, Z. and W. Weiss (1998) "An Architecture for Differentiated Services", RFC 2475, December 1998.

[2]   R. Braden, L. Zhang, S. Berson, S. Herzog, and S. Jamin (1997) "Resource Reservation Protocol (RSVP) Version 1 Functional Specification", IETF RFC 2205, Proposed Standard, September 1997.

[3]   G. Fehér, K. Németh, M. Maliosz, I. Cselényi, J. Bergkvist, D. Ahlard, T. Engborg (1999) "Boomerang – A Simple Protocol for Resource Reservation in IP Networks", IEEE Workshop on QoS Support for Real-Time Internet Applications, Vancouver, Canada, June 1999.

[4]   RFC 1889: Real-time Transport Protocol.

[5]   Schulzrinne, H (1992) "A Transport Protocol for Audio and Video Conferences and other Multiparticipant Real-Time Applications", Internet Engineering Task Force, Internet-Draft, October 1992.

[6]   Lindbergh, Dave (1997) "H.323: Multimedia Conferencing for Packet Switched Networks", Technical Standards Group PictureTel, June 1997.

[7]   M. Handley, H. Schulzrinne, and E. Schooler (1997) "SIP: Session initiation protocol," Internet Draft, Internet Engineering Task Force, Nov. 1997. Work in progress.

[8]   Jacques Cohen (1990) "Constraint Logic programming Languages", Communications of the ACM, July, 1990, v. 33, pp. 52–68.

[9]   N. Björkman, I. Cselényi, A. Latour-Henner, G. Záruba (1997) "The EMMA Multimedia Conference Service", First International Conference on Information, Communications & Signal Processing, Singapore, September, 1997.

Chapter 11

The Token Repository Service: A Universal and Scalable Mechanism for Constructing Multicast Acknowledgment Trees

Christian Maihöfer

11.1 Introduction

Multicast support is a prerequisite for many applications to ensure scalability for large receiver groups. Although multicast support is already available in the Internet, the provided IP multicast service offers only best effort semantics [5]. Several protocols have been proposed to overcome this drawback by a protocol layer on top of IP multicast [7, 10, 16, 19, 20].

All reliable multicast protocols are based on the same concept, controlling the successful delivery by some kind of acknowledgments returned by the receivers to the source. Simple approaches, where all receivers send their acknowledgment messages directly to the sender can cause the well-known ACK implosion problem [9, 13, 15]. To overcome the ACK implosion problem, the most promising approaches are tree-based protocols [4, 7, 10, 19, 20]. They ensure scalability by organising all group members in a so-called ACK tree. Instead of sending an acknowledgment message directly to the sender, each receiver confirms the correct delivery only to its parent in the ACK tree, which is responsible for possible retransmits. Dependent on the concrete protocol, an inner node in the ACK tree sends an acknowledgment to its parent either after it has received the corresponding message correctly or it first collects all acknowledgments from child nodes. This means that in the latter case an inner node sends an aggregated ACK to its parent after it has received the multicast message and the corresponding ACK from each child, confirming the correct message delivery for the entire sub-hierarchy. Since each node in the ACK tree has an upper bound on the number of its children, no node and no part of the network is congested with messages.

Tree-based protocols raise the problem of setting up the ACK tree. A new member joining a multicast group must be connected to the group's ACK tree, which is usually done by a technique called expanding ring search (ERS). ERS is a multicast-based search technique for discovering a suitable parent node in the ACK tree, by gradually increasing the search scope. The advantage of ERS is its simplicity and robustness against node and network failures. However, our performance evaluations will show that the use of ERS on a large scale has several shortcomings, since it results in a large message overhead and causes particular problems in combination with source-based or unidirectional core-based routed networks.

In this chapter we propose an alternative approach for constructing ACK trees, called *token repository service* (TRS). Our approach is based on a distributed token repository. The TRS stores tokens, where a token basically provides the right to connect to a certain parent node in the ACK tree. A node joining a group asks the TRS for a token of this group, which identifies the parent to connect to.

We have developed three strategies to implement the TRS, the proxy-server strategy (TRS-PS) [11, 12], the random-choice strategy (TRS-RC) [17] and the minimal-height strategy (TRS-MH) [14]. The strategies have different characteristics. The proxy-server strategy is easy to implement and to integrate into the Internet structure. The random-choice strategy results in better shaped ACK trees and lower message overhead, but on the other hand needs an infrastructure to be established. The minimal-height strategy is an extension to the random-choice strategy, creating ACK trees with minimal height. In contrast to ERS, all three strategies provide scalability in the ACK tree construction and better shaped ACK trees, necessary for ensuring reliable multicasting with high reliability, low delays and high throughput.

The remainder of this chapter is organised as follows. In the next section the background and related work are discussed. Section 11.3 gives an overview of the token repository service. In Sections 11.4 to 11.6, the three TRS strategies are described in detail. The behaviour of our approach in the presence of failures is considered in Section 11.7. In Sections 11.8 and 11.9, performance evaluations based on theoretical analysis and simulations are presented before we conclude with a brief summary.

11.2 Background and Related Work

When a new member joins a reliable multicast group the question arises how it will be connected to the group's ACK tree. The problem is to connect the new member to a k-bounded parent that is not already *occupied*, i.e. has not already k children. k is the maximum number of children a node can accept. The bound k for a node depends on various characteristics, such as the node's performance, reliability or load.

Most approaches to establish an ACK tree are based on expanding ring search (ERS) [20]. ERS is a common technique to search for resources in a network [2]. With the basic ERS approach for setting up ACK trees, the joining node looks for a parent in the ACK tree by sending multicast search messages with increasing search scopes (see Figure 11.1). The first message is sent with a time-to-live (TTL) of one, i.e. it is limited to the sender's LAN. If a non-occupied group member receives this message it returns an answer allowing the new member to connect to it. If no node answers within a certain time, the TTL is increased and a new search message is sent. The joining node repeats this until an answer arrives or the maximum TTL of 255 is reached. Note that increasing the TTL step-by-step reduces the network load and detects parents that are, preferably, close to the searching node.

Several proposed protocols reverse the method described above by making the non-occupied ACK tree nodes search for child nodes with multicast invitation messages (ERA, expanding ring advertisement) [7, 10] and some protocols use a combination of both approaches [4].

Our analysis and simulation results will show that ERS/ERA result in a large message overhead. An additional drawback of ERS and ERA are their dependency

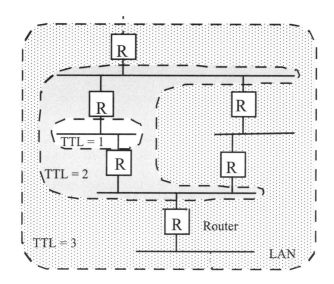

Figure 11.1 Increasing search radius of ERS.

on the various routing protocols, resulting in particular problems with each of them. ERS and ERA with distance vector multicast routing (DVMRP) [18] lead to a vast overhead at all involved routers because a new multicast routing tree has to be built for each sender. This means each node that joins a group via ERS enforces a new, separate routing tree. If ERA is used, a routing tree must be maintained for all non-occupied nodes in the ACK tree. Note that if a member is only a receiver of multicast messages, these trees are only used for the ERS/ERA search. With a unidirectional shared tree approach like PIM-SM [6], the use of ERS and ERA result in a traffic concentration at the core, an even higher message overhead compared with DVMRP and ACK trees of poor quality with respect to tree height and delay.

A further serious drawback of ERA is the message overhead due to the invitation messages, which are sent even if no node wants to join. ERS has the additional drawback that it cannot be used in unidirectional multicast networks. For example, ERS cannot be used in satellite broadcast networks, where there is no multicast backchannel or only an inefficient one.

11.3 Overview of the Token Repository Service

In this section we will describe the interface, concept and implementation idea of the token repository service, which is our proposed infrastructure for building up ACK trees. Then, in Sections 11.4, 11.5 and 11.6, the three strategies TRS-PS, TRS-RC and TRS-MH are described in detail.

Table 11.1 Operations provided by the TRS.

Operation	Description
repCreateGroup (Group, K)	This operation makes *Group* known to the repository service. The caller becomes the root of the ACK tree, which is *K*-bounded.
repDeleteGroup (Group)	This operation deletes all token information of *Group* in the repository.
repJoinGroup (Group, New-Member, K) returns (Token)	*repJoinGroup* is called when the node identified by *NewMember* wants to join *Group*, where *NewMember* is *K*-bounded. The operation returns a token identifying the parent in the ACK tree to connect to.
repLeaveGroup (Group, Member)	This operation deletes all of *Group*'s tokens owned by *Member*.
repAddToken (Group, Owner)	*repAddToken* adds a new token to the repository owned by *Owner*. It is called by *Owner* when a child of *Owner* disconnects from the *Group*'s ACK tree.
repRefreshToken (Group, Owner, Number)	To provide fault tolerance, *repRefreshToken* is periodically called by the tokens' owner. It indicates how many child nodes (*Number*) can still be accepted (see Section 11.7).

11.3.1 Interface and Concept of the Token Repository Service

The basic concept of our approach is tokens that represent the right to connect to a certain node in a given ACK tree. When a k-bounded node has created or joined a group, k tokens are generated and stored in the repository. The creating or joining node is called the tokens' *owner*. A token is defined by a 3-tuple <group, owner, height>, where *group* identifies the multicast group of the *owner*. We define the *height* of a token to be the height of its owner in the corresponding ACK tree. The root node has height 1 in the tree. The height of any other node in the tree is one higher than the height of its parent.

Initially, there are k tokens of a group in the repository, generated on behalf of a *create group* operation. When a node, say N, wants to join a given group, it asks the TRS for a token of this group. The repository service then selects a token of this group, returns it to N and generates new tokens with owner N. The joining node N is now able to connect to the received token's owner in the corresponding ACK tree.

When a node leaves a group, it removes all of this group's tokens out of the repository for which it is the owner. The leaving node has allocated a token belonging to its parent in the ACK tree. This token is returned to the repository, which then can be reused by some other node joining this group later. The operations provided by the TRS are summarised in Table 11.1.

11.3.2 Implementation of the Token Repository Service

In this section, we will describe the basic principles of implementing the TRS. To meet the design goals of scalability and reliability, the token repository service is implemented as a distributed system of token repository servers, *repServers* for short. Each repServer is responsible for a domain, where each domain encompasses a disjoint set of nodes. For example, repServer S_1 in Figure 11.2 is responsible for

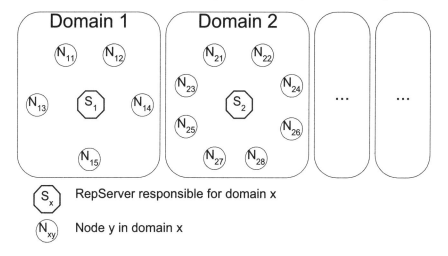

Figure 11.2 Domain structure.

domain 1 consisting of nodes N_{1x}. Domains should structure the network by communication distance, i.e. the communication distance between two nodes in the same domain is typically smaller than between two nodes in different domains. A repServer, responsible for a particular node in its domain, is called this node's *home repServer*. In Figure 11.2, S_1 is the home repServer of the nodes N_{1x}. During normal operation nodes access the token repository service only via their home repServer (see Section 11.7 for failure situations).

Tokens are stored on the distributed repServers. Note that not all tokens of a group are stored at only one repServer, thus several repServers may store tokens for the same group and usually a repServer stores tokens of a number of groups.

If a node requests a token from its home repServer and this repServer possesses a token of the requested group, it simply delivers such a token. Since a token is always stored at the repServer responsible for its owner's domain, a repServer possesses tokens of a group only when a node in its domain has created or joined this group before. As a consequence, usually a repServer does not possess tokens for each group. Therefore, it is possible that a node's home repServer cannot satisfy a token request although another repServer could provide a suitable token. For example, assume that all tokens of a group are stored on a single repServer S_1, responsible for domain 1. If a node in another domain, say domain 2 for example, requests its home repServer S_2 for a token, our approach must ensure that finally S_2 can deliver one of S_1's tokens to the requesting node.

To meet this requirement, a repServer initiates a token search for a group's token if a node in its domain requests a token and none is available locally. In the proxy-server strategy, a token search is processed by ERS. All repServers belong to the same well-known multicast group. If a repServer has to search for a token, it starts an ERS search on the repServers' multicast group. If a repServer receives such a token search message and possesses a token of this group, it hands over one token to the searching repServer.

In the random-choice and minimal-height strategy, all repServers are organised in a tree structure. Nodes access the token repository service only via leaf repServers, which store the token information. Non-leaf repServers are necessary to facilitate the token search procedure, if no local token is available. Each non-leaf repServer maintains a group-specific set of all child repServers that belong to a token-containing sub-hierarchy. A token search is processed by forwarding the search step-by-step to the parent in the repServer hierarchy, i.e. in leaf-to-root direction until one is reached which knows a token-containing sub-hierarchy. Then the search is forwarded in reverse direction, i.e. in root-to-leaf direction to such a child repServer. This is repeated until a leaf repServer is reached which hands over a token to the searching node.

Note that our search mechanism ensures the following:

1. a token is selected whose owner is as close as possible to the joining node and
2. if there are several tokens whose owners are close to the joining node, the one with the lowest height is chosen.

In summary, if a requested token is available locally at the requestor's home repServer, the requestor and the owner of this token are in the same domain. This is the best case in terms of communication overhead between the repServers and communication distance between requestor and owner in the ACK tree. If a token is not available locally, the search procedure tries to find a token in a domain close to the requestor's domain.

11.3.3 Token Information

A repServer stores all tokens of a group in a token basket, i.e. one token basket exists for each group known at the repServer. A token basket has the following structure:

- Group: Unique multicast group identifier.
- SetOfTokenPackets: The tokens are grouped according to their owner into so-called token packets.

Each token packet includes the following information:

- Owner: Unique identifier of the tokens' owner. A node receiving a token from this packet is allowed to connect to owner in the corresponding ACK tree.
- Height: Owner's height in the corresponding ACK tree. The height is used to distinguish the "quality" of alternative tokens. A token with low height is preferable since its use results in an ACK tree with low height and therefore low average path length.
- NoOfTokens: Number of tokens in this token packet.
- ExpDate: Expiration date of the token packet (see Section 11.7).

A token basket is to be established when the first set of tokens associated with the corresponding group is created and it is deleted when the last of this group's token has been removed from it. Each token basket contains a set of token packets. A token packet encloses all of a group's tokens belonging to the same owner.

11.4 The Token Repository Service with Proxy Server Strategy (TRS-PS)

In this section we will describe the group management operations *create group*, *join group*, *leave group* and *delete group* for TRS-PS in more detail. TRS-PS is the first implementation strategy, which is based on ERS. When describing these operations, we assume the absence of failures. Communication and node failures will be considered in Section 11.7.

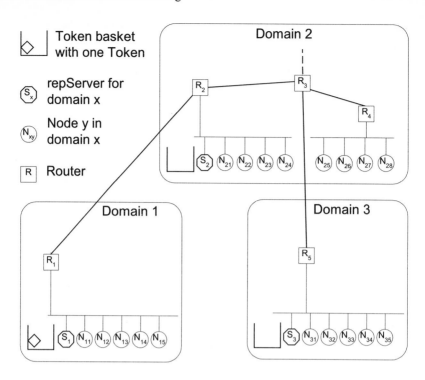

Figure 11.3 A token repository service.

11.4.1 Create Group Operation

A node N creates a new multicast group by initiating a *repCreateGroup (Group, K)* operation at its home repServer S (see Table 11.1). Subsequently, S creates a token basket for *Group* including one token packet with owner N. K specifies the number of tokens in the token packet. The height of the token packet is initialised with 1, because owner N as the root node has height = 1 in the ACK tree. For example, assume node N_{11} in Figure 11.2 sends a *repCreateGroup* operation to its home repServer S_1, responsible for domain 1. Subsequently, S_1 will create a token basket for this group. Figure 11.3 depicts this scenario in more detail and after the token basket is created.

11.4.2 Delete Group Operation

When the operation *repDeleteGroup (Group)* is invoked at a repServer, this server deletes the *Group*'s token basket and sends a *DeleteGroup (Group)* message to all other repServers. Since all repServers belong to a well-known multicast group, this can simply be done by a multicast message. Each repServer receiving *DeleteGroup (Group)* removes the *Group*'s token basket. Note that it is sufficient to send *DeleteGroup* by the best effort IP multicast service since the expiration date mechanism described in Section 11.7 ensures that all outdated state information is finally removed despite node and communication failures.

11.4.3 Join Group Operation

When a node triggers a *repJoinGroup (Group, NewMember, K)* operation at its home repServer *S*, *S* checks whether a token for *Group* is locally available. If such a token exists locally, *S* removes one token with lowest height from the token packet and sends it to the requestor of *repJoinGroup*. Subsequently, *S* creates a new token packet for owner *NewMember* with *K* tokens. The height of the new token packet is the height of the delivered token increased by one. Assume for example that in the scenario depicted in Figure 11.3 a node belonging to domain 1, say N_{12}, sends a *repJoinGroup* operation to its home repServer S_1. S_1 has a locally available token for the requested group that is delivered to N_{12}.

Now we will consider the situation that a repServer *S* has no local tokens for a requested group. If this is the case, *S* initiates a token search by using ERS. The search starts with a multicast *TokenSearch (Group, Requestor)* message to the repServers' group address with a TTL of one. If no repServer returns an answer within a certain time, *S* repeats the search message with an increased TTL, and again waits for an answer. This process is continued until *S* receives an answer or the maximum TTL of 255 is reached.

A repServer receiving a *TokenSearch (Group, Requestor)* message has to check whether it has a token for the requested *Group*. If this is the case, it responds to *Requestor* with an unicasted *TokenAvail (Group, Height, Provider)* message, where *Height* is the minimal height of *Group*'s local tokens at the token *Provider*. Since each ERS search message may result in more than one answer, *S* has to choose one responding node. The *Height* value is used as a token quality metric. *S* chooses the responding token provider *R* with the lowest token height by sending a unicast *GetToken* message to *R*. Finally, *S* receives the requested token with a *Token* message from *R* and *R* removes this token from its token packet.

After *S* has received a token, it establishes a token basket for *Group*, including a token packet for *NewMember,* where *NewMember* was the caller of *repJoinGroup*. Then the received token is handed over to *NewMember*.

To illustrate the token search procedure by means of an example, take Figure 11.3 and assume that node N_{31} wants to join a group and therefore sends a *repJoinGroup* message to its repServer S_3. S_3 checks whether it has a token for this group. Since there is no locally available token, S_3 has to initiate a token search by multicasting *TokenSearch* with increasing TTL until a token is found. The first few multicast messages with a TTL less than 4 do not reach other repServers. The token search message with a TTL of 4 is received by repServer S_2, however S_2 has no tokens and therefore does not reply to S_3. The next search message with a TTL of 5 is received by S_1, which owns a suitable token and answers with a *TokenAvail* message. Subsequently, S_3 stops multicasting *TokenSearch* messages and sends a *GetToken* message to S_1. Finally, S_1 sends the requested token to S_3 that forwards it to the searching node N_{31}. Since S_3 creates new tokens with owner N_{31}, following join requests in domain 3 can be processed by S_3 without further token searches.

During this two-phase token search procedure - phase one includes *TokenSearch* and *TokenAvail*, phase two includes *GetToken* and *Token* messages - the following infrequent situation may occur. If a repServer responds with a *TokenAvail* message, it indicates that at this moment a suitable token is available, i.e. the token will not be reserved for the requesting repServer. Note that this design leads to a stateless and thus light-weight protocol. For example assume that S_1 in Figure 11.3 has only one token and receives two *TokenSearch* messages, one from S_2 at time t_2 and one from S_3 at time t_3, where t_2 is before t_3. S_1 responds to S_2 with *TokenAvail* but also to S_3 since S_1 cannot know whether S_2 will choose S_1's token or has already chosen another one. Therefore, it can occur that both S_2 and S_3 request S_1's token by sending a *GetToken* message. In this case, S_1 hands over its token to the first caller of *GetToken*; all other requestors receive a *NoToken* message, instead.

If a repServer S receives a *NoToken* message it simply chooses another repServer provided that S has received more than one *TokenAvail* message in the first search phase. Otherwise, S simply continues the token search procedure by sending a new *TokenSearch* message with increased TTL.

11.4.4 Leave Group Operation

When a node N leaves a group, all of its tokens are removed. The used multicast transport protocol must ensure that a node is only allowed to leave a group if it has no child nodes in the ACK tree, i.e. is a leaf node. A non-leaf node can leave a group after it has arranged a rejoining for all child nodes at other ACK tree nodes. As we assume that a node has no children in the ACK tree when it leaves the group, all tokens owned by N are in the group's token basket stored on N's home repServer S. When receiving *repLeaveGroup (Group, Member)*, S removes N's token packet from the *Group*'s token basket.

If N leaves a group this affects not only the tokens owned by N, but also the token owned by N's parent in the ACK tree. Conceptually, if N leaves a group it releases its parent's token allocated by N so far. Hence, N's parent adds this token by means of the *repAddToken* operation to the token basket of its home repServer when it recognises that N leaves the group (see Table 11.1).

Note that this mechanism, namely adding tokens by the parent, ensures robustness of our approach. Assume that a node in the ACK tree crashes. The crashed node is not able to return its allocated token to the TRS. Therefore, the parent of the leaving or crashed node has to add the token.

11.5 The Token Repository Service with Random Choice Strategy (TRS-RC)

For the TRS-RC strategy, the network is also structured into domains but in contrast to TRS-PS, the domains are hierarchical. The root domain includes all nodes of the network, while the leaf domains encompass disjoint sets of nodes. Inner domains

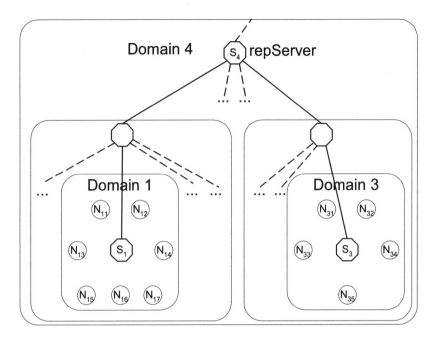

Figure 11.4 Hierarchical domain structure of TRS-RC and TRS-MH.

contain the nodes of their child domains. Figure 11.4 shows the association of nodes to domains. RepServer S_1 is responsible for domain 1 and repServer S_4 is responsible for domain 4, which consists of several subdomains.

A client accesses the token repository service only via the leaf repServers in its domain, called this node's *home repServer*. In Figure 11.4, S_1 is the home repServer for all nodes N_{1x} of domain 1.

All token information is stored on leaf repServers. To facilitate searching for token information for each group a so-called *group tree* is maintained, which is a subtree of the hierarchy of repServers. A group's group tree contains all leaf repServers that store token baskets of this group and all transitive parents of these nodes in the repServer hierarchy. Group tree information is stored in *group records* on non-leaf repServers, where a repServer only stores a group record of a group, say *G*, if one of its transitive (leaf) children store tokens of *G*. A group record of repServer *S* includes the following fields:

- Group: Identifier of the corresponding group.
- Sub: This is a bitmap encoding the list of *S*'s children in the group tree. Each entry in the bitmap corresponds with one child repServer. An entry is set equal to 1 if the corresponding child repServer is part of this group's group tree; otherwise, it is set equal to 0.
- ExpDate: This field defines when the group record expires (see Section 11.7 for details).

Of course, a group tree may grow and shrink during its lifetime, i.e. group records are to be created, updated and deleted dynamically. When a token basket is created, the repServer performing this operation connects to the group's group tree by sending a *TokenAvail* message to its parent in the repServer hierarchy. This message is forwarded in a leaf-to-root direction until it is received by a repServer that already stores a group record or the root node is reached. All non-leaf repServers forwarding this message establish the corresponding group record. When a token basket is removed a *NoTokenAvail* message is sent to the repServer's parent. A non-leaf repServer receiving this message checks whether the message's sender was its only child in the group tree. If this is the case, it deletes the group record and forwards the *NoTokenAvail* message to its parent. Otherwise, it just removes the message's sender from the group record's *Sub* list.

The following sub-sections describe the *create group*, *delete group*, *join group* and *leave group* operations in more detail.

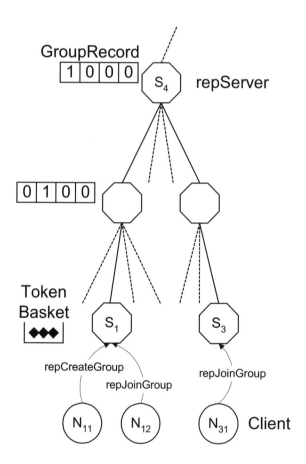

Figure 11.5 Create and join operations at the repServer hierarchy with TRS-RC.

11.5.1 Create Group Operation

When a new group is created, an initial group tree must be established. Assume that S is the leaf repServer at which the *repCreateGroup* operation was issued. The group tree to be established consists of S and all transitive parents of S in the repServer hierarchy. When *repCreateGroup (Group, K)* (see Table 11.1) is issued, S creates a token basket for *Group* with the number of tokens specified by K, where the requestor becomes the owner of these tokens. Subsequently, S sends a *CreateGroup* request to its parent. When receiving a *CreateGroup* request, a non-leaf repServer creates and initialises a group record and sends a *CreateGroup* to its parent.

Figure 11.5 illustrates a scenario where a node creates a group and two other nodes join this group. Node N_{11} creates group G by sending a *repCreateGroup* request to its home repServer S_1. Upon receipt of this request, S_1 creates k tokens $<G, N_{11}, 1>$ in G's token basket, assuming that N_{11} (i.e. the root of G's ACK tree) is k-bounded, i.e. will accept at most k children. The height of the created tokens is 1, since N_{11} is the root node in the created ACK tree and we have defined the root node to have height 1 (see Section 11.3.1). Moreover, group records are established on each non-leaf repServer along the path from S_1 to the root repServer. After their creation they indicate how to find a token containing leaf repServer, starting at the root node.

11.5.2 Delete Group Operation

When the operation *repDeleteGroup (Group)* is issued at a leaf repServer, this server deletes the *Group*'s token basket and sends a *DeleteGroup* request to its parent. Non-leaf repServers forward this request along the edges of *Group*'s group tree, and each repServer receiving this request deletes all state information associated with *Group*. Note that the expiration mechanism ensures that all state information is removed within a certain time despite node and communication failures.

11.5.3 Join Group Operation

When a *repJoinGroup (Group, NewMember, K) returns (Token)* operation is called, the called leaf repServer, say S, checks whether tokens for *Group* are locally available. If this is the case, S removes a token from the token packet with the smallest *height* value in the tokens' 3-tuple <group, owner, height> and returns this token to the caller. It also generates a new token packet for *NewMember* with K tokens and puts it into *Group*'s token basket.

In Figure 11.5, N_{12} resides in the same domain as N_{11}, and hence sends its *repJoinGroup* request also to S_1. When receiving this request, S_1 checks whether tokens for G are locally available. It finds a token $<G, N_{11}, 1>$ and delivers it to N_{12}. In addition, it creates k tokens $<G, N_{12}, 2>$ in G's token basket, assuming that N_{12} will accept at most k children. After receiving token $<G, N_{11}, 1>$, N_{12} can connect to N_{11} in G's ACK tree.

If no token basket exists for *Group* instead, *S* starts the token search procedure, which proceeds in two phases, the leaf-to-root directed and root-to-leaf directed search phase. *S* initiates the leaf-to-root directed search phase by sending a *TokenSearch* request to its parent in the repServer hierarchy. This request is forwarded in a leaf-to-root direction in the repServer hierarchy until a repServer is found that is part of *Group*'s group tree (i.e., it stores the corresponding group record) and has at least one child in this tree being not on the path to *S*. This repServer initiates the downward search phase by sending a *TokenSearch* to one of its children in *Group*'s group tree. This request is forwarded along the edges of the group tree in a root-to-leaf direction until it arrives at a leaf repServer. If a repServer has more than one child in the group tree it randomly selects one of them for forwarding the request. The leaf repServer receiving the *TokenSearch* request removes a token with the lowest *height* value from *Group*'s token basket and delivers the token directly, without using the TRS hierarchy, to *S*.

When receiving the token, *S* establishes a token basket, including a token packet for *NewMember* as described above, and delivers the token to the caller of *repJoinGroup*. In order to connect itself to *Group*'s group tree, it sends a *TokenAvail* message to its parent.

For example, assume that N_{31} in Figure 11.5 wants to join *G*. N_{31} contacts its home repServer S_3, which notices that no tokens are locally available for *G* and hence starts a token search operation. With this search mechanism, the repServer (recursively) asks its parent until the first repServer S_4 is found that belongs to *G*'s group tree, i.e., stores a group record for *G*. *G*'s group tree information stored in non-leaf repServers is used to find the path from S_4 down to S_1. A token <*G*, N_{11}, 1> at S_1 is selected and handed over to S_3. After that, S_3 delivers the token to N_{31}. Finally, group records for *G* are established on the path from S_4 to S_3, and new tokens <*G*, N_{31}, 2> are generated and stored in *G*'s token basket on S_3. The next *repJoinGroup* request concerning *G* can be served by S_3 without involving a search operation.

11.5.4 Leave Group Operation

When a node, say *N*, leaves a group, it conceptually releases a token owned by its parent. Hence, *N*'s parent is requested to add this token by means of the *repAddToken* operation to the token basket of its home repServer when it recognises that *N* leaves the group. As we assume that a node has no children in the ACK tree when it leaves the group, all tokens owned by *N* should be in the group's token basket stored on *N*'s home repServer at the time the *repLeaveGroup* operation is called. When receiving this call, *N*'s repServer removes *N*'s token packet from the group's token basket. If the token basket becomes empty, it is removed and a *NoTokenAvail* message is sent to the parent repServer.

11.6 The Token Repository Service with Minimal Height Strategy (TRS-MH)

In this section we will provide an overview of TRS-MH. The minimal-height strategy is described in detail, including pseudo code, in [14]. TRS-MH creates ACK trees with minimal height that improves reliability and round trip delay in the ACK tree. Note that the reliability of a node depends on its own reliability and the reliability of all nodes on the path from its parent node to the root node, because they are necessary to send a retransmission in case of data loss. Therefore, the lower the number of intermediate nodes on the path to the root, the higher the reliability from this node's perspective. Furthermore, small path lengths usually result in lower delays between the root node and all receivers, which improves throughput of protocols with aggregated acknowledgments [8, 19].

The basic concept of TRS-MH is quite simple. If a client requests a token from the token repository service, a token with minimal height in its 3-tuple <group, owner, height> has to be delivered. Therefore, new nodes connect always as close as possible to the root node in the ACK tree, which results in height-balanced ACK trees. A *height-balanced* ACK tree is a tree with minimal height for a given k-bound, i.e. height=$[\log_k(R(k-1)+1)]$ where R is the number of nodes in the tree (see Section 11.8).

The implementation of TRS-MH is similar to TRS-RC but more complex than the previous strategies. Again, a group tree has to be maintained identifying the repServers that store tokens for a given group. Group tree information is stored in group records with the following structure:

– Group: Unique multicast group identifier.
– MinHeightGlobal: Minimal height of tokens in the entire repository hierarchy.
– MinHeightSub[ ]: Vector determining the minimal token height for each child domain.
– ExpDate: This field defines when the group record expires (see Section 11.7 for details).

In contrast to TRS-RC, leaf repServers store a group record, too, consisting only of *Group*, *MinHeightGlobal* and *ExpDate*. *MinHeightGlobal* determines the minimal height of all tokens in the entire repository hierarchy. If the height of a locally available token is not greater than *MinHeightGlobal*, a local token can be delivered to the requesting client. Otherwise, a token search has to be performed to find a token with minimal height, i.e. a token with height equal to *MinHeightGlobal*.

A token search of TRS-MH consists of two phases, too. In the first phase of the token search, a *TokenRequest* is forwarded in the leaf-to-root direction until a repServer is found that is part of the group tree and the following condition holds: min(*MinHeightSub*) ≤ *MinHeightGlobal*. If this condition holds at a repServer, a minimal-height token can be found in this repServer's subhierarchy, i.e. at one of the transitive children, and hence the search domain needs no further enlargement.

In the second search phase, each repServer forwards the *TokenRequest* message to a child s with *MinHeightSub*[s] = min(*MinHeightSub*) until a leaf repServer is reached. If more than one subhierarchy satisfies this condition, the repServer randomly selects one of them. Finally, the found leaf repServer removes a token with minimal height from *Group*'s token basket and delivers it directly to the searching leaf repServer, without using the TRS hierarchy.

If a repServer delivers a token to another repServer or a client, *MinHeightGlobal* of this repServer is updated to the token's height if it is greater than *MinHeightGlobal*. If this repServer is not already connected to the group tree or *MinHeightGlobal* or the minimal height of all locally available tokens has changed, it sends a *HeightUpdate (minimal local token height, MinHeightGlobal)* to its parent. A non-leaf repServer receiving a *HeightUpdate* message checks whether the corresponding group record already exists and creates one otherwise. Then the receiver updates *MinHeightSub*[i], where i was the sender of *HeightUpdate*, to the received value of the minimal token height and *MinHeightGlobal* to the received value of *MinHeightGlobal*, provided that *MinHeightGlobal* is not decreased. The forwarding of *HeightUpdate (Group,* min*(MinHeightSub), MinHeightGlobal)* to the parent in the TRS hierarchy is then repeated as long as at least one of min(*MinHeightSub*) or *MinHeightGlobal* undergoes a change and the root node is not already reached. The details of TRS-MH are described in [14].

11.7 Fault Tolerance of the Token Repository Service

In the previous sections we have described the group management operations during normal conditions without considering communication and node failures. In this section we will describe the behaviour in such failure situations.

When a group management operation is to be performed and the home repServer is not available caused by a crash or network partition, any other repServer can be selected to execute those operations. To be able to select another repServer, each client maintains a list of some alternative repServers. Of course, when selecting another repServer, those that are in close domains are preferable. Note that using another repServer results in larger distances between parent and child nodes in the created ACK tree, which increases network load and delay for the reliable multicast protocol.

All token information is maintained according to the soft state principle. Token packets are associated with an expiration date. If the expiration date is reached, it must either be extended or the token packet will be discarded automatically. Obviously, the lifetime of a token packet depends on the lifetime of its owner. To prevent a token packet from expiring, the token's owner periodically refreshes the token information of not already used tokens, which extends their expiration date. If no refresh message is received within two refresh cycles, the token packet is discarded. On the other hand, if a refresh message is received without storing the corresponding tokens, these tokens are created. The mechanism for group records used in TRS-RC and TRS-MH is analogous. In most cases the updating of group records through a *TokenAvail* or *HeightUpdate* message due to a change in the group tree is sufficient to extend the group record's expiration date of the parent node. If group tree changes are too infrequent, additional *TokenAvail* or *HeightUpdate* messages are sent to prevent the parent's group record from being discarded.

Although our protocols discard token packets explicitly during normal operations, this mechanism allows to design a robust but nevertheless lightweight protocol, ensuring even in the presence of node and communication failures that eventually all outdated information is removed. In addition, this mechanism allows us to keep token information in volatile memory, which is necessary to provide a high repServer throughput. If the token information is lost due to a repServer crash, the refresh mechanism recovers the lost data.

The mechanisms described above ensure that tokens are not permanently lost. However, token loss can result in a higher overhead for finding a token in the TRS and disadvantageous ACK trees. For example, assume that the home repServer of a node has crashed. Then a token from another domain is used in case the home repServer is not yet available or the tokens are not yet recovered. This leads to larger distances in the ACK tree between parent and child nodes, which increase network load and delay for the reliable multicast transport protocol.

As this refresh mechanism is only necessary to discard outdated information and recover tokens in case of node or communication failures, the refresh cycles can be rather large. Furthermore, only nodes that are not already occupied need to refresh their token information. Therefore, the additional communication overhead is low.

11.8 Performance Analysis

In this section we present some analytical results comparing the TRS strategies with ERS and ERA. We have evaluated the maximum message overhead and the maximum height of the created ACK tree.

11.8.1 Message Overhead

The following message overhead evaluation considers only the overhead for group management rather than the overhead on routing layer or the reliable multicast transport protocol. We assume a scenario in which the join and leave operations are independent, i.e. all join operations are processed before the first leave operation and we do not consider possible rejoining overheads when non-leaf nodes leave the ACK tree. Furthermore, we assume the absence of failures. As the message overhead of ERA depends mainly on the time period, it is not considered here.

Using ERS, create, delete and leave a group is not explicitly done, therefore the message overhead is 0. The worst case for joining a group is that 255 multicast search messages must be sent to find a parent node, since 255 is the maximum time-to-live value in an IP packet and that all nodes that have already joined the ACK tree reply to the searching node. The maximum number of messages n_j for joining a group is therefore as follows:

$$n_j = search\ messages + reply\ messages$$

$$= 255_m\,j + \sum_{i=1}^{j} i$$

$$= 255_m\,j + \frac{j^2 + j}{2} \qquad\qquad (11.1)$$

Index m identifies multicast messages and j is the number of join operations (see Table 11.2). Since there is a square component in the formula, the worst case message overhead is quadratic.

The message overhead for creating a group using TRS-PS is one message, the *repCreateGroup* message. To delete a group, *repDeleteGroup* is sent to the home repServer that sends one multicast *DeleteGroup* message to all other repServers.

To join a group *repJoinGroup* must be sent to the repServer and then a token is replied. If a repServer has no local token for a requested group, a token search is invoked by sending multicast search messages. In the worst case 255 search messages are sent and every other repServer sends an answer message. Finally, the token is handed over, which needs additionally two messages. Such a token search is processed only once per repServer and the repServer at which the group is created needs no token search at all. The maximum number of messages for joining a group is therefore as follows, where B is the number of requested repServers:

$$n_j = 2j + (B-1)(255_m + (B-1) + 2)$$

$$= 2j + 255(B-1)_m + B^2 - 1 \qquad\qquad (11.2)$$

If we assume that we have a large number of join operations, that means if $j \gg B$ then:

$$n_j \approx 2j \qquad\qquad (11.3)$$

This means that the number of messages rises linearly with the number of join operations. To leave a group only one message, *repLeaveGroup* is sent to the repServer.

The message overhead for creating a group using TRS-RC is one message to the home repServer and $(t-1)$ messages to establish the group tree, where t is the height of the TRS tree. To delete a group, *repDeleteGroup* is sent to the home repServer which forwards it along the edges of the group tree. The number of messages is therefore:

$$n_d = \sum_{i=0}^{t-1} k^i \qquad\qquad (11.4)$$

Table 11.2 Notation and summary of analytical results.

Maximum message overhead with ERS:

$$n_c = 0, \quad n_d = 0, \quad n_j = 255_m j + \frac{j^2 + j}{2}, \quad n_l = 0$$

Maximum message overhead with TRS-PS:

$$n_c = c, \quad n_d = d + d_m, \quad n_j = 2j + 255(B-1)_m + B^2 - 1 \approx 2j \quad (j \gg B), \quad n_l = l$$

Maximum message overhead with TRS-RC:

$$n_c = ct, \quad n_d = \sum_{i=0}^{t-1} k^i, \quad n_j = \sum_{i=1}^{t-1} [(k^i - k^{i-1})(3(t-i)+3)] + (j-B+1)2 \quad (j > B), \quad n_l = lt$$

Maximum message overhead with TRS-MH:

$$n_c = ct, \quad n_d = \sum_{i=0}^{t-1} k^i, \quad n_j = \sum_{i=1}^{t-1} [(k^i - k^{i-1})(3(t-i)+3)] + (j-B+1)(2+t-1) \quad (j > B), \quad n_l = lt$$

Maximum tree height with ERS/ERA:

$$h = j - l + 1$$

Maximum tree height with TRS-PS and TRS-RC:

$$h = B - 1 + \lceil \log_k ((j-B+2)(k-1)+1) \rceil$$

Maximum tree height with TRS-MH:

$$h = \lceil \log_k ((j-l+1)(k-1)+1) \rceil$$

nx	Number of messages to create ($x=c$), delete ($x=d$), join ($x=j$) or leave ($x=l$) a group.
c,d,j,l	Number of create, delete, join or leave operations.
B	Number of (leaf) repServers requested for a token.
N	Number of nodes in a complete k-ary tree.
h	Height of the created ACK tree.
t	Height of the TRS hierarchy.

To determine the number of messages for joining a group we distinguish between the first (B-1) joins and the remaining ones. We assume that the first (B-1) joins are issued at different home repServers and therefore result in a token search. In the worst case, the token search must be forwarded to the root node and from the root node to a leaf node which results in $2(t-1)$ messages. If the token is handed over, the group tree must be updated which results in ($t-1$) messages. Three messages are necessary to send *repJoinGroup* to the home repServer, hand over a token to the searching repServer and finally return the token to the client. After the first (B-1) joins all remaining ones involve no further token search and therefore result in only two messages per join operation:

$$n_j = \sum_{i=1}^{t-1} [(k^i - k^{i-1})(3(t-i)+3)]$$
$$+ (j - B + 1)2 \quad (j > B) \tag{11.5}$$

If a client leaves a group this can result in a necessary update of the group record. So, in the worst case t messages are necessary.

Now we want to analyse the TRS-MH strategy. The number of messages to create a group, delete a group and leave a group are equal to TRS-RC. In the worst case the *repJoinGroup* operation results everytime in a token search and update of the group records:

$$n_j = j(3(t-1)+3) \qquad (11.6)$$

Figure 11.6 depicts the maximum number of sent messages for the ERS, TRS-PS, TRS-RC and TRS-MH approaches. The number of join operations ranges from 1000 to 10 000. Note that the y-axis has a logarithmic scaling. In this scenario it is assumed that one group is created, the depicted number of nodes on the x-axis join this group and half the number of joining nodes leave the group. The results show

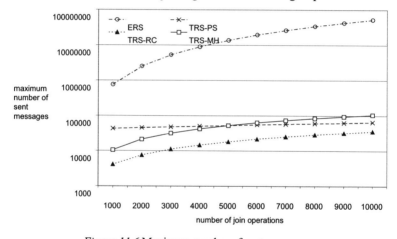

Figure 11.6 Maximum number of sent messages.

that ERS cannot be applied for large receiver groups. The TRS approaches provide significantly better scalability. The best scheme in terms of message overhead is TRS-RC. In contrast to ERS and TRS-PS it sends no multicast search messages and in contrast to TRS-MH it results in less overhead to search for a token in the repServer hierarchy and update the group records.

11.8.2 Tree Height

The height of the created ACK tree influences its reliability and round-trip delay. Trees with low height are desirable (see Section 11.6). Using ERS/ERA, the maximum height of the created ACK tree is only limited by the number of join operations, i.e. in the worst case the height can be equal to $j-l+1$, where j is the number of join operations and l is the number of leave operations.

With TRS the height of the created ACK tree is determined by the number of join operations and the number of requested repServers. If only one repServer is requested, a tree with minimal height is created since for each token request the token with minimal height in the ACK tree is delivered. Therefore, the height can be calculated as follows:

Number of nodes in a complete k - ary tree :

$$N = \sum_{i=0}^{h-1} k^i = k^0 + k^1 + ... + k^{h-2} + k^{h-1}$$

$$N = \frac{(1-k)k^0}{(1-k)} + \frac{(1-k)k^1}{(1-k)} + ... + \frac{(1-k)k^{h-2}}{(1-k)} + \frac{(1-k)k^{h-1}}{(1-k)}$$

$$N = \frac{k^0 - k^1 + k^1 - k^2 + ... + k^{h-2} - k^{h-1} + k^{h-1} - k^h}{(1-k)}$$

$$N = \frac{1-k^h}{(1-k)} \quad \Rightarrow \quad h = \lceil \log_k (N(k-1)+1) \rceil$$

Tree height with j join operations :

$$h = \lceil \log_k ((j+1)(k-1)+1) \rceil \qquad (11.7)$$

If we consider B instead of one repServer, the worst case is that at B-1 repServers only one join operation is processed and that each of these join operations results in a parent with maximum height in the ACK tree. All other join operations are processed by one repServer. The maximum height can be expressed as follows:

$$h = B - 1 + \text{height of a complete k} - \text{ary tree}$$
$$\text{for } (j - (B-1)) \text{ join operations}$$
$$= B - 1 + \lceil \log_k ((j - l - B + 2)(k-1)+1) \rceil \qquad (11.8)$$

The maximum tree height for TRS-RC is equal to the results of TRS-PS. For TRS-MH the tree height is equal to the height of a balanced tree:

$$h = \lceil \log_k ((j - l + 1)(k-1)+1) \rceil \qquad (11.9)$$

Figure 11.7 depicts the maximum resulting ACK tree height of 1000 to 10 000 join operations. The result of TRS-MH is equal to the height of a balanced k-bounded tree and therefore optimal. ERS and ERA can result in large tree heights, which is disadvantageous for round trip delays in the ACK tree and reliability.

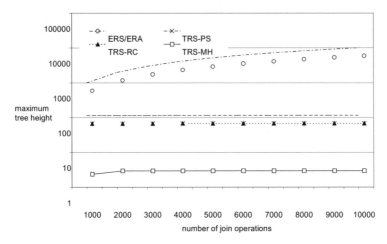

Figure 11.7 Maximum resulting ACK tree height.

11.9 Simulations

We have performed simulations using the NS2 network simulator [1] to compare the token repository service with expanding ring search strategies. The networks are generated with the network generator Tiers [3].

Figure 11.8 depicts the dependency between received messages and various levels of background load. In this simulation study we have used 200 join operations and the routing protocol DVMRP. The background load is measured as the percentage of busy links during the simulation time, i.e. a background load of 100% means that each network link was busy during the entire simulation.

The results show that ERS scales poorly with the background load. If the background load exceeds a certain level, the number of received messages rises strongly. This behaviour is caused by increased message delays due to high background load. When the delay of a search and the resulting answer message exceeds the timeout interval, the sender of ERS starts a new multicast message with increased TTL. Note that the timeout parameter for ERS specifies the time per hop that a node waits for an answer to arrive, before it sends a new search message with an increased TTL. For example, if the timeout is one second and the search scope is ten hops then the node performing ERS waits ten seconds for an answer before it starts a new search. The lower this time to wait is, the sooner a new search message is sent and therefore the earlier the effect of strongly increasing message overhead occurs. However, the timeout parameter can only be increased within a certain range, since this influences the delay of a join operation. Moreover, as can be seen in the figure, increasing the timeout interval also increases the message overhead in case of low background load. For example in Figure 11.8 the message overhead of ERS with 5s timeout interval is up to 6% background load higher than that of the

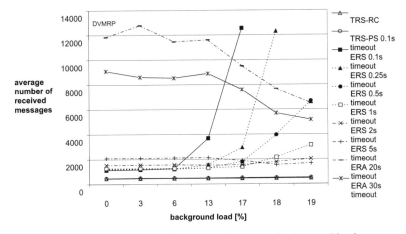

Figure 11.8 Messages received depending on the background load.

other ERS curves with lower timeout intervals. Since it takes longer for a node to join the ACK tree if the timeout interval is increased, it also takes longer before the joining node itself is able to accept child nodes. Therefore, other joining nodes must possibly search in a larger scope to connect to the ACK tree.

ERA results in a high message overhead independent of the background load. With increased background load, the message overhead seems to decrease but this is only caused by our simulation scenario. The use of ERA leads to network congestion and therefore to a high message delay. Since the simulated time period was restricted, not all invitation messages were delivered during simulation time.

The message overhead of both token repository services, with random-choice strategy and proxy-server strategy, is much lower compared with ERS and ERA and moreover, independent of the background load, always constant. The minimal-height strategy, which is not included in the figure, results in about the same message overhead as the random-choice strategy. We have also simulated the proxy-server strategy with various timeout intervals but the results have differed only slightly.

Figure 11.9 shows the results of another simulation study to determine the in-fluence of network size on scalability. Fifty join operations are simulated with DVMRP and PIM-SM routing. The message overhead of TRS-RC, TRS-MH and ERA is constant, independent of the network size and routing protocol. The results show that TRS-PS sends more messages than TRS-RC and TRS-MH and the number of messages increases with larger networks. However, compared with ERS and ERA the number of messages is always smaller and rises only slightly with the network size.

The final simulation results depicted in Figure 11.10 investigate the average path length respectively height of the created ACK trees. The path length affects the reliability of the created ACK tree. The multicast service may be disrupted for a node if one of its parents in the ACK tree becomes unavailable. Therefore, the lower the number of parents the higher the reliability from this node's perspective. So, the

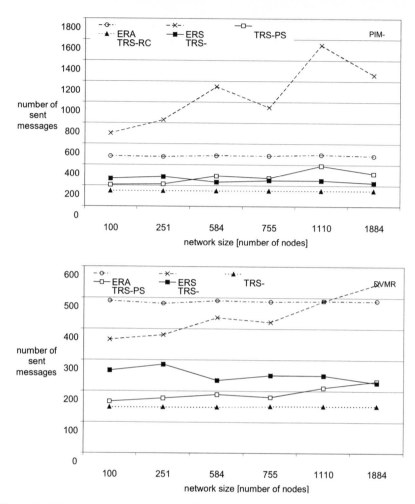

Figure 11.9 Messages sent depending on the network size with DVMRP and PIM-SM.

average path length of the ACK tree can be used as a quality criterion for reliability, since it is equivalent to the average number of nodes that must rejoin the tree if a single ACK tree node fails. Furthermore, low tree height usually results in low delays in the ACK tree.

Figure 11.10 shows that TRS-PS as well as TRS-RC and ERA lead to ACK trees with low path lengths that are near to the theoretical minimum. Note that TRS-MH creates ACK trees with minimal path length. The use of ERS results in unbalanced ACK trees especially in combination with the routing protocol PIM-SM, i.e. the failure of a single node may lead to a vast overhead, for example for rejoining its child nodes. This is caused by the characteristic of PIM- SM that multicast messages are always disseminated from the same core node in the network. Therefore, ERS finds always nodes close to this core and nodes that are far away from the core node get no child nodes, which results in large tree height.

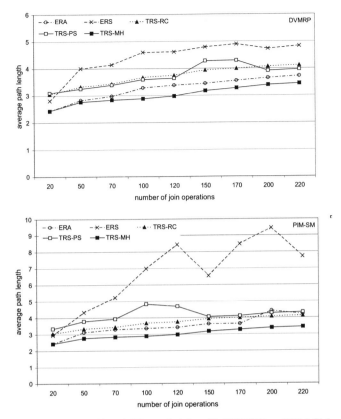

Figure 11.10 Resulting ACK tree height with DVMRP and PIM-SM.

11.10 Summary

In this chapter we have presented the token repository service, which is an efficient and robust approach for constructing ACK trees. The basic concept of our approach is a distributed repository storing tokens, which represent the right to connect to a certain node in an existing ACK tree.

Compared with the various approaches based on expanding ring search, the TRS has several advantages. It needs no bidirectional multicast support for joining nodes and produces network load only when a receiver joins a group. Furthermore, using the TRS, the undesired impact of the multicast routing protocol on the ACK tree construction in terms of scalability and quality of the created ACK trees is almost eliminated. In contrast to ERS with DVMRP, the TRS needs no separate routing tree to be established for each receiver joining the group. In contrast to ERS with PIM-SM, the disadvantageous core-based dissemination of multicast messages hardly influences the results of the TRS. We can conclude from the presented simulation results that the TRS appreciably improves scalability. In addition, in terms of round trip delay and reliability of the created ACK trees, the proposed TRS performs in many cases better than ERS approaches.

References

[1]   Bajaj S., Breslau L., Estrin D., Fall K., Floyd S., Haldar P., Handley M., Helmy A., Heidemann J., Huang P., Kumar S., McCanne S., Rejaie R., Sharma P., Varadhan K., Xu Y., Yu H., Zappala D.(1999). Improving simulation for network research, Technical Report 99-702, University of Southern California, 1999.

[2]   Boggs D. (1983). Internet broadcasting, Ph.D. Th., XEROX Palo Alto Research Center, Technical Report CSL-83-3, 1983.

[3]   Calvert K., Doar M.B., Zegura E.W. (1997). Modelling Internet topology, IEEE Communications Magazine, June 1997.

[4]   Chiu D. M., Hurst S., Kadansky J., Wesley J. (1998). TRAM: A tree-based reliable multicast protocol, Sun Microsystems Laboratories Technical Report Series, TR-98-66, 1998.

[5]   Deering S. (1989). Host extensions for IP multicasting, RFC 1112.

[6]   Estrin D., Farinacci D., Helmy A., Thaler D., Deering S., Handley M., Jacobson V., Liu C., Sharma P., Wei L. (1998). Protocol independent multicast-sparse mode (PIM-SM): protocol specification, RFC 2362.

[7]   Hofmann M. (1996): Adding scalability to transport level multicast, Lecture Notes in Computer Science, No. 1185, pp 41–55.

[8]   Levine B.N., Lavo D.B., Garcia-Luna-Aceves J.J. (1996). The case for reliable concurrent multicasting using shared ACK trees, Proceedings of the fourth ACM International Conference on Multimedia, 1996, pp 365–376.

[9]   Levine B.N., Garcia-Luna-Aceves J.J. (1996). A comparison of known classes of reliable multicast protocols, Proceedings of the IEEE International Conference on Network Protocols, pp 112–121.

[10] Lin J.C., Paul S. (1996). RMTP: A reliable multicast transport protocol, Proceedings of the Conference on Computer Communications (IEEE Infocom), pp 1414–1424.

[11] Maihöfer C. (2000). Improving multicast ACK tree construction with the Token Repository Service, IEEE ICDCS Workshop, pp C57–C64.

[12] Maihöfer C. (2000). Scalable and reliable multicast ACK tree construction with the Token Repository Service, Proceedings of the International Conference on Networks (IEEE ICON), pp 351–358.

[13] Maihöfer C. (2000). A bandwidth analysis of reliable multicast transport protocols, to appear in Proceedings of the Second International Workshop on Networked Group Communication (NGC).

[14] Maihöfer C., Rothermel K. (1999). Constructing height-balanced multicast acknowledgment trees with the Token Repository Service, Technical Report 1999/15, University of Stuttgart, Faculty for Computer Science.

[15] Maihöfer C., Rothermel K., Mantei N. (2000). A throughput analysis of reliable multicast transport protocols, to appear in Proceedings of the Ninth International Conference on Computer Communications and Networks (IEEE ICCCN).

[16] Pingali S., Towsley D., Kurose F. (1994): A comparison of sender-initiated and receiver-initiated reliable multicast protocols, Proceedings of ACM SIGMETRICS, pp 221–230.

[17] Rothermel K., Maihöfer C. (1999). A robust and efficient mechanism for constructing multicast acknowledgment trees, Proceedings of the IEEE Eighth International Conference on Computer Communications and Networks (IEEE ICCCN'99), pp 139–145.

[18] Waitzman D., Partridge C., Deering S. (1988). Distance vector multicast routing protocol, RFC 1075.

[19] Whetten B., Taskale G. (2000). An overview of the reliable multicast transport protocol II, IEEE Network, 14, 1, pp 37–47.

[20] Yavatkar R., Griffioen J., Sudan M. (1995). A reliable dissemination protocol for interactive collaborative applications, Proceedings of the third ACM International Conference on Multimedia, pp 333–344.

Index

3D, 20, 21, 25

access, 139, 158, 159
acknowledgements, 201, 202, 203,
    204, 205, 207, 208, 210, 213, 214,
    215, 216, 217, 220, 221, 223, 224,
    225, 226
ACK-tree, 201, 202, 203, 204, 205,
    207, 208, 210, 213, 214, 215, 216,
    217, 220, 221, 223, 224, 225, 226
adaptation, 119, 162
ADSL, 80
ADUBA, 17, 20, 21, 23, 24, 25, 26,
    28, 29, 30, 31, 32
advertising, 22, 29, 127, 131, 132,
    133, 134
affinity group, 121, 129, 130
affordability, 139, 148
affordance, 11
agent, 20, 54, 60, 61, 121, 128, 129,
    191, 192
algorithm, 101, 162, 163, 164, 165,
    166, 167, 168, 170, 171, 172, 176,
    177, 178, 181, 182, 190, 191, 192,
    193, 194, 195, 196, 197, 198
    compression, 2, 4, 6, 66
architecture, 20, 54, 60, 62, 63, 75,
    91, 93, 94, 95, 97, 98, 104, 105,

106, 107, 108, 109, 111, 113, 114,
    115, 116, 117, 165, 166, 168, 170,
    182, 190
ARPA, 141, 142, 157
artificial intelligence, 20, 22, 23
assembly, 190
ATM, 60, 61, 66, 72, 77, 78, 87, 88,
    91, 92, 95, 97, 113, 171, 182, 183
audio
    clarity, 6, 36, 40

behaviour analysis, 19, 32
blocking, 186, 191, 195, 198
Bond, James, 31
broadcast, 36, 38, 39, 40, 41, 50, 51,
    74, 75, 80, 85, 86, 89, 90, 134,
    141, 143, 152, 204

capacity, 33, 95
channel
    visual, 36, 37, 44
chat rooms, 128
client, 38, 40, 42, 45, 63, 109, 211,
    215, 216, 219, 220
codec, 2, 41
    audio, 61
    video, 50
cognitive science, 21, 22

commerce, 20, 32, 149
communication
  business, 35
  non-verbal, 36, 37, 44, 48, 50
  services, 35, 137, 143
community
  affinity, 130
  online, 127
components
  auditory, 36
compression, 2, 3, 4, 6, 66, 74, 94,
  98, 170
  audio, 8, 9
  video, 2, 4, 6, 8, 9, 12, 60
conference
  distributed, 53, 54, 64, 65, 67, 70,
    88, 89
  video, 91
  virtual, 84, 85
conformity, 94
congestion, 97, 105, 113, 162, 163,
  164, 165, 166, 167, 168, 169, 170,
  176, 182
conspicuity, 23
constrained scaling, 7
constructivity
  architectural, 94
content, 4, 5, 6, 7, 8, 9, 10, 14, 20, 22,
  23, 24, 25, 29, 32, 35, 36, 37, 38,
  39, 42, 44, 46, 48, 49, 50, 56, 65,
  67, 69, 71, 76, 121, 124, 126, 127,
  128, 129, 132, 133, 134, 141, 146,
  167, 170, 191
  emotional, 35
  factual, 35, 37, 41, 42, 43, 44, 46,
    47, 48, 49, 50
  multimedia, 1, 23, 28, 36, 40, 41,
    44, 50
content analysis, 29
continuity, 95, 104
CORBA, 109
CSCW, 51, 54, 60, 67, 72, 76, 77, 92
customer, 22, 23, 32, 130, 133
cyber society, 152, 158

data mining, 18
datagram, 162, 167
delivery, 36, 37, 39, 50, 95, 98, 100,
  113, 201
demographics, 29
deregulation, 138, 140, 143, 145,
  151, 155, 156
design, 9, 10, 18, 37, 38, 42, 46, 51,
  53, 54, 64, 83, 86, 93, 94, 95, 107,
  116, 131, 132, 154, 186, 205, 210,
  217
distribution, 56, 61, 64, 72, 85, 132,
  134, 163, 164, 166, 167, 182
domain, 18, 100, 142, 205, 206, 207,
  208, 209, 210, 211, 213, 215, 217
effectiveness, 36, 50, 162, 172
ETSI, 94, 96, 118, 119
experiment, 4, 5, 41, 42, 45, 48, 49,
  50, 90, 164, 172, 176, 177

feedback, 13, 20, 22, 50, 63, 97, 105,
  106, 107, 110, 162, 163, 164, 165,
  166, 167, 168, 169, 170, 171, 176,
  182
filter
  collaborative, 121, 129, 130, 131

globalisation, 74, 121, 151

hardware, 60, 74, 75, 80
Heidelberg, 94, 107, 112, 115, 118,
  119

IETF, 64, 91, 94, 118, 186, 199
infrastructure, 19, 38, 64, 69, 74, 75,
  77, 78, 83, 86, 91, 104, 116, 128,
  134, 138, 139, 142, 145, 150, 152,
  154, 156, 158, 159, 202, 204
integrity, 95
interaction, 4, 17, 18, 19, 21, 22, 23,
  32, 43, 47, 56, 57, 58, 59, 60, 81,
  84, 85, 89, 96, 105, 107, 115, 140,
  186
intranet, 38

ISABEL, 53, 54, 55, 56, 57, 58, 59, 60, 61, 62, 63, 64, 65, 66, 67, 68, 69, 71, 72, 79, 80, 83, 86, 87, 89, 91, 92
ISDN, 60, 61, 63, 64, 66, 71, 74, 75, 78, 80, 147
ISO, 94, 95, 96, 99, 108, 117, 118, 119
ITU, 6, 14, 74, 118

Lancaster, 94, 111, 115
latency, 95, 98, 164
layer, 59, 60, 61, 63, 97, 101, 107, 111, 112, 113, 114, 115, 116, 161, 162, 163, 164, 165, 166, 168, 169, 170, 171, 172, 176, 190, 201, 217
learning, 23, 24, 29, 35, 37, 50, 51, 92, 131

management, 37, 50, 53, 54, 56, 59, 62, 64, 65, 69, 71, 72, 76, 80, 81, 87, 91, 93, 96, 97, 99, 103, 104, 105, 106, 107, 109, 110, 111, 112, 114, 115, 116, 186, 198, 207, 216, 217
mapping, 7, 100, 111
market research, 17, 18, 19, 20, 21, 131
marketing, 19, 121, 130, 188
Mbone, 79, 80, 85, 87, 89, 91
media
    mass, 17, 18, 32, 85, 122, 134, 136
    meso, 122
millennium, 18
mobile, 147, 157, 186, 192
model, 10, 11, 55, 76, 80, 84, 85, 86, 87, 88, 90, 93, 108, 114, 115, 138, 146, 154, 159, 172, 177, 181
monitoring, 92, 94, 97, 100, 103, 104, 105, 111, 115, 157, 162, 168, 171, 172
motivation, 17, 20
movie, 5, 21, 24, 26, 29, 31, 94, 178
multicast, 40, 60, 61, 63, 72, 80, 83, 87, 91, 101, 102, 112, 161, 162,

163, 164, 166, 167, 168, 170, 176, 178, 182, 201, 202, 203, 204, 205, 206, 207, 208, 209, 210, 215, 216, 217, 218, 220, 222, 223, 224, 225, 226, 227
layered video with retransmission (LVMR), 163, 183
receiver-driven layered (RLM), 163, 164
source-adaptive multi-layered (SAMM), 162, 165, 166, 168, 170, 171, 172, 176, 177, 178, 181, 182
multimedia
    interactive, 22, 93, 95, 99, 104, 116, 117
multimedia learning environment, 37, 50

narrowcasting, 133
navigation, 2, 20, 23, 24
negotiation, 14, 93, 94, 99, 100, 101, 102, 103, 109, 186, 190, 191, 192, 193, 194, 195, 196, 197, 198
network
    communication, 53, 54, 64, 65, 70, 71, 110
    Ethernet, 38, 39, 78
    local area, 203
    Metropolitan Area, 186
    packet-switched, 36
    token ring, 38, 39
network capacity, 36, 38
network congestion, 38, 101, 162, 163, 164, 172, 176, 223
network traffic, 39, 49, 161, 164
NII, 144, 145, 155, 159

ODP, 95, 96, 97, 117
Omega, 94, 114, 115
online, 12, 18, 19, 21, 121, 123, 124, 125, 126, 127, 128, 129, 130, 131, 132, 133, 134, 143, 148, 149, 154
OSI Reference Model, 96

perception, 2, 3, 4, 8, 20, 22, 24, 27, 29, 31, 47
performance, 5, 48, 49, 61, 62, 63, 67, 92, 93, 96, 103, 104, 162, 166, 171, 172, 176, 177, 182, 195, 202, 203
personalisation, 121, 126, 127, 128, 129
prediction, 23, 94, 99
pro-sumer, 121, 128
protocol, 38, 54, 64, 75, 79, 91, 100, 105, 109, 111, 112, 113, 166, 199, 201, 210, 216, 217, 222, 223, 224, 225, 226, 227
    tree-based, 201
prototype, 9, 12, 13
proxy, 223
psychology, 21
psychophysics, 3

quality
    video, 2, 6, 7, 47, 50, 66, 161, 163, 164, 169, 177, 178, 179, 182

radio, 17, 18, 78, 121, 126, 127, 128, 131, 132, 134, 135, 136, 140, 143, 159
real-time, 36, 38, 40, 54, 59, 70, 85, 86, 87, 91, 95, 113, 114
regionalisation, 132
regulation, 137, 138, 141, 147
repository, 202, 204, 205, 206, 211, 215, 222, 223, 225
resolution
    spatial, 2
resource broker, 185, 186, 195, 198
resource reservation, 100
router, 38, 61, 166, 171, 182, 195
routing, 111, 113, 162, 166, 204, 217, 222, 223, 224, 225, 227
RSVP, 97, 112, 117, 118, 199
RTP, 64, 91

saliency, 23
satellite, 61, 66, 74, 78, 147, 157, 204

scalability, 76, 78, 84, 113, 162, 171, 177, 182, 201, 202, 205, 220, 223, 225, 226
scheduler, 62, 63
screen, 1, 12, 37, 42, 55, 81, 83, 86, 87, 155
sensitivity
    application, 94
server, 18, 38, 39, 40, 41, 58, 64, 65, 69, 109, 171, 208, 213, 223
service
    network, 37, 38, 60, 63, 153
    quality, 1, 3, 4, 6, 8, 9, 13, 14, 35, 36, 37, 38, 41, 43, 48, 49, 50, 51, 54, 56, 60, 62, 65, 66, 70, 93, 94, 95, 96, 97, 98, 99, 100, 101, 102, 103, 104, 105, 107, 108, 109, 110, 111, 112, 113, 114, 115, 116, 117, 118, 119, 185, 191, 199
    universal, 139, 140, 143, 144, 145, 148, 149, 150, 153, 154, 155, 156, 157, 158, 159
session, 39, 41, 42, 43, 45, 46, 47, 69, 89, 101, 109, 186, 187, 188, 189, 190, 191, 193
shopping, 123, 128
simulation, 38, 50, 171, 172, 176, 195, 198, 203, 222, 223, 225, 226
SMIL, 22, 23, 24, 26, 28
smiley, 36
software, 2, 40, 55, 61, 66, 71, 74, 75, 79, 80, 83, 89, 128, 129, 130, 131, 132, 136
standard, 7, 8, 54, 56, 59, 60, 63, 64, 70, 74, 78, 90, 96, 108, 181, 186
stream
    audio, 61, 81
streaming, 1, 18, 40, 75, 102, 107, 143, 150
synchronisation, 36, 40, 43, 47, 98, 104, 112, 113, 115

TCP/IP, 59, 60
technique, 7, 38, 65, 130, 202, 203

telecommunications, 78
tele-conference, 55, 79, 81
tele-meeting, 55
tele-service, 185, 186, 187, 188, 189,
    190, 191, 192, 193, 194, 195, 196,
    198
television, 17, 85, 87, 121, 125, 126,
    131, 134, 135, 136, 140, 141
tele-working, 55
Tenet, 94, 107, 113, 114, 115, 118
termination, 94, 104, 105, 115
testing, 8, 9, 11, 13, 65, 78, 80, 88,
    104, 105
timeliness, 95, 104
time-to-live (TTL), 203, 209, 210,
    222
Toffler, Alvin, 126
token, 38, 39, 150, 202, 204, 205,
    206, 207, 208, 209, 210, 211, 212,
    213, 214, 215, 216, 217, 218, 219,
    220, 221, 222, 223, 225
tool, 21, 50, 54, 71, 75, 91, 121, 129,
    130, 145
    predictive, 22
training, 24, 35, 37, 40, 139
transcoding, 163
trend, 19, 121, 132, 133, 138, 140,
    141, 152, 158

tuning, 54, 80, 93, 94, 103, 104, 105,
    106, 107, 143

unicast, 61, 63, 80, 162, 209
usability, 1, 2, 8, 10, 11, 12, 13, 35,
    36, 37, 38, 39, 42, 43, 44, 46, 49,
    50, 96, 139
user behaviour, 17, 18, 19, 20, 21, 22,
    23, 26, 32

video
    clarity, 6
    frame rate, 2, 4, 5, 6, 7, 8, 9, 12,
        14, 64, 97, 98, 115
    smoothness, 6
    streamed, 21
videoconference, 73, 74, 75, 76, 87,
    89, 187, 188, 189, 195
video-on-demand, 94
viewer, 1, 5, 6, 7, 8, 9, 10, 178

watchability, 36
webcast, 121, 134, 137, 138, 139,
    141, 143, 145, 150, 152, 154, 155,
    156
web-site, 19, 20, 21, 23, 24, 126
World Wide Web, 142